# DISTINCTIONS OF BEING

## PHILOSOPHICAL APPROACHES TO REALITY

PUBLICATIONS OF THE

**AMERICAN MARITAIN ASSOCIATION**

General Editors:
Anthony O. Simon (1990 – 2004)
Michael Torre (2009 –)

*Jacques Maritain: The Man and His Metaphysics*
Edited by John F. X. Kansas, 1988
ISBN-13 978-0-268-01205-2, ISBN-10 0-268-01205-9 (out of print)
Distributed by the University of Notre Dame Press

*Freedom in the Modern World: Jacques Maritain, Yves R. Simon, Mortimer J. Adler*
Edited by Michael D. Torre, 1989, Second Printing, 1990
ISBN-13 978-0-268-00978-6, ISBN-10 0-268-00978-3
Distributed by the University of Notre Dame Press

*From Twilight to Dawn: The Cultural Vision of Jacques Maritain*
Edited by Peter A. Redpath, 1990
ISBN-13 978-0-268-00979-3, ISBN-10 0-268-00979-1
Distributed by the University of Notre Dame Press

*The Future of Thomism*
Edited by Deal W. Hudson and Dennis Wm. Moran, 1992
ISBN-13 978-0-268-00986-1, ISBN-10 0-268-00986-4
Distributed by the University of Notre Dame Press

*Jacques Maritain and the Jews*
Edited by Robert Royal, 1994
ISBN-13 978-0-268-01193-2, ISBN-10 0-268-01193-1
Distributed by the University of Notre Dame Press

*Freedom, Virtue, and the Common Good*
Edited by Curtis L. Hancock and Anthony O. Simon, 1995
ISBN-13 978-0-268-00991-5, ISBN-10 0-268-00991-0
Distributed by the University of Notre Dame Press

*Postmodernism and Christian Philosophy*
Edited by Roman T. Ciapolo, 1997
ISBN-13 978-0-8132-0881-7, ISBN-10 0-8132-0881-5
Distributed by the Catholic University of America Press

*The Common Things: Essays on Thomism and Education*
Edited by Daniel McInerny, 1999
ISBN-13 978-0-9669226-0-8, ISBN-10 0-9669226-0-3
Distributed by the Catholic University of America Press

*The Failure of Modernism: The Cartesian Legacy and Contemporary Pluralism*
Edited by Brendan Sweetman, 1999
ISBN-13 978-0-9669226-1-5, ISBN-10 0-9669226-1-1
Distributed by the Catholic University of America Press

*Beauty, Art, and the Polis*
Edited by Alice Ramos, 2000
ISBN-13 978-0-9669226-2-2, ISBN-10 0-9669226-2-X
Distributed by the Catholic University of America Press

*Reassessing the Liberal State: Reading Maritain's Man and the State*
Edited by Timothy Fuller and John P. Hittinger, 2001
ISBN-13 978-0-9669226-3-9, ISBN-10 0-9669226-3-8
Distributed by the Catholic University of America Press

*Faith, Scholarship, and Culture in the 21st Century*
Edited by Alice Ramos, and Marie I. George, 2002
ISBN-13 978-0-9669226-5-3, ISBN-10 0-9669226-5-4
Distributed by the Catholic University of America Press

*Jacques Maritain and the Many Ways of Knowing*
Edited by Douglas A. Ollivant, 2002
ISBN-13 978-0-9669226-4-6, ISBN-10 0-9669226-4-6
Distributed by the Catholic University of America Press

*Truth Matters: Essays in Honor of Jacques Maritain*
Edited by John G. Trapani, Jr., 2004
ISBN-13 978-0-9669226-6-0, ISBN-10 0-9669226-6-2
Distributed by the Catholic University of America Press

*The Human Person and a Culture of Freedom*
Edited by Peter A. Pagan Aguiar and Terese Auer, O.P., 2009
ISBN 978-0-9669226-7-7
Distributed by the Catholic University of America Press

*Maritain and America*
Edited by Christopher M. Cullen, S.J. and Joseph Allan Clair, 2009
ISBN 978-0-9669226-8-4
Distributed by the Catholic University of America Press

*The Renewal of Civilization: Essays in Honor of Jacques Maritain*
Edited by Gavin T. Colvert, 2010
ISBN 978-0-9669226-9-1
Distributed by the Catholic University of America Press

*The Vocation of the Catholic Philosopher: From Maritain to John Paul II*
Edited by John P. Hittinger, 2010
ISBN 978-0-9827119-0-3
Distributed by the Catholic University of America Press

*Reading the Cosmos: Nature, Science, and Wisdom*
Edited by Giuseppe Butera, 2011
ISBN 978-0-9827119-1-0
Distributed by the Catholic University of America Press

*Distinctions of Being: Philosophical Approaches to Reality*
Edited by Nikolaj Zunic
ISBN 978-0-9827119-2-7
Distributed by the Catholic University of America Press

# DISTINCTIONS OF BEING

## PHILOSOPHICAL APPROACHES TO REALITY

EDITED BY

NIKOLAJ ZUNIC

AMERICAN MARITAIN ASSOCIATION

Distributed by the Catholic University of America Press

Washington, D.C. 20064

**Library of Congress Cataloging-in-Publication Data**

Distinctions of being : philosophical approaches to reality / edited by Nikolaj Zunic.
p. cm
Includes bibliographical references and index.
ISBN 978-0-9827119-2-7 (alk. paper)
1. Philosophy. 2. Metaphysics. 3. Ontology. 4. Maritain, Jacques, 1882-1973. 5. Catholic Church and philosophy. I. Zunic, Nikolaj, 1970-
BD21.D57 2012
110--dc23

2012036751

Manufactured in the United States of America

Distributed by the Catholic University of America Press
620 Michigan Avenue, N.E. /240 Leahy Hall
Washington, D.C. 20064

## Acknowledgements

Although a labor of love, this book is the fruit of much dedicated effort and collaboration. No doubt, in the wistful words of Sam Cooke, "it's been a long, a long time coming." In the first instance, I would like to thank John G. Trapani, Jr., the President of the American Maritain Association, for his confidence in my abilities to shepherd this project to the end. My greatest debt of gratitude, however, is reserved for Michael D. Torre, the General Editor of the AMA book series, for his abiding support and guidance throughout this project. His constant words of encouragement and advice, besides his friendly reminders to get the job done, were instrumental in this achievement. Finally, my wife, Erin, deserves the recognition of the stalwart spouse whose regular proddings helped to keep me on track.

## Contents

## PART III
### Maritain's Philosophy of Being



## PART IV
### The Scope of Science

# INTRODUCTION: THE TASK OF THINKING REALITY

NIKOLAJ ZUNIC

## I. THE PERENNIAL PHILOSOPHY

Metaphysics is the science of reality, the study of what things are and how they operate. It is a longstanding view among philosophers that metaphysics is an innate tendency of the human spirit, that people instinctively want to know what reality is. Aristotle famously remarked at the beginning of his *Metaphysics* that "all men by nature desire to know" and about two millennia later Immanuel Kant echoed these same ideas by stating in his *Critique of Pure Reason* that metaphysics is rooted in the teleological movement of reason itself. At first glance the term "metaphysics" can appear a bit daunting and intimidating, conveying the connotation of abstract systematizing, but at its heart the philosophical tradition has always endeavored to tap into and articulate the deepest aspiration of all human beings, which is to live in the truth, the very basis of reality.

With such a formidable tradition standing behind such views one could be forgiven for believing that this desire for truth is a permanent and indelible fixture of the human soul. Yet, when one looks around the world today in the early part of the 21st century, there is much evidence that living in the truth is not the top priority of most human beings. The rapid advances in technology, especially on the communication front (e.g. the Internet), and the increased politicization of society, which more often than not breeds a certain obfuscating and self-serving rhetoric, have created the ideal conditions for the flight from truth and the establishment of a pseudo-reality, often termed a "virtual reality." This is nothing more than a cursory, general observation of the state of humanity in our contemporary age, but the dictum that "truth falters in the public square" (59:14), as promulgated by the prophet Isaiah, is as old as civilization itself and has been witnessed countless times in history, most famously in the case of Socrates, but also throughout the philosophical tradition. Although human beings desire the truth, we also tend to shun and reject it. Although human beings want to embrace and live in reality, we also have an inclination to immure ourselves in falsehoods and even lies. Although human beings are made for happiness, we are prone to sin and to spending our days in sadness. It would not be too outrageous to suggest that human beings are, rightly put, paradoxical creatures.

Despite this contradictory human nature, there is still hope that truth will set us free. As the Irish poet Seamus Heaney remarked, "The mind still longs to repose in what Samuel Johnson once called with superb confidence 'the stability of truth,' even as it recognizes the destabilizing nature of its own operations and enquiries."[1] This confidence in the power of truth to orient the human mind towards its final goal in life and to anchor the soul in the nurturing waters of reality is the backdrop of this present collection of essays, which are devoted to metaphysical themes that take their cue from the original searchings of the ancient Greeks, continued through the Middle Ages, and advanced in contemporary times by figures such as Jacques Maritain. What is at play here is the perceived need to resurrect metaphysical thought and to demonstrate that the unquenchable desire for truth is indeed an aspect of the human condition that cannot be suffocated out of existence.

*Distinctions of Being: Philosophical Approaches to Reality*, as the title itself suggests, bears upon the time-honored insight that philosophical thinking depends upon the making of distinctions. Robert Sokolowski has gone one step further to describe the act of distinguishing as a quintessential philosophical act.[2] Such distinctions include what is essential versus what is accidental, form as opposed to matter, act and potency, the divine and the human, the temporal and the eternal, and so on. No doubt such thinking requires a modicum of talent and skill, for often the realities being distinguished are subtle, abstract, and utterly simple. Nonetheless, it remains a mainstay of philosophical thought itself that the subtleties of sameness and difference be properly recognized and understood. After all, as the cover photo of

1 Seamus Heaney, "Crediting Poetry," in *Opened Ground: Selected Poems, 1966-1996* (New York: Farrar, Straus and Giroux, 1998), 418.

2 Robert Sokolowski, "The Method of Philosophy: Making Distinctions," *The Review of Metaphysics* 51 (1998): 515-32.

this volume perfectly illustrates, in the interplay of the colors of blue and white it is incumbent upon one to be able to pick out the sky from the water and the clouds in the air from their reflection in the sea. In fact, the horizon serves as the limit and boundary for both sky and earth, providing the necessary rupture between two domains of being and offering at the same time the necessary condition for the vision and comprehension itself. To be sure, without a horizon there is no distinction between heaven and earth, and without a perceptive observer there is no recognition of the distinctions of being, the many and various ways in which things exist.

## II. THE THING AS THE BASIS OF METAPHYSICS

The chief inspiration for metaphysical thought is nothing other than the attention paid to the things of the world. We live in a world of things, things that stand apart from us and englobe us in their positioning nature. We orient ourselves by virtue of the reality of objects that act as markers and measures, enabling us to find our bearings. Metaphysics was born from a profound reflection on things. The Ionian and Milesian monists wanted to understand the fundamental essence of the things in the world. St. Thomas Aquinas focused his mind on the being of things, understood in terms of the act of existing. In a more recent development, Martin Heidegger raised the question of being by analyzing the way in which things relate themselves to us, ontological states that he described with the terms *Vorhandenheit* ("present-at-hand") and *Zuhandenheit* ("ready-to-hand"). So intimately connected are things to the act of thinking that one could emphatically announce, along with G. K. Chesterton, that "you cannot think if there are no things to think about."[3]

The importance of things for metaphysics as such has been illuminated in a thought-provoking work by the Canadian philosopher Kenneth L. Schmitz entitled *The Recovery of Wonder*.[4] One of the central theses advanced by Schmitz is that the concept of the thing—*res* in Latin, *to ontos* in Greek—was a hard won achievement. The early, pre-Socratic Greeks did not have a word for a thing as such. What they did

3 G. K. Chesterton, *Orthodoxy* (New York: Image Books, 2001), 31.

4 Kenneth L. Schmitz, *The Recovery of Wonder: The New Freedom and the Asceticism of Power* (Montreal: McGill-Queen's University Press, 2005).

have were the words *ta pragmata* meaning "doable things" or "things that can be done" and *ta chremata* which were "useable or useful things." *Pragma* is related to *praxis*, which has the connotation of an action or deed, whereas *chrema* refers to a useful or needed object, such as money or property, something that one can use in a utilitarian manner. It was not until the advent of Plato and Aristotle, arguably the first significant metaphysicians, that the concept of a thing simply "being"—rather than being done or used—emerged into human consciousness. Thus was the notion of a thing born and the science of reality, known to later ages as metaphysics, given a sustained expression.

It bears noting that the English word "reality" is derived from the Latin *realitas* which is itself linked etymologically to *res*, thing. The thing stands out as a pivotal feature of reality. A thing is an entity residing in the world and capable of being cognized as a unified whole, as a complete some-thing. Trees, houses, tables, dogs, and streams all denote things. But we can also talk about intellectual entities as things, such as thoughts, emotions, and fantasies. Although fraught with problems, we can even speak of God as a thing, as Martin Buber suggests in his concept of the I-It relation. A thing can be either, animate or inanimate, natural or artificial, material or immaterial. The Oxford English Dictionary informs us that the word "thing" has the meaning of "that which exists individually; that which is or may be an object of perception, knowledge or thought; a being, an entity."[5] On one level, the word "thing" is so vague and general as to appear meaningless. We ordinarily use this word to denote just about everything we refer to in our speech: "Give me that thing over there!" or "What was that thing-a-ma-jig you were holding?" or "I did not mean a thing by what I said." Indeed, "thing" has a universal denotation. But, at the same time, a thing marks out what is truly fundamental in our perceptions. Without things which we encounter and use and ponder, there would be no reality to engage with and to reflect on.

---

5 Its first and original meaning is "a meeting, assembly, esp. a deliberative or judicial assembly, a court, a council." The word "thing" originally was related to the proceedings of a court of law, i.e., a suit or cause pleaded before a court.

The careful and even reverential attentiveness to things gives rise to contemplation and thought itself. Schmitz elucidates the origins of the contemplative insight into things that lies at the heart of metaphysics. The Greeks called this approach to things *theoria*, which comes from the word *theoros*, a word which means "one who sees." The "one who sees" is the *theoros*, the individual who has an insight into the things of the world, who can actually "see" what things are. Such a vision, it needs to be stressed, must focus on the nature of the thing as it reveals itself, rather than the perceiver imposing some arbitrary characterization on the thing. This realism, which is nothing other than a deliberate attentiveness to things, is the basis of all metaphysical thinking.

Over time, however, the priority given to things was altered and eventually discarded entirely. Historically speaking, the school known as nominalism—also known as terminism—made its mark in the late Middle Ages. Nominalism was the first major instance in the philosophical tradition of the West in which the thing was separated from the concept. This distance placed between things and ideas proved in the long run to be a ruinous enterprise. The chief problem with nominalism, at least from our perspective here, is that it loses the sense of the inner depth and meaning of things. Jacques Maritain expresses his lament in the following way:

> [The nominalists] have a basic misunderstanding of the value of the abstract, that immateriality which is more enduring than things for all that it is untouchable and unimaginable, that immateriality which mind seeks out in the very heart of things. But why this incurable nominalism? The reason is that while having a taste for the real indeed, they nevertheless have no sense of being. Being as such, loosed from the matter in which it is incorporated, being, with its pure objective necessities and its laws that prove no burden, its restraints which do not bind, its invisible evidence, is for them only a word.[6]

This intellectual and spiritual neglect of the being of the things was furthered in the rationalism of René Descartes. By separating the mind from sensible things in his pursuit of intellectual certainty, Descartes

---

6 Jacques Maritain, *Distinguish to Unite or The Degrees of Knowledge*, trans. Gerald B. Phelan (Notre Dame, Indiana: University of Notre Dame Press, 1995), 1.

transformed the philosophical understanding of the manner by which knowledge is obtained. In the older metaphysics of the ancients and medievals, knowledge always originates in the apprehension of sensible things. But for Descartes it is possible to arrive at a purely intellectual grasp of truth independently of sensation. Because the Cartesian epistemology reflects the Thomistic conception of how angels, which are pure intellectual substances, come to know essences without needing to perceive material things through the senses, Maritain labels Descartes' philosophy an *angelism*. This Cartesian angelism effects a violent separation between mind and reality, between the intellect and experience, and, in so doing, introduces into modernity the principle of idealism.

The modern idealists lose completely the appreciation of things as existing independently of mind. Whereas in the past, in the older metaphysics, the human intellect was attentive to the ontological constitution of things, which it patiently penetrated in its theoretical inquiries, gradually uncovering the rich being of things, idealism stands in stark contrast by abolishing all intrinsic otherness to things. At bottom, for an idealistic standpoint, things are determinations and constructions of the mind. Immanuel Kant represents this idealistic attitude in his attempt to seek the grounds for the validation of scientific knowledge, so that knowledge can meet the demands of scientific rigor, precision, and certitude. What is at stake is not the origination of beings but the justification of knowledge-claims; what is at stake is not the reality of things but the authority of the knower. This issue for idealism is not ontological constitution but epistemic validation. This justification is achieved by Kant on the basis of a priori categories. Things are translated from objects in the early modern sense into phenomena in the sense of Kant's critical idealism. If the material of knowledge could appear only under the actively determining conditions of the knowing subject, objects had in idealism received their definitive emptying: they were no longer that which stands over against the mind as objects (with a diminished, residual independence), but that which appears to the mind as phenomena, under the mind's conditions; that is, they were in effect appearances, not things. Therefore, idealism has the effect of completely desensitizing human intelligence to the presence and meaning of things. It diminishes the human appreciation of reality and radically transforms accordingly the nature of human subjectivity. With such a profound effect on the human spirit, it is not surprising, then, to learn that Maritain regards philosophical idealism as an error of monumental proportions. Idealism, in short, violated the integrity of metaphysics, that is, the human person's capacity to know reality as such.

## III. THE CLAIMS OF KNOWLEDGE

Knowledge is a curious possession, for it is essential to everyday, ordinary living, a veritable commonplace, but its proper nature is usually very little understood. To know something is a reality that speaks to the objective and subjective poles of existence. First, knowledge is of *something* that is grasped by the mind in its truth, and, second, it is the intellect that is modified in some way by the presence of knowledge in it.[7] As regards the subject, knowledge is the ennoblement and elevation of intelligence. What is underlined here is a particular way of being, not a process of producing or making. The knower's very being is ontologically enriched in the act of knowing. However, knowledge is not of oneself, but of an object, a determinate something that can be apprehended by the intellect. It is this object that is taken up into the human mind with respect to its intelligible nature. For Maritain, following Aristotle and Thomas, the knower becomes the object in the act of knowing, which explains how precisely the knower's being benefits from knowledge. Certainly, the person does not actually become a table or chair when he or she knows it, but rather the intellect accepts the object's immaterial form into itself through a process of abstraction and in this way becomes the thing in an immaterial way. This act of the intellect becoming the object is so puzzling, yet awe-inspiring that Maritain rightly describes it as a mystery.[8] In fact, Maritain reserves the term *superexistence* to denote the existence of the knower who has become the thing known.[9] It is

7 See Jacques Maritain, *Réflexions sur l'intelligence et sur sa vie propre* (Paris: Nouvelle Librairie Nationale, 1926), 50-53.

8 Jacques Maritain, *The Degrees of Knowledge*, 118. See also Jacques Maritain, *A Preface to Metaphysics: Seven Lectures on Being* (New York: Mentor Omega Book, 1962), 12–15.

9 *The Degrees of Knowledge*, 123. See also Jacques Maritain, *Existence and the Existent* trans. Lewis Galantiere and Gerald B. Phelan (New York: Image Books, 1956), 21: "True knowledge consists in a spiritual super-existence by which, in a supreme vital act, I become the other as such, and which

clear, therefore, that knowing is not an inconsequential or sterile activity, but is responsible for the enlivening and transformation of the human person as such. On this score, Maritain communicates his thoughts with the utmost clarity: "This entirely immaterial informing, wherein the soul receives or submits only in order to exercise its own vital activity—only in order to bring itself in act to an existence that is not limited to itself alone—is that which constitutes knowing."[10] The human person undergoes a deepening of his being in and through the act of knowledge.

In the foregoing discussion, the term "object" was used rather loosely, but it is necessary to distinguish it carefully from the notion of a "thing."[11] The thing is the physical or material object as it exists independently of the mind, whereas the object is the abstracted, formal object in the intellect. To be sure, the object is derived from the thing as the intellect receives the intelligible species of the thing through sensation. From the initial species received into the mind to the formation of a concept there is a constant reference to the thing which was sensibly perceived. The concept of the object has an intentional function in which it acts as a formal sign of the thing.[12] A formal sign, as Maritain explains, is a sign whose intrinsic nature is to signify, whereas an instrumental sign signifies only accidentally.[13] For instance, smoke signifies the presence of fire, but it does so in a non-essential manner, since it can also exist for its own sake without any reference to a cause. Species and concepts, by contrast, are formal signs in the respect that their very nature points to the thing, the material object, which is housed immaterially in the intellect. Thomas Aquinas emphasizes this

---

corresponds to the existence exercised or possessed by that other itself in the particular field of intelligibility which is its peculiar possession." The notion of super-existence is one that Maritain typically uses to describe the mode of existence of human personality, the being who communicates acts of knowledge and love, as found in *The Person and the Common Good*, trans. John J. Fitzgerald (Notre Dame, Indiana: University of Notre Dame Press, 1966), 40.

10 *The Degrees of Knowledge*, 125.

11 Ibid., 26, 96-107.

12 Ibid., 129.

13 Ibid., 127.

same function of the intellect to refer back constantly to phantasms in order for the universality of the concept to be adequate to the particularity of the thing.[14] Without this intentional function, concepts of objects would have no intrinsic connection with the things from which they are derived. Put in even stronger terms, it is precisely this intentionality of concepts that enables our knowledge of things to be assuredly of real things.

The categorical mistake, or, as Maritain expresses it, "the original sin" of modern idealism, is that it separated the object from the thing.[15] Descartes and Kant, to single out the two mightiest representatives of the idealistic tradition, misunderstood fundamentally the nature of human knowledge, which is that when the human intellect comes to know an object it always refers to an underlying or original thing, this being the bedrock of all philosophical realism. As Maritain makes unambiguously clear in *The Degrees of Knowledge*, realism and idealism in philosophy represent two wholly incommensurable and diametrically opposed attitudes towards reality. There is no third alternative, no higher perspective than these two which could overcome the divide and put to rest the quarrel between them. In the final analysis, the philosopher must make a decision as to which of these two standpoints he or she wishes to adopt. There is no doubt which position Maritain chooses. In his denunciation of idealism, he writes:

> One cannot think about a 'thought thing' until after one has thought about a "thinkable thing"—a thing "good for existing", i.e., at least a possible real. The first thing thought about is being independent of the mind. The *cogitatum* of the first *cogito* is not

---

14 Thomas Aquinas, *The Treatise on Human Nature: Summa Theologiae 1a75-89*, trans. Robert Pasnau (Indianapolis: Hackett Publishing Company, 2002), 84.7, 154: "The nature of a stone, for example, is by definition in this stone; and the nature of a horse is by definition in this horse, and so forth. Accordingly, the nature of a stone, or of any material thing, cannot be completely and truly cognized except by being cognized as existing in a particular. But we apprehend the particular through sense and imagination. And so it is necessary, in order for intellect actually to understand its proper object, that it turn toward phantasms so as to examine the universal nature existing in the particular."

15 *The Degrees of Knowledge*, 115.

> *cogitatum*, but *ens*. We do not eat what has been eaten; we eat bread. To separate object from thing, the objective *logos* from metalogical being, is to violate the nature of intellect, to flee from the first evidence of direct intuition, and at the same time, to mutilate reflexive intuition (the very reflexive intuition on which we would make everything depend) in the very first of its immediate data. Idealism sets an original sin against the light at the beginning of the whole philosophical edifice.[16]

Philosophical realism, the critical realism of Maritain's metaphysics, can only be supported if the thing is permitted to play a role in philosophy. Without the thing we cannot have the option of realism, which positions itself against idealism. "As long as the value of the thing or of the subject is not fully restored, it is useless to try to be a realist."[17] It is for this reason that Maritain assiduously defends the notion of the thing and gives it pride of place in his metaphysics. For he is painfully aware that without the thing, idealism is victorious!

## IV. THE INNER MEANING OF REALITY

In a striking passage in *The Degrees of Knowledge*, Maritain writes: "The mystery of creation alone can allay the scruples of idealism."[18] By this statement, Maritain wishes to express his firm conviction that the main error of idealism is that it accords to human intelligence a power over things that it really does not possess. The fact of creation, the reality that the universe and the things in it derive their being from a divine act, reminds us all that the human intellect is finite and created, and, furthermore, that it does not bring things into being. To be sure, creation reveals to us that things have an existence independently of us.

Kenneth Schmitz picks up on this idea of creation as crucial for a proper understanding of the being of things. Creation informs us that things are not only *given*, but that they are a *gift*.[19] Things are the

---

16 Ibid., 115.

17 Ibid.

18 Ibid., 116.

19 See Kenneth L. Schmitz, *The Gift: Creation* (Milwaukee: Marquette University Press, 1982).

products of an infinite, divine generosity and possess this fecundity of spirit in their very ontological constitution. Recognizing things as created, as gifts, opens our minds to the interiority, integrity, and depth of things. Schmitz speaks of the intrinsic immateriality of things that is situated in form. This immaterial, formal aspect of things, as mentioned earlier in this introduction, reveals a profound depth of meaning in things, as witnessed in their relations with other things that constitutes a community of things, what we can call a holistic network of meaning. The openness towards the things that we have not made is the core of the attitude of *theoria*, the contemplative insight into the heart of things. This theoretical disposition towards things, penetrating their interior essence, instills in the observer the feeling of wonder, which, as Plato and Aristotle both asserted, is the principle of all philosophizing. On this score Schmitz writes:

> Through the interior depth in things, then, there is a shared bond for mutual relations between us and things: an openness for meditation, for *theôria*, and for a wonder that grows upon us as a kind of realization of the *significance* of each thing (*res*). From that should follow a new behaviour towards things.[20]

This theoretical attentiveness to things should lead to a transformation of the human subject and ennoble human intelligence. Instead of seeking to control and manipulate things, which is the general tendency of the modern, technological, and scientific disposition towards the world, the generosity of the gift of things calls us to be loving stewards of creation, faithful to our solidarity with things. And, with this reverential disposition towards the world, the hope is born of a renewed acknowledgement in the human heart of the ultimate origin of things in God's creative act.

## V. OVERVIEW OF THE PRESENT VOLUME

The essays collected in this volume all deal with metaphysical themes. They all share a common engagement with the traditional metaphysics of the ancient Greek philosophers and medieval Schoolmen. To be sure, the thought of Jacques Maritain looms large in these pages. The basic thrust of this book is to bring into sharp relief

---

20 Kenneth L. Schmitz, *The Recovery of Wonder*, 123.

the questions and topics that philosophy has dealt with from time immemorial: being, form, matter, truth, knowledge, and God. Such ways of considering things may be on the wane in our contemporary age, but this volume serves to reignite the spark of this mindfulness for the inner nature of things.

The book is divided into four thematic sections. The first part, "Foundations of Aristotelian-Thomistic Metaphysics," contains papers which examine the basic concepts of Aristotle's and Aquinas' understanding of metaphysics. In the first paper, "Why the Senses Cannot Have Truth: The Need for Abstraction," Steven J. Jensen develops the Thomistic notion that truth resides in the intellect, despite the senses' ability to perceive empirical objects as they really exist. His discussion revolves around the intellect's ability to make judgments of reality, expressed in propositions, which reveal the truth of things. In this treatment of truth, the proper focus is the intellect's relationship with reality, traditionally subsumed under the correspondence theory of truth.

This systematic approach is continued in Joshua P. Hochschild's paper, "Form, Essence, Soul: Distinguishing Key Principles of Thomistic Metaphysics." The point of departure for Hochschild's essay is the many confusions that permeate the different terms used to describe living things, such as human persons. What is a person's substantial form? And does this differ from the person's essence? Above all, what exactly is the soul? By elucidating the different uses and understandings of the terms form, essence, and soul—ultimately gauged with respect to grades of actuality—Hochschild has provided a valuable service in setting the record straight.

The concept of being—the very heart of metaphysics—is the subject matter of Lawrence Dewan, O.P.'s, stimulating paper, "First Known Being and the Birth of Metaphysics." This is a rigorous and sustained reflection on the nature of metaphysics itself in dialogue with Plato, Aristotle, and Aquinas. How does metaphysics begin? Some philosophers and theologians, notably Ralph McInerny and Benedict Ashley, have argued that metaphysics only comes into existence with the demonstration of separate, immaterial being. Dewan respectfully disagrees. His paper aims to contradict these views by showing that metaphysics is already present in the apprehension of sensible substances. As Dewan affirms, "we have a notion from the start that is maximally universal." Metaphysics is born the moment we start to question the being of things as such, not just immaterial being.

Giuseppe Butera's paper, "Incomplete Persons: Thomas Aquinas on Separated Souls and the Identity of the Human Person," is devoted to a critical assessment of Elenore Stump's views on the distinguishing mark of human nature. Stump challenges the constitution view of human nature, which holds that the identity of the human person is a composite of matter and form, body and soul. Instead, she argues that that constitution is not synonymous with identity, a proposition that opens the door to the thesis that the separated soul after death could be construed as being the person him- or herself. Butera argues that this anti-constitution view is an error and a misreading of Aquinas. He takes Stump's ideas to task by arguing that she has confused what is accidental in human nature with its substantial being. Moreover, by downplaying the notion of personhood, which has received greater emphasis in the modern age than it ever had in Aquinas's day, some of the puzzles surrounding the characteristics of the separated soul can be solved.

The next major thematic section of the book is entitled "Analogies of the Divine." The papers here deal principally with the topic of God, exhibiting both theological and philosophical perspectives. In his splendid essay, "'The Great Visible God': Socrates, Aristotle and Thomas Aquinas on the Way from Nature to Nature's God," Christopher S. Morrissey presents a reflection on natural theology. Morrissey argues that Aquinas' Five Ways, which are arguments demonstrating God's existence, ones borrowed directly from Aristotle, owe much to Socrates' own argumentative method. Socrates inquired into the origin of creatures and the world by positing a fourfold pattern of investigation that examined the existence, essence, properties, and causes of things. According to Morrissey, this Socratic Method influenced Aristotle and later Aquinas in their arguments for God's existence. From observations of physical nature we can, through reason alone, deduce the existence of an immaterial first cause, this being God. Considerations about the interplay of the physical and the metaphysical domains run throughout Morrissey's careful analyses.

"From the Relative to the Absolute: Louis de Raeymaker's 'Metaphysical Proof' for the Existence of God" is William P. Haggerty's contribution to this volume. Haggerty's paper is an incisive study of Louis

De Raeymaker's proof for God's existence, as conveyed in his book *The Philosophy of Being*. We are certainly in Haggerty's debt for this presentation of this largely overlooked "retrieval of Thomistic metaphysics" from a former professor of philosophy at the Higher Institute of Philosophy at the Catholic University of Louvain in Belgium. De Raeymaker develops a unique standpoint by emphasizing the absolute status of being in the context of the relativity of particular or finite beings. The overall order of being is due not to particular beings themselves, which present relations or relativities, but to an external cause of this order of being, which is identified as God. The doctrine of participation is a key element in this ontology. Although Aquinas may have confused logical and real participation in his Fourth Way, Haggerty is convinced that de Raeymaker's treatment of God's existence is quite compelling—more compelling even than many traditional cosmological and teleological arguments.

The Christian philosophical and theological traditions have taught that human beings have a natural appetite or desire for God. In his essay, "Maritain on the Natural Desire to See God: Reflections Appreciative and Critical," Michael D. Torre engages with the thought of Jacques Maritain on precisely this subject. At issue is the relationship between nature and grace. The human person can know that God exists through philosophical reasoning and this cognition spurs one on to know God fully. But can this natural desire to know or see God be fully realized and perfected? Or is it forever unfulfilled until the moment when grace is bestowed? By scrupulously poring over Maritain's texts, Torre argues that in the early part of his career Maritain maintained that the beatific vision was incomprehensible to reason, whereas he gradually changed his mind in the later stages of his life. By suggesting that the possibility of the beatific vision was a truth within reach of reason and philosophy, Maritain came to adopt a position that fell in line with the views of Aquinas himself on this point.

John Marson Dunaway examines the deficiencies of the modern theory of the subject in his paper, "The Majesty of Intersubjectivity: Maritain and Marcel *Contra* Cartesian Subjectivity." Through his self-reflective posturing, Descartes bequeathed a narrow image of the self to his disciples in the West, an image appropriated wholeheartedly by Jean-Paul Sartre. The problem with Sartre's doctrine of subjectivity, according to Dunaway, is that it isolates the person in a solipsistic universe. To counter this view, Dunaway presents Maritain's idea of subjectivity as an unfathomable mystery and complements it with Maritain's doctrine of connatural knowledge—knowledge by inclination—which opens persons up to otherness and allows for an intimate relation with God. Dunaway perceives a harmony between Maritain's views and Gabriel Marcel's championing of the reality of intersubjectivity. For Marcel, intersubjectivity is grounded in participation, the human person's embodied existence, in which the bonds with others are recognized and affirmed. Indeed, the notion of intersubjectivity straddles the boundary of metaphysics; Dunaway in fact believes that it has more to do with poetry and mysticism, that is, the participatory mode of existence.

Jacques Maritain was a magnificent metaphysician and his *magnum opus, Distinguish to Unite or The Degrees of Knowledge*, attests to this claim. The third major section of the book deals directly with Maritain's metaphysical thought that falls under the rubric of "Maritain's Philosophy of Being." John G. Trapani, Jr., opens this section with his paper, "Difficult Acrobatics: 'Gravitating Head First to the Midst of the Stars,' " a title whose inspiration is taken from the introductory essay of *The Degrees of Knowledge*. Maritain was keenly aware of the poverty of metaphysics, which was exhibited in its inability to deliver the human person unto a union with God. Yet metaphysics does possess a majesty, which allows human reason to rise up to the highest heights of being itself in its pursuit of utter fulfillment. Ultimately, metaphysics is in need of grace; the metaphysician must work together with the poet. In and through the intuition of being, human nature can achieve its greatest accomplishment: the love of God.

As a fitting segue, James G. Hanink discusses some key concepts in Maritain's metaphysics in his paper, "In Defense of the Intuition of Being." Maritain is well known for having advanced the doctrine of the intuition of being—the view that the intellect can have an immediate grasp of or insight into being itself prior to any conceptualization of being. Some philosophers, such as Étienne Gilson and John F. X. Knasas, have denied that such an intuition could ever take place. Their objecttions are summarized by Hanink under the term *the sensory limit objection*, which stipulates that the intuition of being is impossible because our cognitive categories are restricted to the sensible and not the metaphysical domain. Hanink attempts to argue against this objection by citing three sources of the intuition of being: the experience of irreducible singularities, the phenomenon of free and intelligent acts of persons, and the reality of having being (*habens esse*). Whether Hanink succeeds in debunking the sensory limit objection is something that the reader must decide for him- or herself.

Raymond Dennehy's paper, "How Maritain May Have Bridged the Gap Between Metaphysics and Activism," takes these reflections in a new direction by attempting to link Maritain's metaphysics with his social activism. A perennial conflict in Western philosophy is that between the life of intellectual contemplation and the life of practical action. Maritain sought to integrate both orientations into this own life. Dennehy shows how in his youth Maritain achieved a superficial union of thought and action by using Spinoza (the contemplative) and Nietzsche (the anti-rationalist agitator) as models, which proved to be a short-lived experiment. Eventually, Thomism was the prime recipe for this holism Maritain was looking for. Dennehy wishes to emphasize the continuity that existed between Maritain's metaphysics and his activism, a continuity that was made possible by the intuition of being, which allowed Maritain to be liberated from mere concepts and to come into contact with reality both in thought and in action. To be sure, Maritain stressed in his maturity that being is not a concept, but rather an act exercised by a subject. This is precisely the intuition that permitted him to be both a metaphysician and an activist.

In "Maritain, Ratzinger, and the New Era of Intellectual Culture," John Deely, a philosopher who has written much in the area of semiotics, argues that scholars of Maritain's work have typically neglected the importance of signs for his metaphysical thought. The question that opens his essay is Maritain's musings on the point of unity between epistemology and metaphysics, or, in other words, what could bridge the divide between the philosophy of mind and the philosophy of being. Deely claims by echoing the words of Joseph Cardinal Ratzinger—Pope Benedict XVI—that the age when the notion of substance was considered the fundamental category of reality has expired. What is as fundamental as substance is the sign. John Poinsot—otherwise known as John of St. Thomas—was an early modern thinker who developed a theory of signs that exercised an enormous influence on Maritain. According to Deely, epistemology and ontology come together under the dominion of the sign. In this sense, semiotics offers a more encompassing vision of reality than a traditional metaphysics, which is anchored in the doctrine of substance. As Deely himself expresses it: "the *whole* of our awareness depends upon signs."

The fourth and final section of this present volume is entitled "The Scope of Science." It deals with topics that lie at the intersection of philosophy and theology with science. Jean de Groot's paper, "Distinguishing Between Natural Philosophy and Science: The Case of Ancient Mechanics," evaluates Maritain's claim that an unbridgeable divide exists between modern experimental science and the philosophy of nature, particularly as developed and practiced by Aristotle. De Groot wishes to argue that Maritain's judgment is too harsh in this regard. In fact, in her essay, de Groot attempts to show the lines of continuity between the ancient philosophy of nature and modern science. She does this by discussing how Aristotle developed his notion of *dunamis* (power, potentiality) from his observations of the mechanism involved in a lever. *Dunamis*, according to de Groot's account, incorporates both a receptivity (passive power) and an activity (active power). The concept of *rhopê* (force, impetus) is presented as a contrast to *dunamis*. By latching onto the concept of *rhopê* at the expense of *dunamis*, practitioners of science paved the way for the gradual disappearance of the ontological understandings enshrined in the latter term, which were replaced by a more entitative interpretation of nature as represented by the former term. In this way, de Groot convincingly illustrates the transition that happened in the West from the philosophy of nature to modern experimental science, a movement which Maritain discusses at some length in *The Degrees of Knowledge.*

The final essay in the collection is by Peter A. Pagan and bears the title "Faith, Physical Determinism and Scientific Method." This paper deals principally with the limits of science and the value that philosophy offers for scientific research. Pagan sets up the paper by introducing some of the views of the American physicist Stephen M. Barr, who asserts that science is not restricted only to the sensible world, but can go beyond it. An aspect of Barr's position that Pagan contests is the rejection of a physically deterministic understanding of the universe and the embrace of the Heisenberg indeterminacy principle at the centre of the Copenhagen interpretation of quantum mechanics. In short, according to Pagan, Barr maintains that only the

Copenhagen interpretation and the concomitant rejection of physical determinism is compatible with Biblical faith. At issue in this discussion is the view that classical determinism rides roughshod over free will and that the denial of free will is simply at variance with the Christian understanding of reality. Pagan believes that Barr's scientific pretensions go too far. For Pagan, a proper understanding of physical determinism, grounded in an Aristotelian-Thomistic theory of causality, rather than a mechanistic or Humean one, is more than compatible with Christianity. Miracles are a good illustration of this: miracles are premised on the idea that violations of physical laws happen, and, even when they occur, that physical laws remain in place. The main problem here, according to Pagan, is that science, although well intentioned, often neglects to be properly informed and guided by philosophical principles. And that is a lesson that all scientists should heed!

This present volume brings together a wide variety of topics and perspectives, from the nature of intellect and knowledge to philosophy's ability to prove God's existence to the relationship of social justice and science to the metaphysical domain. Despite this plurality of voices, there is a unified and concerted attempt throughout to grasp the nature of reality in its unadulterated being. Some thinkers have suggested that metaphysics and belief in a supersensible reality have disappeared with Nietzsche's proclamation of the death of God. Others, such as Bertrand Russell, A. J. Ayer, and W. V. O. Quine, have advocated the view that science has replaced philosophy in the modern age because of its ability to provide reliable, empirical knowledge, whereas philosophy endlessly dawdles in inconclusive theorizing. It is unmistakable that philosophy and metaphysics have received a "bum rap" over the last century and that many philosophers and non-philosophers alike have lost their confidence in the power of thought to penetrate to the truth of things. What the essays in this collection have hopefully demonstrated is that, contrary to all this misleading and confused rhetoric, metaphysical thinking is alive and well in the 21st-century and continues to generate insights into the very nature, structure, and purpose of reality. But what is more, the *perennial philosophy*, the thoughts of the ancient Greeks and the medieval Schoolmen, still has the power to awaken a dormant mind to lofty reflections on being itself. The skeptics have neglected the indomitable restlessness of the human spirit that is the root and animus of the search for truth. And the modern mind, which has conformed to the deleterious principles of epistemological idealism, has lost the sense of the mystery and grandeur of the things of the world that nurture and sustains metaphysical thinking. Truly, if reality is based upon God's creative act, then metaphysics is born of a certain disposition of gratitude towards the world, receiving all things as gifts, a reverential attitude evoked splendidly by the modern poet W. B. Yeats in these uplifting words:

> When such as I cast out remorse
> So great a sweetness flows into the breast
> We must laugh and we must sing,
> We are blest by everything,
> Everything we look upon is blest.[21]

---

21 W. B. Yeats, "A Dialogue of Self and Soul," in *Selected Poetry*, ed. A. Norman Jeffares (London: Pan Books, 1962), 145.

# PART I
## FOUNDATIONS OF ARISTOTELIAN–THOMISTIC METAPHYSICS

# Why the Senses Cannot Have Truth: The Need for Abstraction

Steven J. Jensen

Thomas Aquinas maintains that truth is not found formally in the senses but only in the intellect.[1] If by truth we mean merely the conformity of the mind to the reality known, then the senses do possess truth, as when the sense of sight perceives the color black as it actually is. In general, says Aquinas, the senses correctly perceive their proper object, so that the sense of sight perceives colors, the sense of hearing sounds, and so on. The senses often err, on the other hand, for common sensibles, such as shape, perceiving them as they are not. When viewed from an angle, for instance, a circle is perceived as an ellipse.

If the senses do conform to reality, even if only for the proper sensibles, then why reserve truth to the intellect? Because, says Aquinas, truth is formally realized and completed only by becoming aware of one's conformity to reality.[2] While the perception of the color black truly corresponds to black in things, the senses are not aware of this correspondence. Only the intellect attains such awareness. Indeed, the intellect itself attains it only in its second act, the act of composing and dividing, and not in the first act of simple apprehension. When the intellect grasps the nature of the color black, then it has a correspondence with reality, but it does not yet recognize this correspondence. Only when it makes a judgment, such as, "The bird is black," does it formally attain truth through an awareness of conformity with the thing known. We do not say, after all, that the word "black" is true or false, but we do say that the sentence "The bird is black" is true or false.

---

[1] St. Thomas explicitly addresses this issue in *De Veritate* q. 1, a. 9 & a. 11; I, q. 17. a. 2; he refers to it in I *Sent.*, d. 19, q. 5, a. 1 ad 6 ; I, q. 16, a. 2; I *Peri Hermeneias*, l. 3, n. 9.

[2] See I, q. 16, a. 2; *De Veritate* q. 1, a. 3 & a. 9; I *Sent.*, d. 19, q. 5, a. 1 ad 7; I *Peri Hermeneias*, l. 3, n. 6; VI Metaphysicae, l. 4.

## I. SECOND ORDER TRUTH

One way to imagine the awareness of conformity is to picture the intellect viewing its own act of understanding, laying it up against the reality known, and comparing the two for similarities. When it perceives that its own action is similar to the reality, then it attains to truth most formally, for it is aware of its own correspondence to the reality. In the same way, we might place a portrait of an individual near to the individual and then compare the two, looking for similarities or dissimilarities. If it is similar, then we say it is a true representation.

Such seems to be our procedure when we are presented with a questionable proposition. When it is suggested, for instance, that "The butler did it," we might consider what it means for the butler to kill, and then consider the reality of the matter, trying to discern whether he really did kill. When we come to the conclusion that the reality of the matter did involve the butler killing, then we recognize that the proposition with this meaning corresponds to the reality, and so we declare the proposition true.

Such declarations of truth involve what Maritain called, following Cajetan, a reflective awareness of conformity *in actu signato*, a kind of stepping back and looking at our own acts of knowing. The contrast is to a reflective awareness *in actu exercito*, which is an immediate awareness of our own awareness.[3] In the latter, we are aware of a black bird, and by the very same act we are aware of our awareness; the direct object of our thought is the bird, but, by being aware of the bird, we also become aware of our awareness. In the former, we form a new idea, a conception of our conception, whose direct object is our act of knowing.[4] Because we have become aware of our act of understanding *in actu exercito*, we can make that act of understanding the object of a new conception, a conception that bears upon our own act of understanding, discerning its nature and properties. Such is the work of logic, which reflects upon so-called second intentions; that is, it reflects upon things as they are in our understanding.

---

[3] Jacques Maritain, *Distinguish to Unite or the Degrees of Knowledge*, trans. Gerald B. Phelan (Geoffrey Bles: London, 1959), 89, n. 1.

[4] Maritain, *Degrees*, 89, n. 1 and 394.

Truth and falsity are certainly a central focus of logic, which lays out propositions as objects to be examined. Similarly, we consider the truth of the proposition "The butler did it," by examining it *in actu signato*. We step back and form a conception of the proposition, then consider whether the proposition corresponds with the reality. In such judgments, the proposition itself becomes the subject of another proposition. "The butler did it" becomes the subject of the larger proposition " 'the butler did it' is true" in which the predicate "is true" simply means that the proposition corresponds to reality. Indeed, if we adopt the convention of calling first acts of understanding "concepts" and second acts of understanding "propositions," then it becomes plain that we must form a concept of a proposition. We have a simple act of understanding whose object is the judgment "The butler did it," and which we can in turn pass judgment upon, predicating of it various attributes, such as its being true, false, a complete thought, and so on.

We conceive the proposition, of course, as a mental act referring to a certain state of affairs, the state of the butler killing. The proposition turns out to be true, then, just so long as this state actually is the case. In other words, we must first judge that the butler actually did kill before we can judge that it is true that the butler killed.

When Aquinas states that we become aware of the conformity between our mental acts and reality only in the second act of the intellect, he might mean that only in the second act do we reflect *in actu signato* upon the relationship between our acts of understanding and the thing known. Only then do we step back and form an idea of our idea, comparing it to the reality it represents. Such seems to be a plausible interpretation of Aquinas's explanation, in the *De Veritate*, why the senses do not have truth. He explicitly acknowledges that even the senses have a self-reflective awareness of their own awareness. What distinguishes the intellect, he claims, is the ability to comprehend the nature of its own actions, thereby allowing it to compare its actions as conforming or not to reality.

> Truth is in the intellect...as known by the intellect...but it is known by the intellect insofar as the intellect reflects upon its own act, not simply insofar as it knows its own act but insofar as it knows its relation to reality, which cannot be known unless the nature of its very actions are known. This nature, in turn, cannot be known unless the nature of the active principle is known,

> which is the intellect itself, whose nature is to conform to things. In this manner, the intellect, which reflects upon itself, knows the truth.[5]

Such comprehension of its own actions fits well the description of reflection *in actu signato*. It would follow, then, that the senses have a reflective knowledge *in actu exercito* but not *in actu signato*. While viewing a bird, there is a kind of awareness of the viewing, but no conception of what it means to view, no second-order analysis of the act of seeing. Consequently, the senses cannot consider whether their actions conform to the reality. The senses cannot make their own actions the direct object of consideration, so as to recognize their various attributes, such as their conformity to reality. For convenience, let us call this reading of Aquinas the second order view of truth.[6]

## II. THOUGHT BEARING ON REALITY

Maritain rejects this interpretation of truth, with good reason.[7] He acknowledges that we can become aware of the conformity between our mind and reality *in actu signato*, but he denies that truth is found only in such judgments. The truth is found also through reflection *in*

---

[5] Aquinas, *De Veritate* q. 1, a. 9: "Dicendum, quod veritas est in intellectu et in sensu, sed non eodem modo. In intellectu enim est sicut consequens actum intellectus, et sicut cognita per intellectum. Consequitur namque intellectus operationem, secundum quod iudicium intellectus est de re secundum quod est. Cognoscitur autem ab intellectu secundum quod intellectus reflectitur supra actum suum, non solum secundum quod cognoscit actum suum, sed secundum quod cognoscit proportionem eius ad rem: quae quidem cognosci non potest nisi cognita natura ipsius actus; quae cognosci non potest, nisi natura principii activi cognoscatur, quod est ipse intellectus, in cuius natura est ut rebus conformetur; unde secundum hoc cognoscit veritatem intellectus quod supra seipsum reflectitur."

[6] Francis M. Tyrrell seems to hold this position in his "Concerning the Nature and Function of the Act of Judgment," *The New Scholasticism* 26 (1952), 393-423; for he claims that the second act of the intellect is primarily an act of reflecting and only secondarily an act directed to reality (398, 402), but then he explicitly rejects the view (404).

[7] As does John Wippel in "Truth in Thomas Aquinas: Part 2," *Review of Metaphysics* 43 (1990): 543-67, at 562-63.

*actu exercito*.[8] Without stepping back and forming a conception of our own ideas, we can become aware of the conformity between our understanding and reality. In the very act of judging "The bird is black" we become aware of the conformity between the idea and the thing known. We need not go on to form, *in actu signato*, a further judgment that " 'the bird is black' is true." Indeed, only through the prior awareness, *in actu exercito*, of some propositions conforming to reality can we go on explicitly to ask, *in actu signato*, whether a given proposition conforms to reality.

If truth were found only in explicit truth judgments, in judgments containing the predicate "is true," then most of our judgments would not attain truth, any more than do the senses, since usually we do not make such second-order judgments. We judge that "the butler killed" not that " 'the butler killed' is true;" we judge that "The bird is black," not that " 'the bird is black' is true." We do not usually pass judgment upon the conformity of our acts of understanding to reality; we pass judgment upon that which the proposition addresses, determining whether this predicate applies to this subject. Indeed, even second-order judgments consider whether conformity, expressed by the predicate "is true," applies to a certain proposition, the proposition being conceived as a reality known.

The second order view reserves truth and falsity not to the second act of the intellect but to a particular subset of second acts, to those in which we directly judge the conformity of our mind to reality. We are left to draw the absurd conclusion that the very propositions we judge to be true are not true most formally. They are no more true than simple acts of apprehension, such as our understanding of the color black, to which we can also apply the predicate "is true," for we recognize the correspondence between the concept and reality. They are no more true than the senses; for we can also judge that the senses conform to reality. Admittedly, it is not the senses themselves that recognize the conformity, but neither, on this interpretation, do we recognize, *in actu exercito*, the conformity of our second acts to reality. On this reading, there is no good reason for saying that propositions can be true but concepts cannot. "The bird is black" can be true or false, but "black" can be neither. Why? Both of them can conform to

---

[8] Maritain, *Degrees*, 97, n. 2.

reality; neither of them–on this reading–recognizes its own conformity. The conformity is always recognized in a second-order judgment upon the idea itself.

We must seek to discover, then, in what way the intellect can recognize its own conformity to reality *in actu exercito*. We must show how the intellect, while directly passing judgment upon something else, becomes aware of its own conformity. While judging that "The bird is black," we become aware that our conception of the bird being black conforms to reality. Since the senses also have a reflective awareness of their own awareness, we must show in what way the intellect's awareness, in its second act, is distinct from the self-awareness of the senses. The option of turning to a reflective awareness *in actu signato* is excluded. We cannot consider those cases in which the mind gazes upon the content of its own act as a direct object of knowledge; we must consider those cases in which the mind gazes directly upon some external reality. We cannot consider the case in which the mind contemplates the proposition "The bird is black" wondering whether it is true; we must consider the case in which the mind contemplates the bird, relating it to the attribute of being black. We are left, in short, with a reflective awareness *in actu exercito*, an awareness possessed also by the senses. The senses, however, must lack something found in the intellect.

## III. WHAT IS PROPER TO THE INTELLECT

Aquinas provides few clues indicating what is distinctive of the intellect's reflective awareness, but he does say that only in the second act of the intellect does the mind have something of its own, proper to it but not to the reality known. When the act of knowing is in all ways similar to the reality, then no comparison can be made between the two, but when the two are similar and yet distinct, then a comparison can be made.

> The notion of truth consists in a conformity [adaequatio] of the thing and the intellect. The very same thing, however, does not conform to itself; rather, a conformity is of diverse things. It follows that the formality of truth is found in the intellect first where the intellect first begins to have something proper to itself, something which the reality outside the mind does not have. Nevertheless, this external reality, having something

corresponding to the intellect, can then be taken to conform to the mind. When the intellect forms the quiddity of things, it has only a likeness of the thing existing outside the mind, even as do the senses when they receive a sensible likeness. But when the intellect begins to pass judgment upon the reality understood, then, this very judgment of the intellect is something proper to it, something not found in the external reality.[9]

Only in combining and dividing, then, do we find a significant difference, allowing us to compare our understanding to the reality. Neither the first act of the intellect nor the senses, says Aquinas, has anything additional beyond what is found in the reality known. The act of judging, however, provides something additional.

A likely candidate for the element proper to judgment is the combination of two concepts, for Aquinas says that even what he calls a division, that is, a negative proposition, involves a psychological union of two concepts, although they refer to a separation in reality.[10] For instance, the proposition, "The bird is not white," brings together in the mind the concepts of "bird" and "white" although it does so only to signify that the two are separate in reality. Perhaps this union of

---

[9] Aquinas, *De Veritate* q. 1, a. 3: "Veri enim ratio consistit in adaequatione rei et intellectus; idem autem non adaequatur sibi ipsi, sed aequalitas diversorum est; unde ibi primo invenitur ratio veritatis in intellectu ubi primo intellectus incipit aliquid proprium habere quod res extra animam non habet, sed aliquid ei correspondens, inter quae adaequatio attendi potest. Intellectus autem formans quidditatem rerum, non habet nisi similitudinem rei existentis extra animam, sicut et sensus in quantum accipit speciem sensibilis; sed quando incipit iudicare de re apprehensa, tunc ipsum iudicium intellectus est quoddam proprium ei, quod non invenitur extra in re." It is difficult to translate adaequatio. It has the notion of a conforming or a making equal. Elsewhere, however, he uses the word conformitas (e.g., I, q. 16, a 2). Since Aquinas grants that conformitas can be found between the first act of the intellect and reality while he states here that adaequatio cannot, it may be that "conformity" is too weak of a translation. A sense of making to conform or recognizing a conformity might be needed. We might distinguish between two senses of conformity, one which merely has similarity, perhaps exact likeness, the other which involves a difference that contains a similarity.

[10] Aquinas, I *Peri Hermeneias*, l. 3, n. 4

concepts is the distinctive feature that allows the intellect to make a comparison with reality.

Unfortunately, a sort of union can be found in the first act of the intellect and even in the senses. We can take the concepts "bird" and "black" and unite them into a new concept "black bird." This new concept, although a kind of union of two simpler ideas, is not susceptible of truth, as is the proposition "The bird is black," for we would not say that the combination "black bird" is either true or false. It simply signifies a reality. That which is signified and the reality are one and the same. No comparison between the two is possible.

In a similar manner we can bring together in the imagination the image of the bird and the color black; conversely, we can join the image of the bird with some other color, such as white. These images unite diverse features, and yet we would not call them true or false. The mere union of ideas, then, cannot explain the uniqueness of combining and dividing. What is distinctive of the second act is not a psychological union, says Aquinas, but the very judgment, the very predication of one thing to another.

## IV. ABSTRACTION

Since a proposition contains both a subject and a predicate, it might be seen as referring to two objects, for instance, both to a bird and to the color black. In contrast, the combination "black bird" refers to two features melded into a single object.[11] In the proposition, the two are kept distinct, although one is applied to the other. That which the concept "black" signifies is applied to that which the concept "bird" signifies. A proposition, then, signifies two objects, but in reality there is only one thing. In other words, what is distinctive in the union of a proposition is that the elements remain in some sense separate, each signifying its proper object, but they are united through an application of one to the other.

While the complex concept "black bird" narrows the reference to just those birds that are black, the proposition "The bird is black," maintains the distinctive reference of the concept bird and, rather than narrowing it, provides additional information. We learn of "bird,"

---

[11] Maritain, *Degrees*, 395.

which has a distinctive reference of its own, that it is black. We learn of "black" that it applies to bird. In contrast, for the concept "black bird" we have a whole new complex nature or essence under consideration. We are not considering "bird" and know in addition that it is black; rather, we are considering "black bird." Such a consideration does not reveal whether bird is anything separate from black or black is separate from bird. The union here is too tight. Predication, on the other hand, considers two objects as separate, but one applying to the other. In other words, the element of combination and division that might allow self-reflective awareness of conformity is not its union, but the distinctiveness of its elements.

Maritain suggests as much in the title of his work, *Distinguishing in Order to Unite.* The union found in predication first distinguishes and then unites. The distinction that Maritain later identifies as essential to the second act is the abstraction carried out in the first act. In some way, the truth realized in the second act requires the abstraction of the first act. Simple apprehension, he says, prepares the mind for judgment.[12] Evidently, the second act, by joining two or more simple apprehensions, reconstructs the original unity within reality, a unity that was broken through abstraction: "The judgment restores to the transobjective subject the unity that simple apprehension (by laying hold of different objects of thought in it) has shattered. That unity could not hold precedence in the mind since, quite to the contrary, the mind undoes it only to reconstitute it afterwards."[13]

Through abstraction, we comprehend some form or feature by itself, apart from the conditions in which it exists. We can grasp "bird," for instance, apart from any particular colors it might have, apart from some particular size, or apart from any particular weight. Similarly, we can grasp the color "black," apart from its being realized in a bird or a dog or in any particular thing.[14] Even the senses have some measure of abstraction, since they know only a slice of a reality, for example, the sense of sight knows colors apart from sounds and odors, and so on.

---

[12] Maritain, *Degrees*, 98, n. 2.

[13] Maritain, *Degrees*, 98.

[14] Although, when conceived concretely, it is conceived as an existing thing, just not in this or that particular thing.

Nevertheless, the senses always know an object with its concrete conditions, in some concrete realization. In contrast, the intellect can know the color black apart from its concrete realizations. It knows the color black as it might exist under this condition, in a bird, or in some other condition, in a bear, or in any other possible condition. The sense of sight knows the color black apart from sounds, but it always knows the color black under this or that particular condition.

The combination involved with predication maintains this distinction, this abstraction, in a way that complex concepts such as "black bird" do not. In this concept, we are no longer considering a bird as a kind separate from color, for black has been incorporated into our concept. These complex concepts, then, do not reconstruct reality, but merely provide a different abstraction of reality. In contrast, propositions take the shattered reality and put it back together again, applying one piece to another.

Each of the elements is referred to, but as united or applied to one another. We are referring to "bird," but with "black" applied to it. We are referring to "black," but as applied to "bird." These two views of what is one in reality provide the perspective of truth. Just as two different visual perspectives provide the added dimension of depth, so the two formalities directed to the same reality provide the added dimension of truth.[15] Our understanding has the depth of truth because we perceive that which is a bird, as something coherent in itself, apart from being black, yet we see that this thing referred to is also black. The diverse references become united in something beyond themselves.

> In any true affirmative proposition, the predicate and subject must signify what is in some way the same in reality and diverse in formality, which is evident in propositions which have accidental predication as well as in those which predicate essentially. It is plain that "man" and "white" are in the same subject but differ in formality, for the notion of man is distinct from the notion of white. Similarly, when I say "Man is an

---

[15] Maritain (*Degrees*, 97, 395) says that the predicate and subject, which differ in notion, are identical in the thing; the two formalities are one within the object.

> animal," the very thing that is a man is truly an animal. In the very same supposit is found both sensible nature, from which it is called animal, and rational nature, from which it is called man. Therefore, the subject and predicate are the same in supposit but diverse in formality....To the diversity of formality corresponds a plurality of subject and predicate, while the intellect signifies the identity in reality through composition.[16]

A distinction must be drawn between the thing "out there" and the formality in which it is understood.[17] In reality, the bird is one thing with many features or aspects. In our knowledge, however, we know the bird piecemeal, abstracting this or that feature of it: for instance, we know it insofar as it is a bird or we know it insofar as it is black. What is one materially, as thing, is many formally, as object known. As Aquinas says, the subject and predicate refer to diverse formalities but to what is one in reality.

If all we know is "bird," then we have no notion that there is a difference between this formality that we know and the thing; if all we know is "black" then also we cannot perceive that there is a difference between this formality known and the thing. Only when we know both "bird" and "black," yet as united, do we perceive that there must be

---

[16] Aquinas, I, q. 13, a. 12: "In qualibet propositione affirmativa vera, oportet quod praedicatum et subiectum significent idem secundum rem aliquo modo, et diversum secundum rationem. Et hoc patet tam in propositionibus quae sunt de praedicato accidentali, quam in illis quae sunt de praedicato substantiali. Manifestum est enim quod homo et albus sunt idem subiecto, et differunt ratione, alia enim est ratio hominis, et alia ratio albi. Et similiter cum dico homo est animal, illud enim ipsum quod est homo, vere animal est; in eodem enim supposito est et natura sensibilis, a qua dicitur animal, et rationalis, a qua dicitur homo. Unde hic etiam praedicatum et subiectum sunt idem supposito, sed diversa ratione. Sed et in propositionibus in quibus idem praedicatur de seipso, hoc aliquo modo invenitur; inquantum intellectus id quod ponit ex parte subiecti, trahit ad partem suppositi, quod vero ponit ex parte praedicati, trahit ad naturam formae in supposito existentis, secundum quod dicitur quod praedicata tenentur formaliter, et subiecta materialiter. Huic vero diversitati quae est secundum rationem, respondet pluralitas praedicati et subiecti, identitatem vero rei significat intellectus per ipsam compositionem."

[17] Maritain, *Degrees*, 93.

more to the bird than just "bird" and more to the black thing than just "black." There must be some thing that is both "bird" and "black." The dual perspective of grasping "bird"–as distinct in itself–and "black"–also as distinct–yet realized in this one thing, provides the realization that the formality known is distinct from the thing.

In contrast, the complex concept "black bird" does not separate the thing from the formality known. Rather, a complex formality is now known. "Bird" and "black" are not known as two distinct formalities but as a single complex formality. Without the separation, the abstraction of one from the other, the mind does not recognize the thing beyond the formality. It gazes upon the nature as a simple unit, without anything additional coming to it. Or, says Aquinas, it is aware of the thing that has the nature;[18] in so doing, however, it knows nothing of the thing beyond its having the nature. Even the combined concept "black bird" does not consider bird as separate from black, requiring something beyond its meaning to bring in black; rather, it considers bird precisely as black. Similarly, when the imagination forms an image of a black bird, there is but a single complex formality known. Predication, on the other hand, keeps bird distinct but adds black onto it. Or, rather, it keeps the black thing distinct, and applies it to the thing that is a bird. When the world is not shattered into diverse formalities, then it cannot be seen as distinct from the formalities.

## V. PREDICATION

Abstraction itself, of course, cannot be that which is proper to the intellect, allowing it to perceive a conformity with reality, for abstraction is found in the first act. The judgment or predication itself, says Aquinas, is that which is distinctive of the intellect. Still, abstraction is necessary, in order to provide the two perspectives upon a single reality. Predication goes beyond abstraction, applying one

---

[18] See *Expositio De Hebdomadibus*, lect. 2: "Aliter autem se habet in his quae significantur in concreto. Nam homo significatur ut qui habet humanitatem, et album ut quod habet albedinem. Ex hoc autem quod homo habet humanitatem vel albedinem, non prohibetur habere aliquid aliud, quod non pertinet ad rationem horum, nisi solum quod est oppositum his: et ideo homo et album possunt aliquid aliud habere quam humanitatem vel albedinem."

thing to another. It is this application that is distinctive of the intellect. We must not suppose, however, that the psychological act of understanding is itself the something distinctive, for all acts of understanding, whether first or second, are quite distinct from the object known. Aquinas cautions us against looking for a conformity between the psychological act of the intellect and the reality. Rather, we must look for a conformity between reality and that which the intellect says.

> The truth of the intellect is a conformity between the intellect and reality, insofar as the intellect says to be what is or not to be what is not; therefore, the truth pertains to that which (in the intellect) is said, not to the operation by which it is said. The intellect is not determined to the truth such that the very act of understanding is conformed to the reality, since the reality is sometimes material while the understanding is immaterial. Rather, that which the intellect says and knows in its act of understanding must be conformed to the reality, so that things are such in reality as the intellect says.[19]

We must distinguish, then, between the act of understanding and that which it says or signifies. The act of understanding a bird is one thing; what it refers to is another, namely, a bird. We will be sorely disappointed if we seek a conformity between a bird and our act of understanding a bird, for the one is material and the other immaterial. What we should seek, rather, is a conformity between the bird and what we understand or assert of it, for although our understanding is immaterial, it means or signifies something material.[20]

---

[19] Aquinas, *Summa Contra Gentiles*, 59, n. 2: "Cum enim veritas intellectus sit adaequatio intellectus et rei, secundum quod intellectus dicit esse quod est vel non esse quod non est, ad illud in intellectu veritas pertinet quod intellectus dicit, non ad operationem qua illud dicit. Non enim ad veritatem intellectus exigitur ut ipsum intelligere rei aequetur, cum res interdum sit materialis, intelligere vero immateriale: sed illud quod intellectus intelligendo dicit et cognoscit, oportet esse rei aequatum, ut scilicet ita sit in re sicut intellectus dicit."

[20] Maritain (*Degrees*, 392) says concepts differ from reality according to *esse in*, that is, insofar as they exist in the mind, not according to *esse ad*, that is, according to their intentional content or meaning.

Any conformity involves a comparison between two things. We must drop the supposition that the conformity of truth is between an act of the mind and some reality, as if we view our act of mind and then we view the reality, comparing the two as similar to one another. Rather, says Aquinas, truth involves a conformity between what the intellect knows or says and some reality. Little wonder, then, that the full sense of conformity is lacking for the first act of the intellect. In this simple act of understanding, the intellect grasps some feature of reality. That which the mind knows *just is* this feature. There are not two things here, one of which may be said to be similar to the other. There is only one thing: that which the intellect knows, which is also some reality. Even a complex concept, such as "black bird," involves only one thing known.

The second act of the intellect, on the other hand, gives us a subject and predicate, two things that now can be compared with one another. It does not compare them, however, according to their formal notions, as if it were considering the similarities and differences between the nature of bird and the nature of black, the way we might compare birds and mammals. Rather, it compares the application of one to the other, and this very application is a construct or activity of the mind. We have something *of the mind*, not so much *in the mind*, that can be compared to the reality, namely, the saying of one thing of another. The saying "is black" is compared to the reality of the bird, which is known through the subject, and found to be in conformity. We are aware, then, that what we say conforms to the reality.

Abstraction allows this comparison, in part, because the subject and predicate have distinct content, so that what is known as black is distinct from what is known as bird, and yet they are perceived to coincide. They are different yet one, so there must be something beyond these formalities by which they are united, some reality beyond what is known in abstraction. More profoundly, perhaps, abstraction allows this comparison because it frees our knowledge from the material conditions of things. With our senses, we must always know things as bound to the singular. Our senses cannot free up the quality "black" so that it can be applied to something else, such as a bird. Even our imagination knows the quality black as concrete, and if it first imagines a black square and then a black bird, it has not applied the first image of black to a second image of bird, but has rather formed a new concrete image of black in the shape of bird. With our intellect, on the other hand, we can separate out "black," knowing it apart from the concrete conditions of existing in this bird or in that cat; consequently, we are free to apply "black" to diverse subjects, for the conception of it is not bound to this or that subject.

Without abstraction, then, there could be no predication. We could not know two objects as distinct, and we could not take one object and apply it to another. This application is something peculiar to the mind; it signifies a union not found in the bare formality of the subject. The predicate "is black," for instance, when applied to "bird" signifies a union, but the very idea of a bird does not contain this notion. We are able, then, to compare this application, this saying of the moment, to the reality; when we perceive conformity, then we have the truth.

The judgment we pass is upon some reality, for example, upon a bird that is black. We are not judging that our act of mind conforms to reality; this we do only *in actu signato. In actu exercito* we pass judgment upon things such as birds. When we judge, however, that black applies to bird, we are judging that that which we say, this union or application known in the predicate, corresponds to the reality as known in the subject. No comparison, nor even any saying, could be made without abstraction.

The senses, forever bound to concrete realizations, are unable to apply one thing known to another. All they perceive is in the concrete, unable to be lifted and applied to another. Even though the senses grasp the world in slices, they cannot pull the world apart, freeing one slice to unite it with another. The senses can never take one reality and lay it against another, knowing them as distinct yet united. What the senses know, then, does indeed conform to reality, but the senses can never recognize this conformity. They always know the reality they dwell upon, but never know something about it to compare with another.

## VI. SELF-AWARENESS

The intellect is aware that what it says corresponds to reality. Prior to combining and dividing the mind does not recognize a difference between the reality known and the thing in reality, for the simple reason that there is no difference; the first act of the intellect can refer to an object under only one formality, even if it is a complex formality.

When diverse formalities signified converge upon one thing, however, then we become aware of a difference. We can also become aware that, despite this difference, there is correspondence. Truth and falsity may now be found in that which is signified by the mind. To judge that the reality is so is also to become aware that the proposition that refers to this reality conforms to it.

> [The second act of] the intellect can know the relation of conformity, so that in it alone can truth be known. Therefore, the philosopher says in book vi of the *Metaphysics* that the truth–in the sense of becoming aware of the truth–is only in the mind. To know this relation of conformity is nothing other than to judge that something is so or not so in reality, which is to compose and divide. Therefore, the intellect knows the truth only by composing and dividing in its judgment, which is itself true if it conforms to reality, as when the intellect judges to be what really is or not to be what is not.[21]

The senses can attain none of this. While they have a kind of self-awareness, a kind of consciousness, they are not aware that their actions are about some reality. They do not recognize anything distinct from what they grasp. As such, they cannot sort out the object they know from the thing in reality. In no way, then, are they aware of any conformity between the object of their awareness and some reality beyond their actions.

What makes all of this possible to the intellect is the power of abstraction. The senses always know concrete individual things and are

---

[21] Aquinas, I *Peri Hermeneias*, l. 3, n. 9: "Intellectus autem potest huiusmodi habitudinem conformitatis cognoscere; et ideo solus intellectus potest cognoscere veritatem. Unde et philosophus dicit in VI *Metaphysicae* quod veritas est solum in mente, sicut scilicet in cognoscente veritatem. Cognoscere autem praedictam conformitatis habitudinem nihil est aliud quam iudicare ita esse in re vel non esse: quod est componere et dividere; et ideo intellectus non cognoscit veritatem, nisi componendo vel dividendo per suum iudicium. Quod quidem iudicium, si consonet rebus, erit verum, puta cum intellectus iudicat rem esse quod est, vel non esse quod non est. Falsum autem quando dissonat a re, puta cum iudicat non esse quod est, vel esse quod non est."

unable to separate out one aspect of a thing from another.[22] They grasp a black bird as a single whole, without identifying its being black as distinct from its being a bird. "Black," therefore, cannot be said of "bird," for there is no separate awareness of black to be said of anything.

In contrast, the intellect distinguishes the color black from being a bird. Since it does not belong to the notion of a bird that it be black and it does not belong to the notion of the color black that it be a bird, these two are truly known distinctly. If a bird should be black, then, it can only be on account of something beyond what is known in bird, only because the bird is more than just bird. It must not merely be such; it must also be. Only because "bird" is distinct from "black" can one be said of another. Without separation, there is no application of one thing to another, for there is only one thing. This very application of one thing to another, however, is not found in reality, where various features of reality simply exist together. We find a bird that is black, not black being applied to a bird. Abstraction, then, allows the intellect to perceive its own distinct "saying" or application. The mind asserts something about reality; when the reality, known in the subject, is such, then the mind is in conformity.[23]

As we are self-reflectively aware of our knowledge that the bird is black, we are also aware that we have asserted black of the bird. We are aware of something in our thought not found in the reality. Prior to this point, our thought has always focused on the reality. A knowledge of "bird" or black" is a knowledge of things, not of our awareness of things. Now, however, while still focusing upon the reality, such as the bird being black, our self-awareness might be better called *self-consciousness*, a distinct recognition of our minds as different, not simply as present, but as unique and active.

---

[22] Except that their proper objects are limited, for example, sight knows colors while hearing knows sounds. Because the proper object of imagination is the sensible as absent, it must "abstract" from both time and place.

[23] As Patrick Lee argues in his "Aquinas on Knowledge of Truth and Existence" (*New Scholasticism* 60 [1986]: 46-71, at 65-67), the second act of the intellect makes an assertion of one thing to another, becomes aware of some distinct existence, and recognizes its own conformity, all in a single act.

The life of the senses divorced from reason is rather flat. Objects present themselves, animals are aware of them and respond. While they are conscious of objects, they do not clearly distinguish the object from their awareness of them. While they know realities, they do not know them precisely as realities. They can be familiar with objects from past experience, but they cannot assert that one object *is* something else. Faced with a Humean stream of perceptions, they can react, but they cannot ask whether anything is true. Like Hume, they cannot even know their own minds, for they perceive nothing distinctive of their minds.[24] While they have a self-reflective awareness of their own awareness, they cannot step back, *in actu signato* and consider the nature of their thoughts. Whatever notion they might have of themselves, if any, is not of a mind self-aware of other realities.

Reason's power to abstract, then, opens the doorway to truth. It distinguishes so that it might then unite. Pulling the world apart into abstract formalities, it is then able to put the world together again through assertions of one thing to another. The fragmentation of the world is a prerequisite to recognize the world around us.

[24] Maritain (*Degrees*, 89, n. 1) states that only in judging do we have reflective knowledge of our existence.

# Form, Essence, Soul: Distinguishing Principles of Thomistic Metaphysics

Joshua P. Hochschild

## I. INTRODUCTION

What is the difference between the substantial form, the essence, and the soul of a living material substance? Each of these three items would normally be considered in a course in Thomistic philosophy. In my experience, there reaches a point where students begin to wonder how these terms are related and even whether it is necessary to describe the metaphysical principles of things in so many different ways. I have found it useful, for my own understanding and my teaching, to exploit, even to foster, some potential confusions precisely in order to focus on them, and in the process illuminate certain distinctions and insights in Thomistic philosophy.

## II. CONFUSIONS

Presentations of Thomistic metaphysics can tend to present the substantial form, essence, and soul as if they are basically the same thing. Aquinas himself, after all, sometimes treats "form" as synonymous with "essence,"[1] and they seem to serve the same basic metaphysical task: both are causes not only of a thing's being the kind of thing it is, but of its just being.[2] And, as causes, the causality exercised by both the essence and the form is *formal*, not material or efficient.[3] As for the soul, Aquinas of course adopts its Aristotelian

---

[1] Aquinas, *De Ente et Essentia*, ch. 1: "Dicitur etiam forma secundum quod per formam significatur certitudo uniuscuiusque rei, ut dicit Avicenna in II Metaphysicae suae."

[2] Aquinas, *De Ente et Essentia*, ch. 1: "Et hoc est quod Philosophus frequenter nominat quod quid erat esse, id est hoc per quod aliquid habet esse quid." *De Principiis Naturae*, ch. 1: "omne a quo aliquid habet esse, quodcumque esse sit sive substantiale, sive accidentale, potest dici forma."

[3] D.Q. McInerny treats essence and substantial form as the same in his *Metaphysics* (Priestly Fraternity of St. Peter, 2004), 219-20, 237.

definition as the form of (a certain kind of) a body, i.e. as that kind of body's substantial form. He even says, on at least one occasion, that the soul can be called the essence (or the *quod quid erat esse*) of the body.[4] So, surely, one might be forgiven for beginning to treat "essence," "substantial form," and "soul" as different words for the same metaphysical principle. The words may not be synonymous, but perhaps they are co-extensional, picking out the same item but in virtue of different connotations: we talk about a *substantial form* when we want to emphasize the natural philosopher's contrast between form and matter; of *essence* when we want to emphasize the common whatness or quiddity of something, or else when we want to talk about the famed Thomistic real distinction between *esse* and *essentia* in created beings; and we speak of the *soul* when we are considering living things as living things—explaining either their various powers as living things or their very life itself.

On the other hand, it is not very difficult to show that these three cannot be identified, that as metaphysical principles they play different roles that should not be confused. For consider the following metaphysical equations, each describing in different ways the compositionality[5] of an individual living material substance, such as Socrates, and each well attested in the works of Aquinas:

> (1) Socrates is a composite of a *substantial form* and *prime matter.*
>
> (2) Socrates is a composite of an *essence* and some *designated matter.*

---

[4] Aquinas, *In Metaph.* Bk. 7, lect. 10 (§1484): "Corpus enim organicum non potest definiri nisi per animam. Et secundum hoc *anima dicitur quod quid erat esse* tali corpori."

[5] Note that these "compositions" are not to be thought of as the mixing together of material elements, or the incidental joining of components that have independent existence in their own right. A consistent emphasis in Aquinas is that a material substance, like Socrates, is really one substance, and so when we speak of Socrates as a composite we are distinguishing in him metaphysical principles which are "parts" of Socrates in the sense that they are not identical with Socrates and they are not beings in their own right, but taken in combination they can be said to constitute the really one substantial whole.

(3) Socrates is a composite of a *soul* and a *body*.

Now, given the metaphysical equations listed here, it should be quite clear that in referring to Socrates' substantial form, soul, and essence we are not referring to exactly the same things. For each of these is said to constitute Socrates together with respective, complementary, metaphysical principles that are not identical with each other: *prime matter*, which is matter in pure potentiality, lacking any actuality, is not the same as *designated matter*, which is matter with some actuality, namely that actuality which determines it to particular dimensions; and neither prime matter nor designated matter is the same as the relevant *body* which is composed with the soul; for that body is not prime matter, and it has even more actuality than designated matter, enough actuality to make it "an organized body having life potentially in it." But then, if prime matter, designated matter, and an organized body capable of life are clearly distinct, then the three principles with which they respectively compose the same one substance cannot be identical.

## III. FURTHER CONFUSIONS

One proposal for making sense of a difference between essence and substantial form would describe the essence as universal or specific and the substantial form as individual or particular. But will this do? The essence or nature or quiddity, considered absolutely or according to its proper *ratio*, abstracts from existence in particular individuals (but this also is not the universal, as Aquinas famously makes clear in *De Ente et Essentia*, ch. 4). The essence or nature or quiddity can also be considered insofar as it has being in individuals, but in this case it is multiplied–the quiddity as it has *esse* in Socrates is only specifically the same, but remains numerically distinct, from the quiddity as it has *esse* in Plato. (This is why it sometimes seems appropriate to speak of "individual" essences or "individualized" essences, or singular or particular essences, although this is controversial.[6]) Likewise, substantial forms can be spoken of as numerically distinct actualities in individual things; but by abstracting from their individual determinations in individual things, we can speak of a common form—e.g. the substantial form of

[6] Cf. Joshua P. Hochschild, "Kenny and Aquinas on Individual Essences," *Proceedings of the Society for Medieval Logic and Metaphysics* 6 (2006): 45-56.

man common to Socrates and Plato and all other human beings—as specifically one, that is, in a sense as "universal." So it does not seem that we can distinguish essence and substantial form just as universal vs. particular.

Nor can we distinguish form from essence simply by availing ourselves of Aquinas's point that essence includes both form and matter.[7] After all, Aquinas says essence only includes "undesignated" or "common" matter. *Designated* or determinate matter is the principle of individuation; the *undesignated* "matter" that we are including in the essence—because it is formulated as part of the definition of the thing—is, as part of the essence, occupying the role of a formal principle.[8] The essence of man "includes matter" only insofar as we can't define man except as a *kind* of material thing; but then, doesn't *materiality* enter into the essence of man formally, as a part of the determination of the kind of thing a man is?[9] It seems that, proceeding up the Porphyrian tree, we simply spell out that man is a rational, sensitive, living, *material* substance. But if this is what is meant by the "universal" or "common" matter that is included in the essence of man "along with" the form, it is hard to see how this matter *adds* anything to the form. Especially given the thesis of the unicity of the substantial form, the form by which something is a material substance, made up of some kind of matter, must be that very form by which the material substance is the specific kind of material substance it is. If this is all that is meant

---

[7] The claim is sustained throughout Aquinas's career. See e.g. *De Ente et Essentia*, ch. 2 and *Summa Theologiae* I, q. 75, a. 4; the claim will be discussed further below.

[8] In the words of Fr. John Wippel, the essence is "the formal part" of that of which it is the essence. *The Metaphysical Thought of Thomas Aquinas* (Washington, D. C.: the Catholic University of America Press, 2000), 205.

[9] Jacques Maritain, *An Introduction to Philosophy* (New York: Sheed and Ward, 1935), 211, n. 3 (continued to 212): "This unindividuated or common matter [included in the essence of man], taken simply as receiving the form and determined by it, and not as the primary root of certain characters (the individual characters) of the subject, is made known to us by the form: *materia cognoscitur per formam, a qua sumitur ratio universalis* (St. Thomas, *loc cit.* [*In VII Metaph.*, lect. 10] Cf. *De Verit.*, q. 10, 1, 4 & 5), and is part of that which we have here termed the *immaterialized being* (*archetypal being*) or *formal being* of the thing (*forma totius, seu potius forma quae est totum*)."

by affirming that an essence of a material being "includes matter," it is hard to see how essence and substantial form differ at all.

As for the difference between substantial form and soul, this too seems problematic. As a good Aristotelian, Aquinas frequently invites us to identify the soul of a living material substance with its substantial form. But if we identify them with each other, why do we say that Socrates is composed of soul and *body*? Perhaps someone would argue that we should instead say that Socrates is composed of his soul and *prime matter*? After all, in calling the soul substantial form, Aquinas says that it is the form *of* the body. To say that does not imply that the soul is composed *with* the body; the soul as substantial form of the body could be composed *with* prime matter, thus producing the body *of* which it is the form. Given that such a body obviously must have a substantial form by virtue of which it is a body, and again, given the thesis of the unicity of substantial forms, this substantial form by which the body is a body must be the soul that has already been identified as its substantial form.[10] So, in referring to the body of which the soul is the form, we are referring to something that has that relevant form.[11] It is like when we refer to such-and-such a shape as the *form of the statue*. The statue is a statue because of the form, and we don't say that it is composed of form and statue; we say it is composed of form and, say, bronze.

But this line of argument is inadequate. Because, if we attend to what Aquinas says about soul and body, we have to admit that in addition to saying that the soul is the *form of* the body, he does say, quite clearly, that the individual living substance is *composed of* soul *and* body, as a whole is made from distinct parts. In *De Ente et Essentia* for instance, he says: "Man is said to be [composed] from soul and body, *as*

---

[10] Aquinas, *Quest. de Anima*, q. 9: "since a soul is a substantial form because it constitutes a human being in a determinate species of substance, there is no other substantial form intermediate between a soul and prime matter; but it is the soul itself which perfects a human being according to diverse levels of perfection, so that he is a body, and a living body, and a rational animal." Cf. *Summa Theologiae* I, q. 76 ad. 4.

[11] Frederick C. Copleston, *Aquinas* (Penguin, 1955), 155: "...to call the soul the form of the body is to say that the soul is what makes the body a human body."

*from two things some third thing is constituted* which is neither of those [two]; for a man is neither soul nor body."[12]

## IV. CLARIFICATIONS

To address the puzzle of how to understand the difference between substantial form, soul, and essence, I will proceed by considering each of these principles in their own right.

### 1. Socrates = substantial form + prime matter

The language of form comes from the context of natural philosophy and the analysis of change. Change involves matter—an underlying subject—receiving form. And because all physical things come to be, that is, are a result of change, each can be conceived as a composite of matter and form. Form is that by which something has being; it is the principle of actuality. What it actualizes, the principle of potentiality, is matter. In the case of accidental change, the form is an accidental form and what receives it or is actualized by it is something that already has some substantial being: it is a substance. In the case of substantial change, the underlying subject or matter that receives the form cannot already be a substance. In *De Principiis Naturae*, Aquinas first introduces that which is in potency to substantial being as matter *from which*, as opposed to matter *of which*—then simply as matter in its proper sense, as opposed to the looser sense of matter that includes the subject that is in potency to accidental being. Eventually, he introduces the notion of *prime matter*, that which is only in potency to being without any actuality of its own; only this can be the subject of the substantial form by which the individual substance comes to be. So, an individual material substance is said to be composed of substantial form and prime matter. Since the substantial form is the principle of all grades of actuality of the composite, the other, material, principle that it informs in itself has no actuality; it only has potency. That is why the material substance is said to be composed of substantial form and prime matter.

---

[12] Aquinas, *De Ente et Essentia*, ch. 2: "ex anima enim et corpore dicitur esse homo sicut ex duabus rebus quaedam res tertia constituta quae neutra illarum est, homo enim neque est anima neque corpus." Cf. *Summa Contra Gentiles* II, 69: "Non enim corpus et anima sunt duae substantiae actu existentes, sed ex eis duobus fit una substantia actu existens."

Notice, however, that there are different ways of signifying what something is, according to the different grades of actuality for which the substantial form is responsible. Socrates is a man, and he is an animal, and he is a body. In each case here, the predicates—"man," "animal," "body"—are substantial predicates; they speak of what Socrates is essentially, but with greater or lesser specificity. Indeed, we can even name the grades of actuality that these terms signify in Socrates—his humanity, his animality, his corporeity. We could even speak of each of these as distinct forms, but the distinction between them is merely rational, not real. That is the point of the thesis of the unicity of substantial forms already mentioned: there is not a plurality of substantial forms in a substance, one for each grade of substantial actuality; rather, the one substantial form of the substance communicates all grades of substantial actuality. So, while in *ratio* corporeity, animality, and humanity all differ, they are in reality all the same one substantial form, only conceived in different respects.

**2. Socrates = soul + body**

We speak of a soul in the context of that part of natural philosophy that seeks to account for why some material things are alive and have certain vital functions. In a pre-philosophical sense, the soul is the principle of life, whatever that may be. The philosopher seeks an analysis of what kind of thing or principle the soul is.

Now, by speaking of life, we are logically isolating one grade of actuality, the vital perfections of the living material substance, from other grades of actuality, like its materiality. But this grade of actuality is a substantial actuality, which is why the Aristotelian philosopher is so keen to identify the soul with the substantial form. The soul is the substantial form named insofar as that form is the principle of life; but then it differs only rationally and not really from that substantial form by virtue of which the living body is a body.

Thus, Aquinas can even say that a living substance's bodiliness or corporiety is its soul,[13] insofar as both name the one substantial form by

---

[13] Aquinas, *Quaestiones disputate de Spiritualibus Creaturis*, a. 3 ad 14: "Corpus autem quod est in genere substantiae, habet formam substantialem quae dicitur *corporeitas*, quae non est tres dimensiones, sed quaecumque forma substantialis ex qua sequuntur in materia tres dimensiones; *et haec forma in*

virtue of which the living material substance is a living material substance.

This must be the sense of bodiliness signified by "body" when we say that the soul is the *form of* the body. For, as we saw above, when we say that the soul is the form of the body, the body we are talking about is the genus of the being of which the soul is the soul.[14] In everyday terms, in this sense, Socrates *is* the body.

But we also speak of a body that Socrates *has*. In this sense, the body of Socrates is not his genus, but his part. True, this part of him is what it is thanks to the same one substantial form of Socrates; but it is referred to as a part insofar as it can be conceived of not only apart from, but in a sense *excluding*, the further perfections—life, rationality, etc.—that make Socrates the kind of thing he is. Recognizing this—for there is the same ambiguity in Latin between the *corpus* that Socrates is and the *corpus* that he has—Aquinas described two different senses of

---

*igne est igneitas, in animali anima sensitiva, et in homine anima intellectiva.*" *Summa Contra Gentiles*, Bk. IV, ch. 81: "Non enim sunt diversae formae substantiales in uno et eodem, per quarum unam collocetur in genere supremo, puta substantiae; et per aliam in genere proximo, puta in genere corporis vel animalis; et per aliam in specie puta hominis aut equi. Quia si prima forma faceret esse substantiam, sequentes formae iam advenirent ei quod est hoc aliquid in actu et subsistens in natura: et sic posteriores formae non facerent hoc aliquid, sed essent in subiecto quod est hoc aliquid sicut formae accidentales. Oportet igitur, quod *corporeitas*, prout est forma substantialis in homine, *non sit aliud quam anima rationalis*, quae in sua materia hoc requirit, quod habeat tres dimensiones: est enim actus corporis alicuius." Cf. *Compendium Theologiae*, Bk. I, ch. 154.

[14] Aquinas, *Summa Theologiae* I, q. 76, a. 4 ad 1: "Aristotle does not say that the soul is the act of a body only, but 'the act of a physical organic body which has life potentially'; and that this potentiality 'does not reject the soul.' Whence it is clear that when the soul is called the act [of the body], the soul itself is included [in the body]; as when we say that heat is the act of what is hot, and light [is the act] of what is lucid; not as though lucid and light were two separate things, but because a thing is made lucid by the light. In like manner, the soul is said to be the 'act of a body,' etc., because by the soul it is a body, and is organic, and has life potentially. Yet the first act is said to be in potentiality to the second act, which is operation; for such a potentiality 'does not reject'—that is, does not exclude—the soul."

"body." One is an exclusive sense, which names the body Socrates has (body as a part) and the other a non-exclusive sense, which names the body Socrates is (body as a whole).

Corresponding with this, we can distinguish exclusive and non-exclusive senses of "soul." The non-exclusive sense indicates the substantial form as principle of life, but not excluding other perfections, including corporeity, communicated by the form; these other perfections then do not have to be added to it, for they are virtually or implicitly included. The exclusive sense of "soul" indicates the substantial form exclusively as principle of life, leaving outside of its meaning the perfection of corporeity, which therefore has to be considered as something added.

This helps us make sense of how we can say that Socrates' soul is his substantial form, and also that his soul is composed with body and not prime matter. Socrates' soul is his substantial form, but when I refer to it as his substantial form, I am implying every grade of actuality, and its complementary metaphysical principle is prime matter—this is "soul" in the non-exclusive sense. When I refer to Socrates' soul as a part of him, which constitutes the whole together with his body, I am implying only the grade of actuality of life in the exclusive sense, and so distinct from the bodiliness, in the exclusive sense, by virtue of which he has a body. Of course that body is a body by virtue of the same substantial form by which it is alive. But the soul considered in its exclusive sense differs from the substantial form as one grade of actuality to the full grade of actuality communicated by that form.[15]

---

[15] The position sketched here is explored in much greater detail in Gyula Klima, "Man = Body + Soul: Aquinas's Arithmetic of Human Nature," in Brian Davies, ed., *Thomas Aquinas: Contemporary Philosophical Perspectives* (Oxford University Press, 2002), 257-73. [Also available online at: http://www.fordham.edu/gsas/phil/klima/ BODYSOUL.HTM.] Incidentally, Klima's distinction of different ways of signifying the one substantial form by which a living body is a body and alive solves the difficulties raised in the last section of another article in Davies' anthology, Christopher Hughes, "Matter and Actuality in Aquinas," 61-76.

### 3. Socrates = essence + designated matter

In what context do we speak of *essences*? In the sense used by Aquinas, *essentia* pertains to answering the question of *what* something is (and hence it is paired with *esse* which answers to the question of whether something is or that by which it is); it is what is captured by a definition. (It is also called quiddity, and more typically corresponds to the Greek *to ti ein einai* than *ousia*.) And it is also called nature, or common nature.

It is true that Aquinas will loosely refer to the essence as "form," but only loosely.[16] As we have seen, form, as principle of actuality in an individual thing, is individual; we can speak of Socrates and Plato having "the same form," but their forms are only *specifically* the same–the form of Socrates is something that exists[17] and by which Socrates exists; the form of Plato is something that exists and by which Plato exists, and these are clearly distinct forms—one can exist while the other does not. Indeed, although I find this rarely emphasized, since forms are principles of actualization, which make actual individual beings to be, forms themselves have an aspect of particularity or individuality about them.[18]

In contrast to this, the essence, in its intelligibility, must not have in it anything that is individual and therefore unintelligible; as something common to many, determining species, it must abstract altogether

---

[16] Aquinas very carefully handles those passages in Aristotle's *Metaphysics* where form seems to be identified with essence; see Armand Maurer, "Form and Essence in the Philosophy of St. Thomas," *Mediaeval Studies* 13 (1951): 165-76. But Aristotle's position may not be as unambiguous as Maurer describes; Aristotle suggests composition in the essence of material things in *Metaphysics* IX, ch. 10 (1051b17). See Thomas Aquinas, *In IX Metaph.*, lect. 11 (§§1901-1903) and Cajetan's *In De Ente et Essentia*, §29.

[17] Of course, material forms exist not as *quod est* but as *quo aliquid est*—but then, so long as we keep in mind the analogical senses of being, it is not inappropriate to say that forms exist.

[18] Also perhaps relevant here is that, while forms are principles of actuality corresponding with matter as principles of potentiality, Aquinas conceives of essences as principles of potentiality, corresponding with being (*esse*) as a principle of actuality.

from particularity.[19] Only then can it be *understood* and *defined* as something common to many.

The non-particularity of the essence is why the individual qua individual does not have an essence, because the individual qua individual does not have a definition;[20] or, if an individual does have an essence qua individual, that essence could not be defined.[21] A definition is formulated and understood as something common—at least potentially common—to many. The individual qua individual can be sensed, but not understood, and so is not subject to definition. Given the non-particularity of the essence, it would seem that for Aquinas it is

---

19 Famously, the nature absolutely considered also must abstract from universality. But, as Aquinas explains in his careful handling of the problem of universals in *De Ente et Essentia*, it is the fact that it is conceived absolutely, that is in abstraction from particularity, which makes it possible to speak of the nature in an individual mind—directing that mind to attend to the nature absolutely considered as one thing common to many—to acquire universality as an accident.

20 *De Ente et Essentia*, ch. 2: "Haec autem materia in diffinitione hominis, in quantum est homo, non ponitur, sed *poneretur* in diffinitione Socratis, *si* Socrates diffinitionem haberet."

21 *Summa Contra Gentiles*, IV. 65: "the essence of a singular [qua singular] is made up of signate matter and an individual form: thus the essence of Socrates [qua Socrates] is made up of this particular body and this particular soul, even as the essence of man in general is made up of soul and body, as stated in 7 Metaph. Wherefore, since the latter are included in the definition of man in general, so would the former be included in the definition of Socrates, if he could be defined." (Singularis autem essentia constituitur ex materia designata et forma individuata: sicut socratis essentia ex hoc corpore et hac anima, ut essentia hominis universalis ex anima et corpore, ut patet in VII Metaphysicae. Unde, sicut haec cadunt in definitione hominis universalis, ita illa caderent in definitione socratis si posset definiri.) Cf. *De Veritate* 2.7: "Intellectus autem cognoscens essentiam speciei, per eam comprehendit omnia per se accidentia speciei illius: quia, secundum philosophum, omnis demonstrationis, per quam accidentia propria de subiecto concluduntur, principium est quod quid est: unde et cognita propria essentia alicuius singularis, cognoscerentur omnia accidentia singularis illius: quod intellectus noster non potest: quia de essentia singularis est materia signata, a qua intellectus noster abstrahit, et poneretur in eius definitione, si singulare definitionem haberet."

only in a very qualified sense that we can speak of an essence of an individual qua individual.[22]

The non-particularity of the essence is also why we speak of it being in need of a principle of *individuation*.[23] The general Aristotelian position is clear, that the essence is individuated by matter. But there are difficulties with this position. First, the essence can't be individuated by prime matter, which is not actually anything on its own. Second, there also has to be a sense in which matter is included in the essence, since it is part of the nature of material beings to be material beings. So the matter that individuates can neither be prime matter, nor can it be the formal materiality already included in substantial form.

Here Aquinas's solution is well-known, and has already been mentioned: the essence is individuated by *designated* matter. Designated matter is matter with the first grade of actuality that marks it out as some particular bit of matter and not some other. As noted, Aquinas recognizes designated matter also to distinguish it from undesignated matter or common matter, the matter included in the essence. But what does it mean that non-designated matter is included in the essence? It is not obviously clear.[24] The form of a material being is

---

[22] We should distinguish two things that could be meant by "individual essence": one, the common nature as it has being in an individual (we could call this "the individual*ized* essence"); the other, the particular essence of an individual qua individual (we could call this "the singular essence"). [For one account of individual essences, see Hochschild, "Kenny and Aquinas on Individual Essences."]

[23] As far as I can tell, Aquinas does not address the problem of individuation as a problem for *forms*, but as a problem for *common natures* or *essences*. On the different kinds of questions which "a principle of individuation" might serve to answer, see Peter King, "The Problem of Individuation in the Middle Ages," *Theoria* 66 (2000): 159-84. [Also available online here: http://individual.utoronto.ca/pking/ articles/Mediaeval_Individuation.pdf.] See also Georgio Pini, "Scotus on Individuation," *Proceedings of the Society for Medieval Logic and Metaphysics* 5 (2005): 50-69.

[24] Maurer seems to suggest that *prime matter* is also included in the essence: the composite includes prime matter, and so, "Although unintelligible in itself, prime matter is thus essential to the full intelligibility of the composite and enters in full right into the essence of a material being" (Maurer, "Form and Essence," 175).

called a material form, not in the sense that it is made up of matter, but in the sense that for it to be is for it to be in, or to actualize, matter. But then, as we saw previously, it seems as if materiality is already included in the very nature of such forms; why then, when it comes to describing the essence, do we have to say that it doesn't include "only" form but "also" matter? How does the essence differ from the substantial form?

I think we can make sense of this if we recall that the designated matter is matter with the first grade of material actuality. What communicates this first grade of actuality to the designated matter that individuates the essence must be the substantial form. The essence, therefore, which is individuated by designated matter, cannot be the same as the substantial form which actualizes designated matter.

In fact, it is Aquinas's clear and considered position that there is a real distinction between the essence and the substantial form. For reasons that remain somewhat obscure, Aquinas consistently expresses this as the distinction between the *forma totius* and *forma partis*, attributing the distinction to Avicenna (and occasionally opposing it to the doctrine of Averroes).[25] The terminology is confusing, inviting explanations that themselves are not always clear.[26] The literal

---

[25] E.g. *In IV Sent.*, d. 44, a. 1b ad 2; *Quodlib. Quest.*, II, q. 2, a. 2; *SCG* IV.81; *In VII Metaph.*, lect. 9 (§§1467-69).

[26] E.g. Peter King, "The Problem of Individuation in the Middle Ages": "Aquinas distinguishes two kinds of forms: those including matter in their definition, and those not. The form 'humanity' includes matter in its definition, since it is rational animality; since animals are physical objects, matter must be involved in some fashion. On the other hand, the forms of immaterial objects clearly do not involve matter; more exactly, certain forms need not be enmattered to exist. Now forms occurring in material objects can be viewed either as the form of the whole object (*forma totius*), in which case the form is the complement to the *matter* of the object, or as the form of part of the object (*forma partis*), specifying only the formal principle of the object, in which case the form is the complement of the *material principle*" [English italics added]. I am not sure what difference King means to indicate between the matter and the material principle. Jorge J.E. Gracia's "Towards a Metaphysics of Existence" (in *The Classics of Western Philosophy: A Reader's Guide*, ed. Jorge J.E. Gracia, Gregory M. Reichberg, and Bernard N. Schumacher [Blackwell, 2003], 137-42) says: "In one sense, 'an essence'

translations–form of the whole and form of the part—are only partly illuminating. The *form of the whole* is the form of the whole composite—but not including designated matter; so it is the form of the whole of what something is. The *form of the part* is the form of one part of the composite–the part left over being prime matter.

To complicate matters, Aquinas says that the *forma totius* (essence or quiddity) can itself be referred to according to different modes of signification: *as a whole* (by the concrete term, e.g. "man") or *as a part* (by the abstract counterpart term, e.g. "humanity"). In the first case, it can be predicated of that whole individual (qua member of a species); in the second case, it can only be predicated of that principle by which the individual is made a member of the species, but not of the individual itself.

---

means everything that is expressed in the definition of the substance in question; this is why it can be predicated of the individuals who have such an essence. Accordingly, the essence of man embraces everything that is part of the definition of man, including materiality. In another sense, however, 'an essence' means just the form that, united to matter, constitutes the individual substance. Accordingly, the essence of this man, for example, refers only to the form of this man, which joined to this matter constitutes the individual man. Aquinas calls the first *forma totius*—generally translated as 'form of the whole,' but better expressed as 'the whole form'—and the second *forma partis*—again generally translated as 'the form of the part,' but better expressed as 'the form that is a part.' The status of the second is quite clear, for it is the individual essence of an individual being (*ens*)" (140). I do not find Aquinas treating the *forma partis* or substantial form as the "individual essence." Also, consider Gyula Klima, in "Man = Body + Soul": "if we distinguish corporeity as that substantial form on account of which whatever has it exists in a material, spatio-temporal manner, whether the thing in question is alive or not, then the corporeity thus distinguished will clearly coincide in all living bodies with their soul, conceived as that substantial form on account of which whatever has this form is alive, whether it is a body or not. Therefore, in this non-exclusive sense, both the corporeity thus conceived and the soul thus conceived are nothing but the form of the whole, that is, the essence or quiddity of a living body." But if soul or substantial form are the *forma totius*, how does Klima account for the real distinction between the essence (*forma totius*) and the substantial form (*forma partis*), which he acknowledges earlier in the paper?

So, when we *name* the essence (i.e. with the abstract term, such as "humanity") we signify the *form of a whole* (i.e. the whole essence) *as a part* (i.e. as a part of the whole individual being). When we *signify* the essence in *naming* a *member of the species* (i.e. with the concrete term, such as "man") we signify the form of the whole (the whole essence) *as a whole* (i.e. as designating the whole composite individual).

Aquinas, of course, says that the essence differs from the form because it includes, in addition to form, also matter. On my account, however, it seems that in a sense the substantial form "includes" more than the essence—it implies being (actually), and it implies particularity, communicating even the first grade of actuality to prime matter (pure potentiality) to make the individual actual not only as the *kind* of thing it is but as the *particular* thing that it is. (I think this is why Aquinas makes the survival of the soul the basis for the survival of the whole individual in the resurrection: *SCG* IV. 81.) On this account, what is included in the individual's essence that is not included, or is obscured, in the substantial form is not *matter* but *intelligibility*.

## V. CONCLUSION

These reflections lead to the following account of how the substantial form, soul, and essence differ when considered as components of an individual living material substance, united respectively with prime matter, body, and designated matter. The individual's soul is the grade of actuality of the individual's life. The individual's essence is every grade of actuality of the individual excluding its particularity. And the individual's substantial form is the whole range of the individual's actuality, including not only what places it in a species but what makes it that particular individual.

# First Known Being and the Birth of Metaphysics

## Lawrence Dewan, O. P.

### I. Introduction[1]

The organizers of the American Maritain Association annual meeting are to be congratulated for having planned this year's event to bear on metaphysics, its greatness and its humble condition. Were it only to mark the publication last year of Fr. Ashley's remarkable book, *The Way Towards Wisdom*, and to express our gratitude and admiration for all that Fr. Ashley has been doing now these many years, we would have reason enough and to spare.

However, this is a Maritain Association, and Fr. Ashley's approach to the question of the "way towards wisdom," while it agrees in spirit with Jacques Maritain, is notably different from the approach of Jacques. And so it is fitting that there be discussion, even argument, about such an issue. Indeed, it is one of the great benefits of an association such as this one, that we are all united in that "magis amica veritas"[2] principle

---

[1] Some abbreviations for works of St. Thomas Aquinas: "*SCG*" for *Summa Contra Gentiles*; "*ST*" for *Summa Theologiae*; "*CM*" for *Commentary on Aristotle's Metaphysics*; "*BT*" for *Commentary on Boethius' On the Trinity*.

[2] Cf. Aristotle, *Nicomachean Ethics* 1.6 (1096a13-16): "Yet it would perhaps be thought to be better, indeed to be our duty, for the sake of maintaining the truth even to destroy what touches us closely, especially as we are philosophers or lovers of wisdom; for, while both are dear, piety requires us to honour truth above our friends [Oxford tr.; Sir David Ross]." Cf. St. Thomas, *In Ethic.*, 1.6 (paras. 4 and 5)(Pirotta #77-78):

> Quod autem oporteat veritatem praeferre amicis, ostendit hac ratione. Quia ei qui est magis amicus, magis est deferendum. Cum autem amicitiam habeamus ad ambo, scilicet ad veritatem et ad hominem, magis debemus veritatem amare quam hominem, quia hominem praecipue debemus amare propter veritatem et propter virtutem ut in VIII huius dicetur. Veritas autem est amicus superexcellens cui debetur reverentia honoris; est etiam veritas

which urges us to spell out our disagreements as well as our agreements, for the common good of all.

I do not mean to present myself as *altogether* in agreement with Maritain,[3] but what I propose concerning the coming into being of metaphysics has more in common with his views than with those of Fr. Ashley.

When I speak of the coming into being of metaphysics I identify as metaphysics the science that considers things precisely as beings (and mean by "science" demonstrated conclusions and the ability to draw

---

quiddam divinum, in Deo enim primo et principaliter invenitur. Et ideo concludit, quod sanctum est praehonorare veritatem hominibus amicis.

Dicit enim Andronicus peripateticus, quod sanctitas est quae facit fideles et servantes ea quae ad Deum. Juxta hoc etiam est sententia Platonis, qui reprobans opinionem Socratis magistri sui dixit quod oportet de veritate magis curare quam de aliquo alio; et alibi dicit: amicus quidem Socrates sed magis amica veritas; et in alio loco: de Socrate quidem parum est curandum, de veritate autem multum.

[But that one ought to prefer truth to friends he shows by this argument: because to him who is the greater friend preference is to be given. Now, since we have friendship as regards both, viz. towards the truth and towards a human being, we ought to love the truth more than the human being, because we ought to love the human being especially because of truth and virtue, as is said in the 8th book of this work. But truth is a surpassing friend to which one owes the reverence of honour; truth is also something divine, for it is found primarily and principally in God. And so he concludes that it is a holy thing to honour by priority truth over human friends.

For Andronicus the Peripatetic says that holiness is that which makes [us] faithful and servants of those things relating to God. In this connection there is also the view of Plato who, criticizing the opinion of his master Socrates said that "one must care more for truth than for anything else" and in another place he says: "Socrates is a friend, but truth a greater friend." And in still another place: "One should care little about Socrates, but much about truth."]

[3] I have expressed some disagreement with Maritain on this in my paper: "Jacques Maritain, St. Thomas, and the Birth of Metaphysics," *Études Maritainiennes\Maritain Studies* 13 (1997): 3-18.

them). And I see myself as asking a perennial question. Plato, in the *Republic*, for example, offers us an account. He asks: "What, then, Glaucon, would be the study that would draw the soul away from the world of becoming to the world of being [*epi to on*]?"[4] He had already proposed the nature of the educational task: not to "put true knowledge into a soul that does not possess it, as if they were inserting vision into blind eyes..." but rather "an art of the speediest and most effective shifting or conversion of the soul, not an art of producing vision in it, but on the assumption that it possesses vision but does not rightly direct it and does not look where it should, an art of bringing this about."[5]

His general description of what draws the soul towards being is that "some reports of our perceptions do not provoke thought to reconsideration because the judgment of them by sensation seems adequate, while others always invite the intellect to reflection because the sensation yields nothing that can be trusted."[6] He illustrates what he means by considering, let us say, the last three fingers of the hand, so that the middle of the three is seen as big relative to the smallest and as small relative to the biggest. Thus, the *same* finger is viewed as *both small* and *big*. And he asks: "And is it not in some such experience as this that the question first occurs to us, *what* in the world, then, *is* the great and the small?"[7] Plato moves us through an entire curriculum of subjects, e.g. arithmetic, geometry, physics, etc., always from the viewpoint of their stimulating questions about *what is* and *entity*. In the end, he says:

> But all the other arts [other, i.e., than "dialectic" or metaphysics] have for their object the opinions and desires of men or are wholly concerned with generation and composition or with

---

[4] Plato, *Republic* 7.6 (521D), trans. Paul Shorey, The Loeb Classical Library (London/Cambridge: Heinemann/Harvard University Press, 1935). Allan Bloom (Plato, *Republic* [New York: Basic Books, 1968], Book 7, 521D) translates: "What, then, Glaucon, would be a study to draw the soul from becoming to being?"

[5] Plato, *Republic* 7.4 (518B-D).

[6] Plato, Republic 7.7 (523A-B).

[7] Plato, *Republic* 7.7 (524C).

> the service and tendance of things that grow and are put together, while the remnant which we said did in some sort lay hold on reality [*tou ontos*]-geometry and the studies that accompany it-are, as we see, *dreaming about being* [*peri to on*], but the clear waking vision of it is impossible for them as long as they leave the assumptions which they employ undisturbed and cannot give any account of them.[8]

As Socrates had already said in presenting the Divided Line, mathematics leaves its starting-points unexamined, while the power of dialectic explores all such "starting-points" and rests only in what can be seen to be absolute beginnings.[9]

Plato's point on the less than full awareness of being in the sciences lower than dialectic, i.e. lower than metaphysics, finds its continuation in Aristotle's view, in *Metaph.* 6.1 (1025b7-17). As Thomas says in explaining this passage:

> All these particular sciences, which have just been mentioned, are about some one particular domain of being, for example, about number or magnitude, or something of that order. And each one treats circumscriptively about its own subject-domain, i.e. so [treats] of its own domain, that [it treats] of nothing else; for example, the science which treats of number does not treat of magnitude. For none of them treats of being unqualifiedly, that is, of being in its generality [*de ente in commune*], *nor even about any particular being inasmuch as it is a being.* For example, arithmetic does not determine about number inasmuch as it is a being, but inasmuch as it is number. For to consider *any* being, inasmuch as it is a being, is proper to metaphysics [italics mine].[10]

## II. WHAT DOES METAPHYSICS LOOK LIKE? THOMAS' ANSWER

To judge the birth of something, one must have knowledge of the authentic appearance of that thing. Let us ask St. Thomas for a

---

[8] Plato, *Republic* 7.13 (533B-C).

[9] Plato, *Republic* 6.20-21 (510C-511D).

[10] Cf. St. Thomas, *CM* 6.1 (1147), concerning Aristotle at 1025b7-10.

description of metaphysics. I will use for this, to begin with, *CM* 4.2. There, with Aristotle, Thomas is calling metaphysics simply "philosophy." We read:

> [563] Here [Aristotle] shows that the parts of philosophy are distinguished in keeping with the parts of "a being" and "one." And he says that the parts of philosophy are as many as the parts of substance, about which the terms "a being" and "one" are principally said, the principal consideration and aim of this science being about [substance]. And because the parts of substance are ordered to one another in a certain order, since immaterial substance is naturally prior to sensible substance, therefore it is necessary that among the parts of philosophy there be some first. Nevertheless, that [part] which is *about sensible substance* is *first in the order of teaching*, because it is necessary to begin teaching from what are more known to us; and concerning that there is treatment in the seventh and eighth books of this work. However, that [part] which is *about immaterial substances* is prior in *dignity* and in the *aim* of this science; concerning which there is treatment in book twelve of this work. And nevertheless whatever are first must be continuous with the other parts, because *all the parts have for genus "one" and "a being."* Hence, in the consideration of "one" and "a being" the diverse parts of this science are united, even though they are about *diverse parts of substance:* in such a way that it is *one* science inasmuch as the aforementioned parts are following on this, i.e. *"one" and "a being," as what are common to substance.* And in this respect the philosopher is like the mathematician. For mathematics has diverse parts, one principal, viz. arithmetic, and one secondary, viz. geometry, and others following upon these, such as optics, astronomy, and music.[11]

---

[11] Aquinas, *CM* 4.2 (563), commenting on Aristotle, *Metaph.* 4.2 (1004a2-9):

> Et tot partes hic ostendit partes philosophiae distingui secundum partes entis et unius; et dicit, quod tot sunt partes philosophiae, quot sunt partes substantiae, de qua dicitur principaliter ens et unum et de qua principalis est huius scientiae consideratio et intentio. Et, quia partes substantiae sunt ordinatae adinvicem, nam substantia immaterialis est prior substantia sensibili naturaliter; ideo necesse est

Thus, while Thomas, as the teacher, presents the whole project, he also indicates the order of teaching, i.e. *the order according to which the human mind properly enters into metaphysics.* It aims for the heights, whatever they may be, from the start, but it takes its rise from the study of sensible substance, study of such substance from the viewpoint of being.[12]

---

> inter partes philosophiae esse quamdam primam. Illa tamen, quae est de substantia sensibili, est prima ordine doctrinae, quia a notioribus nobis oportet incipere disciplinam: et de hac determinatur in septimo et octavo huius. Illa vero, quae est de substantia immateriali est prior dignitate et intentione huius scientiae, de qua traditur in duodecimo huius. Et tamen quaecumque sunt prima, necesse est quod sint continua aliis partibus, quia omnes partes habent pro genere unum et ens. Unde in consideratione unius et entis diversae partes huius scientiae uniuntur, quamvis sint de diversis partibus substantiae; ut sic sit una scientia inquantum partes praedictae sunt consequentes hoc, id est unum et ens, sicut communia substantiae. Et in hoc philosophus est similis mathematico. Nam mathematica habet diversas partes, et quamdam principaliter sicut arithmeticam, et quamdam secundario sicut geometriam, et alia consequenter se habent his, sicut perspectiva, astrologia et musica.

[12] We might recall *CM* 7.11 (1525-6-7):

> He [Aristotle] shows what remains besides to be determined concerning substances. And he posits that two [things] remain to be determined. The first of which is that, since it has been determined that the substance and quiddity of sensible and material things are the very parts of the species, it remains to determine *whether of such substances, i.e. material and sensible, there is any substance separate from matter [praeter materiam]*, such that it is necessary to seek some substance of these sensibles other than that which has been determined, as some people say numbers existing outside matter, or something like that, i.e. species or Ideas, are the substances of these sensible things. And concerning that *there must be inquiry later*.
>
> For *this inquiry is proper to this science*. For in this science we try to determine concerning sensible substances for the sake of this, that is, because of immaterial substances, because *the theorizing concerning sensible and material substances in a way pertains to physics*, which is not first philosophy, but second, as was established in book 4. For *first philosophy is about the first substances, which are immaterial substances,*

Because many of our friends have said that metaphysics only comes into existence with the discovery of the existence of immaterial substance,[13] a view that does not seem to me correct, I was led further to focus on what Aristotle says in *Metaphysics* 7, at the end of the second of the two introductory chapters. In that beginning of book 7, it is first established that the focus of the science is to be on being as found in *substance*. There is then a review of the opinions of some other people regarding substance. First, evident substance is reviewed, i.e. sensible substances; and the question is raised whether these are the only substances (as the ancient physicists thought), or whether there are other substances besides these, such as those proposed by the Platonists, or whether sensible substances are not substances at all, but only some non-sensible substances are such. Aristotle then reviews the opinions concerning non-evident substance, mentioning Pythagorean views and the Platonic doctrines of mathematicals as distinct from the Ideas, etc.

We then move to a statement of what is to be done with regard to all this. Notice where Thomas, paraphrasing Aristotle, says that *it must be asked* whether the mathematicals and the [Platonic] Forms are anything other than sensible things or not, and if not, whether there are any other separable substances, and why and how: "...or whether there is no substance other than the sensibles." And he goes on to say that *this will be determined in the 12th book and beyond.* The text reads:

---

*about which it theorizes not merely inasmuch as they are substances, but inasmuch as they are such substances*, i.e. inasmuch as they are immaterial. *About sensible substance* it does not theorize inasmuch as they are such substances, but inasmuch as they are *substances*, or even *beings*, or inasmuch as *through them we are led to the knowledge of immaterial substances*. But the physicist, conversely, determines about material substances, *not inasmuch as they are substances*, but inasmuch as they are material and [as] having in them a principle of movement.

[13] Most recently we have Benedict Ashley, O.P., *The Way toward Wisdom: An Interdisciplinary and Intercultural Introduction to Metaphysics* (Notre Dame, Indiana: University of Notre Dame Press, 2006); and also Ralph McInerny, *Praeambula Fidei: Thomism and the God of the Philosophers* (Washington, D.C.: the Catholic University of America Press, 2006).

Then when he says: "Therefore, concerning these things..." [Aristotle] shows what is to be said concerning the aforesaid: ... what about the aforesaid is said well or not well, and *which* are substances, and whether the aforementioned mathematicals and forms are something apart from sensible things or not. And [as regards] those substances, if they are apart from sensibles, what sort of being they have. And if these are not apart from sensible substances, *whether there is any other substance that is separable, and why, and how, or whether there is no substance other than sensible [substances].*

For this he will determine in this work, *in book 12 and beyond.* But nevertheless, *before he determines this,* it is *necessary* to propose and describe what substance is in these sensible things, in which substance is *manifestly* to be found. This he does in this seventh [book] and in the following eighth.[14]

*We see, here, that the exclusive concern in this part of metaphysics will be substance as found in sensible things.* The question as to *whether there is any substance besides this, any "separable" substance, belongs to the second part of metaphysics.*

This is the conception of both Aristotle and Thomas as to how the human mind enters into metaphysics.[15]

---

[14] Aquinas, *CM* 7.1:

[1268] Deinde cum dicit: "De his igitur..." ostendit quid circa praedicta dicendum sit; dicens, quod dicendum est quid de praedictis dicitur bene aut non bene, et quae sunt substantiae, et utrum praedicta mathematica et species sint aliquid praeter res sensibiles, aut non. Et illae substantiae si sint praeter sensibiles, quem modum essendi habeant. Et si ista non sunt praeter sensibiles substantias, utrum sit aliqua alia substantia separabilis, et quare et quomodo; aut nulla est substantia praeter sensibiles.

[1269] Hoc enim determinabit in duodecimo huius et infra. Sed tamen antequam haec determinentur, oportet primo ponere et describere quid sit substantia in istis sensibilibus, in quibus substantia manifesta invenitur. Quod quidem facit in hoc septimo et in octavo sequenti.

[15] The question, of course, is often raised as to whether Thomas, in his commentaries, is expressing his own views as well as what he takes to be

## III. THE NATURE OF FIRST KNOWN BEING

St. Thomas has a description of our first knowledge of being that is at odds with what we find suggested by both Fr. Ashley and Ralph McInerny. The difference this makes as regards the coming into existence of metaphysics will become clear as we proceed.

In his book *Praeambula Fidei: Thomism and the God of the Philosophers*, McInerny in his first chapter on metaphysics leads off with a section on "establishing the possibility of a science of *ens inquantum ens*" [191]. We read:

> On many occasions Thomas makes the point that until and unless there is proof of the existence of immaterial being, *to be and to be material will be synonymous.* It is *only* a proof of the existence of im-material being that opens the possibility of a science whose subject would be being as being [my stress].

Now, this is not true. Thomas never says or implies a situation (other than error) in which the human mind takes "to be" and "to be material" as *synonymous.* And we have already seen Thomas present the first part of metaphysics, the study of *being as being* in sensible substances, as existing even when it is not known whether there is any immaterial being. How can McInerny have read him the way he has?

At the beginning of the chapter he raised the question: how can there be need for a science of "being," in the light of the doctrine that being is what we all first know. His section is called "*ens primum cognitum.*" In exposing the puzzle, he asks how there can be need for sciences *presupposed* to metaphysics (considered as science of being). McInerny distinguishes our knowledge of *ens primum cognitum*, i.e. first known being, from the consideration of *ens* "*inquantum ens*", i.e. being as being.[16] *He contends that "until and unless it is known that there is*

---

Aristotle's; I believe that he is, particularly because he does indicate differences on occasion.

[16] He mentions the distinction made by Cajetan in his *Commentary on De Ente et Essentia*, and also refers to a text of John of St. Thomas on our first knowledge. I am glad to note that I have seen no such distinction in Capreolus's defense of St. Thomas against Scotus and Peter Aureol concerning the notion of "*ens*:" cf. my paper "Does Being Have a Nature? (Or: Metaphysics as a Science of the Real)," published in *Approaches to Metaphysics*,

*immaterial being, the predicable range of 'being' will be material things*" [190]. This, again, is not so. Of course, if "the predicable range" means merely the items of which we can here and now predicate "being," then it is true, but trivial. It means simply that we know of no immaterial beings. However, we are from the outset able to pose the question: "are all beings material beings?" and this question is only intelligible because "being" is not limited in its "predicable range" at all. Human intellection has the nature of intellection right from the start, and its object is "*ens universale*, universal being."[17] That is why intellection in its very nature is *infinite* [*ST* 1.54.2]. There is no doubt that, in the case of the human intellect, the object must first be encountered in material things: "*ens et verum consideratum in rebus materialibus*" ["a being" and "the true" considered in material things][*ST* 1.87.3.*ad* 1]. St. Thomas uses this expression when explaining that, while the human intellect can know its own operation, it can only do so by *reflection* back from an operation bearing upon a material being. Now, the very possibility of such *reflection* as resulting in knowledge is based on the essential *universality* of the object, "*ens*" ["*commune quoddam*," ibid.].[18]

As Thomas teaches, the very universality of the object, "*ens*," indicates that the rational creature that possesses such knowledge is in immediate relation with the universal cause of being [*ST* 2-2.2.3]. Indeed, the knowledge of the very terms of the absolutely first principle of understanding *known to all* pertains to *wisdom*, since it is a

---

ed. William Sweet (Dordrecht, Holland: Kluwer Academic Publishers, 2004), 23-59.

[17] Cf. *SCG* 3.25 (Pera #2066 [para. 12]); *ST* 1.78.1; 1.79.2c and ad 3; 1.105.4; 1-2.9.1; 1-2.10.1.ad 3.

[18] This object is also spoken of in the body of the same article as "*natura materialis rei*." Obviously, "*natura*" here is the same as "*essentia*" and "*quidditas*," and all such items, *understood*, have an infinite reference, a reference to being as such. (That is why the essence of the angel is not a principle of *understanding* even the angel's very own self, save as seen under the aspect of "*ens et verum*" [1.54.2.ad 2].) Cf. also *SCG* 2.83 (paras. 28 and 29; Pera ed. #1677 and #1678) on the powerful generative role of our natural knowledge of "*ens*" [a being].

knowledge of the proper effect of the highest cause, that effect being *ens commune.*[19]

It is quite true that at first we do not know whether there is any immaterial being. Thus, the proper answer to the question (already a truly metaphysical question): "is there immaterial being?" is "I do not know." *At that stage already* the statement: "to be is to be material" is *simply false*. It is a *metaphysical error*.

This[20] is a point made clearly by Thomas in his *Commentary on the Nicomachean Ethics*. There we read that metaphysics is most certain, i.e. more certain than any other science, inasmuch as it attains to the

---

[19] On this, see "St. Thomas, Physics, and the Principle of Metaphysics," ch. 4 in my book: *Form and Being* (Washington, D.C.: the Catholic University of America Press, 2006), at 57-60. The climax is in *ST* 1-2.66.5.ad 4:

> Ad quartum dicendum quod veritas et cognitio principiorum indemonstrabilium dependet ex ratione terminorum, cognito enim quid est totum et quid pars, statim cognoscitur quod omne totum est maius sua parte. *Cognoscere autem rationem entis et non entis*, et totius et partis, et aliorum quae consequuntur ad ens, ex quibus sicut ex terminis constituuntur principia indemonstrabilia, pertinet ad *sapientiam*, quia *ens commune* est proprius effectus causae altissimae, scilicet Dei. Et ideo sapientia non solum utitur principiis indemonstrabilibus, quorum est intellectus, concludendo ex eis, sicut aliae scientiae; sed etiam iudicando de eis, et disputando contra negantes. Unde sequitur quod sapientia sit maior virtus quam intellectus. [The truth and knowledge of the indemonstrable principles depends on the notion of the terms [*ex ratione terminorum*]; for, it being known what a whole is and what a part is, at once it is known that every whole is greater than its own part. But to know the notion of "a being" and "not a being" [*entis et non entis*], and of "whole" and "part," and of the other [items] that follow upon "a being," out of which as out of terms the indemonstrable principles are constituted, *pertains to wisdom*; because "a being, universally" [*ens commune*] is the proper effect of the highest cause, viz. God. And so wisdom does not merely make use of the indemonstrable principles, on which [the virtue of] understanding [bears], concluding from them, as do the other sciences; but also [it treats of them] as judging about them and as disputing against those who deny them. Hence, it follows that wisdom is a greater virtue than understanding.]

[20] This paragraph is taken from the just-mentioned book *Form and Being*, 55-56.

primary principles of beings. Though some of these principles are *less* known to us than other things (thus placing in doubt metaphysics' claim to being "most certain"), nevertheless this claim is well founded, inasmuch as the most universal principles, pertaining to being as being, are *both best known in themselves and best known to us.* And these pertain to metaphysics.[21] Obviously, if the first principles, as first known, were *at first limited to corporeal being as corporeal,* they would not be known as they pertain properly to metaphysics. Thomas sees the principles, precisely as known first of all and to all, as having the properly metaphysical character. This does not make the beginner a finished metaphysician, but it does mean that the principles of metaphysics are precisely those very first known principles, not some newly constructed conception of being resulting from the study of physics. If we did not start with metaphysical principles, no particular science would ever provide them. Nor can we *improve on* what is *best known to us and in itself.*[22]

Now McInerny goes on, very properly, to say: "let us have the texts before us." The text he selects from Thomas bears on the ancient

---

[21] Thomas Aquinas, *Sententia libri* ETHICORUM *Aristotelis* 6.5, Leonine edition (Rome: Ad Sanctae Sabinae, 1969), tome 47-2, lines 102-06 (concerning Aristotle at 1141a12-17), Pirotta edition, #1181:

> ...existimamus quosdam esse sapientes totaliter, idest respectu totius generis entium...illa quae est sapientia simpliciter est certissima inter omnes scientias, inquantum scilicet attingit ad prima principia entium, quae secundum se sunt notissima, quamvis aliqua illarum, scilicet immaterialia, sunt minus nota quoad nos. Universalissima autem principia sunt *etiam quoad nos magis nota, sicut ea quae pertinent ad ens inquantum est ens*: quorum cognitio pertinet ad sapientiam sic dictam, ut patet in quarto Metaphysicae [my italics]. [We judge that some people are universally wise, i.e. with respect to the entire field of beings... that which is wisdom unqualifiedly is the most certain among all the sciences, inasmuch as it attains to the first principles of beings, which in themselves are most known, though some of them, i.e. the immaterial things, are less known to us. However, the most universal principles are *more known even to us, such as those which pertain to being as being*: whose knowledge pertains to the "wisdom" so said, as is clear in *Metaph.* 4.]

[22] Cf. *ST* 1-2.51.2 (979b31-35 and 46-48).

philosophers who thought that all being is material, and who accordingly thought that it belonged to natural science to treat of the first principle, the principle of contradiction. They were wrong because there is immaterial being, and so their science was not the most universal, having being as being as its subject. In order to confirm this point, Thomas notes that in *Physics* 8 it is proven that immobile being exists.[23]

Quite so. However, this does not mean that until such proof is forthcoming, "to be and to be material will be *synonymous*." It rather means that, since people spontaneously think metaphysically,[24] until one proves the existence of immobile being or immaterial being, *one stands in danger of making the erroneous metaphysical judgment*: "All being is mobile and material." One further stands in danger of confusing the science of mobile being with the science of being as being. It is significant that Thomas, in speaking of the ancients here concerned, says: "...the ancients did not opine [*non opinabantur*] that any substance other than mobile corporeal substance existed...." That is, they *opined* that no such substance exists. The word "opine" is a propos. They were making a metaphysical error.

And such people did act confusedly, making metaphysical judgments on insufficient evidence. Thus, they really did treat what they studied from the viewpoint of being, treating of being as being. That is why *Aristotle* singles out those same naturalists as his *predecessors* when he is introducing the idea of a science of being as being. The early cosmologists had the ambition to seek the highest causes, and they sought the causes of being as being![25]

Notice that it is never said in the text of Thomas offered to us that until one proves the existence of the immobile or immaterial, "being" and "being material" are *synonymous*. One could say that *some early*

---

[23] The text is *CM* 4.5 (593).

[24] Consider *ST* 1-2.94.2 (ed. Ottawa 1226a3-8), teaching that the human being has a natural inclination to know the truth about God. Cf. also *SCG* 3.25 (Pera #2066 [para. 12]).

[25] Aristotle, *Metaph.* 4.1 1003a26-32, and Thomas, *CM* 4.1 (533).

*thinkers thought so*. They said, as reported by Plato in the *Sophist*: "To be is to be a body."[26] They were already in error.

Thomas uses the establishment in *Physics* 8 of immobile and incorporeal being as *making evident* the greater universality of "being" as contrasted with "mobile being" and thus the distinction of the two sciences.[27] However, this is not the same as saying that until such a proof is made, no one is asking truly metaphysical questions, or reaching truly metaphysical conclusions. We have seen Thomas himself present the first part of metaphysics as treating of being in sensible, material substance and still not knowing whether there is any immaterial substance. (If one took our opponents' point of view, one would have to say that Thomas thought he was doing metaphysics when in fact he was in physics!)

McInerny refers also to *CM* 6.1 (1170), to 11.7 (2267), and to 3.6 (398). This last in part reads: "Just as, if there were no other substances prior to mobile corporeal substances, natural science would be prime philosophy, as is said below in book 6."[28] This encapsulates exactly what all these texts say, namely that if there were no substances ontologically prior to mobile corporeal substance, natural science would be *first philosophy*.

---

[26] Plato, *Sophist* 246a-b. In the translation of H.N. Fowler [Loeb Classics, *Plato* , vol. VII (Cambridge, Mass. and London: Harvard University Press/ Heinemann, 1921)], the passage runs: "... for they ... maintain stoutly that that alone exists which can be touched and handled; for they define existence and body, or matter, as identical, and if anyone says that anything else, which has no body, exists, they despise him utterly, and will not listen to any other theory than their own."

[27] We should note that Fr. Ashley's book (cf. p. 19) is meant to develop a "dialogue" in a mode of "reconciliation" as the approach to metaphysics most appropriate for our place and time in culture. It is thus "dialectical" in the Aristotelian sense. Thomas, too, sees the proving of the existence of separate entity as overcoming a confused situation. Indeed, no one doubts the importance for metaphysics and so for humanity of a proof of the existence of immaterial reality.

[28] Aquinas, *CM* 3.6 (398): "Sicut si non essent aliae substantiae priores substantiis mobilibus corporalibus, scientia naturalis esset philosophia prima, ut dicitur infra in sexto."

McInerny claims, in concluding, that all these texts show that "metaphysics as a science of being as being, where being has more reach than sensible being, depends upon knowing that there are immaterial beings." [193] Again, "reach" is ambiguous, as was "predicable range." If it means: "is actually predicated of," then it is trivial: all admit that people who are ignorant of the existence of immaterial being cannot be talking about it. Still, such a person can say: "I do not know whether there are immaterial beings." "Being," for them (as for everyone), "reaches beyond" the material. Thus, what McInerny contends is simply not so. The texts he refers to only say and show that if there were no separate entity, physics would be primary philosophy (obviously, such "first philosophy," such "science of being as being," would not be suitably named "meta-*physics*."). They say nothing about a need to *know* that such entity exists *in order to bring into existence* metaphysical science.[29]

It is certainly true that if, *per impossibile*, there were no immaterial entity, no immobile, incorporeal substance, then the science that treats of material substance would be altogether universal and first. However, there does exist separate entity, and that means that our intellects are different from any intellect that would exist, *per impossibile*, in that hypothetical world. Real intellect is something which we have by participation from immaterial substance (*ST* 1.79.2 and 4). Its first notion, of *ens universale*, is a sapiential seed: 1-2.66.5.*ad* 4 and 2-2.2.3 (ed. Ottawa, 1416a6-17).

This does not mean that we are full-fledged metaphysicians from the start, but it does mean that from the start we are equipped to ask the question: "Is to be to be a body?" This is a question which would

---

[29] This also applies to what he says in n. 12, p. 194. There he refers to *CM* 1.12 (181): this merely asserts the insufficiency of the doctrine of causes in the earliest philosophers, since they made no provision for incorporeal realities, and such reality exists, as is seen in the book *De anima*. There is no doubt of the importance of such doctrines for metaphysics, but that does not mean that the thinker who is still in ignorance of such being cannot, while still in such a condition of ignorance, be a metaphysician. He is considering being as being when he asks the question as to whether there is separate entity, and he need not give the wrong answer; he may confess ignorance and keep working on an answer.

have no sense if "being" simply meant "body," i.e. if they were *synonyms*. And we are equipped from the start to refrain from the wrong answer. The early philosophers really were guilty of *metaphysical error*.[30]

McInerny's scenario does not capture the true situation of the early philosophers, viz. that they were actually *confusing two different sciences*, unbeknownst to themselves. That is why Aristotle can *both* criticize them and *take them as models*: "*they* were seeking the causes of being as being, and so I should do so."[31] Thus, we see that things are not so easily presented as McInerny thinks.

Consider the following passage from Thomas, where he is speaking again of the first principles known to all human beings. It is of the *terms* of these very principles that he says:

> But of some propositions the *terms* are such that they are in the knowledge of all, such as "a being", "[something] one", and the others which pertain to a being precisely as a being [*entis, in quantum ens*]: for "a being" is the first conception of the intellect. Hence, it is necessary that such propositions not only in themselves, but even relative to *everyone*, stand as known by virtue of themselves: for example that "it does not happen that the same thing be and not be," and that "a whole is greater than its own part," and the like. Hence, such principles all sciences receive from metaphysics, to which it belongs to consider being, just in itself [*ens simpliciter*], and those things which belong to being.[32]

---

[30] One can, of course, contend that their error was understandable.

[31] I dramatize the text of Aristotle, *Metaph.* 4.1 (1003a26-32).

[32] Aquinas, *Expositio libri* POSTERIORUM 1.5 (Leonine lines 120-130; ed. Spiazzi, #50):

> Sed quarundam propositionum termini sunt tales, quod sunt in notitia omnium, sicut ens, et unum, et alia quae sunt entis, in quantum ens: nam ens est prima conceptio intellectus. Unde oportet quod tales propositiones non solum in se, sed etiam quoad omnes, quasi per se notae habeantur. Sicut quod, non contingit idem esse et non esse; et quod, totum sit maius sua parte: et similia. Unde et huiusmodi principia

It is these terms, *as known by everyone*, that pertain to the metaphysician. This is hardly a scenario in which "being" first has a narrow meaning, limited to the physical, and then is widened by physics proving the existence of the incorporeal. What characterizes the group Thomas is speaking of in the text quoted above is that they are known from the start to all. These belong to metaphysics.

As regards the scientist in a particular discipline such as physics, St. Thomas views the mind of the physicist as using what is *known to all*, but using it *in a narrower* way. He says (speaking of the principles used by all the sciences):

> Now, the reason why all the sciences use them [Aristotle] assigns thusly, that *each* subject genus of a particular science receives the predication of "a being." However, the particular sciences use the aforementioned principles not according to *their own community,* inasmuch as they extend to *all beings,* but rather as much as suffices for themselves; and this is according to the limit of the genus that has the role of subject in the science, concerning which the science provides demonstrations. For example, natural philosophy uses them inasmuch as they extend to mobile beings and no farther.[33]

*The doctrine is not* that we have first a narrow notion and then it gets broadened by proof of separate entity; it is rather that *we have a notion from the start that is maximally universal ("their own community"),* but that the physical scientist "uses" only part of its range. The first notions are

---

omnes scientiae accipiunt a metaphysica, cuius est considerare ens simpliciter et ea, quae sunt entis.

[33] Aquinas, *CM* 4.5 (591):

> Rationem autem, quare omnes scientiae eis utuntur, sic assignat; quia unumquodque genus subiectum alicuius scientiae recipit praedicationem entis. Utuntur autem principiis praedictis scientiae particulares non secundum suam communitatem, prout se extendunt ad omnia entia, sed quantum sufficit eis: et hoc secundum continentiam generis, quod in scientia subiicitur, de quo ipsa scientia demonstrationes affert. Sicut ipsa philosophia naturalis utitur eis secundum quod se extendunt ad entia mobilia, et non ulterius.

known from the start to all human beings and known in their *universality*.[34]

I am pleased to note that Jacques Maritain taught that our first notions are such as to reveal their wider applicability. Speaking of the transcendentals he says:

> Such objects are trans-sensible, because while having reality in the sensible where we grasp them first of all, they present themselves to the mind as transcending every genus and every category, and as able to have reality in subjects of a quite other essential nature than those subjects wherein they are apprehended. It is most remarkable that the first object attained by our mind in things, i.e. being—which cannot deceive us because, being the first, it cannot involve the mind's own construction and thus possibility of false composition—bears within it the sign

---

[34] Ashley [*The Way*, 148] says:

> I have argued in chapter 4 that such first principles as that of non-contradiction and of causality are shown *in via inventionis* to be directly evident principles only as principles of natural science restricted in its scope as a science of the sensible. Only when natural science has proved that immaterial being exists can these principles be extended analogically to become universal principles common to all the sciences. Thus, if taken in this universal sense, they are first principles of all the sciences and are proved by Metascience *in via resolutionis*.

I say that the physicist uses the first principles in a limited way (and so does Thomas: e.g. *CM* 4.5 [591], just seen). That does not affect the question of their *intrinsic power* right from the start. It affects their *scientific use*. Indeed, for Thomas, in the pedagogical order, their first scientific use is in *mathematics* (or even logic), not physics or metaphysics. Cf. e.g. Thomas Aquinas, *Super Librum de causis expositio*, ed. H. D. Saffrey, O.P. (Fribourg\Louvain: Société philosophique Nauwelaerts, 1954), 2, lines 14-24; English translation: St. Thomas Aquinas, *Commentary on the Book of Causes*, trans. Vincent A. Guagliardo, O.P., Charles R. Hess, O.P., and Richard C. Taylor (Washington, D.C.: the Catholic University of America Press, 1996), 3-4. I note, though, that the reason given for placing metaphysics last in this text relates properly only to *the second part of metaphysics*: i.e. it is that it "treats of the highest causes."

that beings of another order than the sensible are thinkable and possible.[35]

This is certainly not McInerny's conception of a notion of "being" which is *synonymous* with "corporeal being." It corresponds well with what I have pointed out in St. Thomas's texts about the first notion.

## IV. THE NATURE OF FIRST KNOWN BEING (PART 2)

It could be that a source of confusion is the presentation of "*separatio*" in St. Thomas's *Commentary on Boethius' De Trinitate*.[36] If one uses as the *only possible statement* of the nature of the metaphysical object the Avicennian statement,[37] i.e. that metaphysics bears upon "what is separate from matter," in the sense that "[the objects] do not necessarily have being in matter, as do the mathematicals," it may seem to follow that metaphysics can be known to be possible only when some being apart from matter is proved to exist.

---

[35] Cf. Jacques Maritain, *Les degrés du savoir*, 5th ed. (Paris: Desclée de Brouwer, 1946), 423-24 [the translation is mine, but I find it is essentially the same as that made from the 4th ed. under Fr. G.B. Phelan's direction, viz. *The Degrees of Knowledge* (New York: Scribners, 1959), 214]:

> De tels objets sont trans-sensibles, puisque réalisés dans le sensible où nous les saisissons d'abord, ils s'offrent à l'esprit comme transcendant tout genre et toute catégorie, et pouvant être réalisés dans des sujets d'une toute autre essence que ceux où ils sont appréhendés. Il est extrêmement remarquable que [424] le premier objet atteint par notre esprit dans les choses, l'être, - qui ne peut pas nous tromper parce qu'étant le premier il ne saurait envelopper de construction effectuée par l'esprit, donc de possibilité de composition fautive – porte en lui le signe que des êtres d'un autre ordre que l'ordre sensible sont pensables et possibles.

[36] Aquinas, *Commentary on Boethius'* ON THE TRINITY, 5.3: cf. Thomas Aquinas, *Expositio super librum Boethii De trinitate*, ed. Bruno Decker (Leiden: Brill, 1959); English translation in: Thomas Aquinas, *The Division and Methods of the Sciences: Questions v and vi of his Commentary on the De Trinitate of Boethius*, translated by Armand Maurer, 4th revised edition (Toronto: Pontifical Institute of Mediaeval Studies, 1986). This work is hereafter abbreviated as *BT*.

[37] It is so called, as we shall see, in e.g. *CM* 6.1 (1165).

It is certainly true that if, as in the time of Aristotle, there is confusion of physics and metaphysics, proving the existence of separate entity makes it clear that they are two distinct sciences (one might just as well say that it is thus that physics is revealed as a science distinct from metaphysics, as the converse). Aristotle thus made the point that if there is separate entity, then there is a science distinct from physics and prior to it in intelligibility. This step, historically, has even led many readers to hold that Aristotelian metaphysics is *solely about* separate entity.[38]

Thus, we see St. Thomas, at the very moment when Aristotle makes this case for first philosophy as considering separate entity, insist in his commentary quite simply that *metaphysics is also about material substance.* So serious is the possibility of misreading here that Thomas, after following out Aristotle's presentation, sees the need to comment:

> *It is to be noted, however* [*Advertendum est autem*], that though to the consideration of first philosophy pertain those things that are separate as to being and notion from matter and motion, nevertheless not just those things, but rather the philosopher studies sensible things as well, inasmuch as they are beings.[39]

Only after making this point clear does he recall the Avicennian description:

> *Unless perhaps we say* [*Nisi forte dicamus*], as Avicenna says, that the sort of common items that this science studies are called "separate as to being" not because they are always without

[38] For a review of the variety of readings of Aristotle's *Metaphysics* in this regard, cf. Joseph Owens, *The Doctrine of Being in the Aristotelian* METAPHYSICS, second edition (Toronto: Pontifical Institute of Mediaeval Studies, 1963), 35-68 (summary at 66-68).

[39] Aquinas, *CM* 6.1 [1165]: "*Advertendum est autem*, quod licet ad considerationem primae philosophiae pertineant ea quae sunt separata secundum esse et rationem a materia et motu, non tamen solum ea; sed etiam de sensibilibus, inquantum sunt entia, philosophus perscrutatur (my bold letters)." I was glad to see that John Wippel, in his book: *The Metaphysical Thought of Thomas Aquinas* (Washington, D.C.: the Catholic University of America Press, 2000), 54-55, treats the "Advertendum est autem..." passage as seemingly expressive of Thomas's own view.

> matter, but because they do not necessarily have being in matter as do the mathematicals.[40]

The Avicennian presentation is an *option*, not the necessary presentation of the doctrine of the nature of metaphysics. There is no objection to this formulation, but Thomas's own first statement is to be noted, as a protection against being misled by Aristotle's procedure.

One could say, with Avicenna, that metaphysics is about "what is without matter and motion" because being can *sometimes* be found without these. The Avicennian formulation, *so taken, is made in the context of already knowing that there is separate entity.* Thomas's own first statement, i.e. "metaphysics is also about material substance," expresses his position, as we have seen him spell it out, that one can be in the science of metaphysics ("the first part of metaphysics"), and not yet know whether there exists any immaterial substance.

This is indeed, I would say, how one should read *ST* 1.85.1.ad 2, on the three levels of abstract objects. Notice that one is in a discussion of human intellectual knowledge *of corporeal things*. This is the topic of qq. 84-86.[41] Q. 85 presents the mode and order of knowing such things. A. 1 of q. 85 bears on the understanding of corporeal and material things through abstraction from the images in the imagination, as the introductory paragraph makes explicit: "Thus we proceed to the first [article]. It seems that our intellect does not understand corporeal and material things through abstraction from the phantasms."[42] The second objection reads:

> Besides, material things are natural things, in whose definition matter is included. Now, nothing can be understood without that which is included in its definition. Therefore, material

---

[40] Ibid.: "*Nisi forte dicamus,* ut Avicenna dicit, quod huiusmodi communia de quibus haec scientia perscrutatur, dicuntur separata secundum esse, non quia semper sint sine materia; sed quia non de necessitate habent esse in materia, sicut mathematica (my italics)."

[41] Cf. *ST* 1.84.1.prologue (ed. Ottawa, 511a23-27).

[42] Aquinas, *ST* 1.85.1: "Ad primum sic proceditur. Videtur quod intellectus noster non intelligat res corporeas et materiales per abstractionem a phantasmatibus."

> things cannot be understood without matter. But matter is the principle of individuation. Therefore material things cannot be understood through abstraction of the universal from the particular, which is to abstract the intelligible likenesses from the phantasms.[43]

Consider, now, the reply to the objection itself. Thomas begins by pointing out that some people have held that the species of the material thing is the form alone; however, Thomas himself holds that the definition of the material thing includes matter. He accordingly distinguishes between individual matter and common matter. This allows him to resolve the problem as regards the objects of natural science. However, he does not stop there. In keeping with Aristotle himself in *Metaphysics* 7 (to which Thomas refers here), who also spoke of a matter within mathematical objects,[44] Thomas continues with the distinction between sensible matter and intelligible matter. This allows him to distinguish not only between the natural and the mathematical, but also between the intellectual objects of mathematics and the objects of mathematical imagination. One can abstract from individual intelligible matter, but not from common intelligible matter.

In this same line of discussion we are introduced to the objects that Thomas elsewhere calls "metaphysical."[45] We read: "But there are some [objects of intellectual consideration] which can be abstracted even from common intelligible matter, such as 'a being,' 'something one,' 'potency' and 'act,' and other such items, which also can exist without any matter, as is clear in the case of immaterial substances."[46] Now, I

---

[43] Aquinas, *ST* 1.85.1.obj. 2: "Praeterea, res materiales sunt res naturales, in quarum definitione cadit materia. Sed nihil potest intelligi sine eo quod cadit in definitione eius. Ergo res materiales non possunt intelligi sine materia. Sed materia est individuationis principium. Ergo res materiales non possunt intelligi per abstractionem universalis a particulari, quod est abstrahere species intelligibiles a phantasmatibus."

[44] Cf. Aristotle, *Metaph.* 7.10 (1036a10).

[45] Cf. *ST* 1.11.3.ad 2: "quoddam metaphysicum."

[46] Aquinas, *ST* 1.85.1.ad 2 (525b32-37): "Quaedam vero sunt quae possunt abstrahi etiam a materia intelligibili communi, sicut ens, unum, potentia et actus, et alia huiusmodi, quae etiam esse possunt absque omni materia, ut patet in substantiis immaterialibus."

would say that we should read as essential here the text up to the words: "other such items." This presents the mode of abstraction we are to consider, taking "abstraction" as pertaining to *absolute intellectual consideration*. "*Ens*" and its associates abstract, i.e. by leaving it out of consideration, from *all* matter, individual and common, sensible and intelligible. The idea is that we mine *sensible things* for three modes of intelligible object, the third of which abstracts completely from matter.

Thomas then continues with the point that *these* objects *also* pertain to the discussion of the sort of "abstraction" that occurs in the intellect's compositions and divisions. One can see that this is so because of the case of immaterial substances.

Thomas, in the reply to the previous objection, had distinguished the abstraction pertaining to our intellect's acts of simple and absolute consideration from the abstraction pertaining to its acts of composition and division.[47] In the present reply to obj. 2, "*ens*" is presented as the product of an abstraction according to absolute consideration: it leaves out all matter. However, if one has knowledge of the existence of immaterial substances (which knowledge the body of the article noted as possible, starting from knowledge of material things), then it is clear [*patet*] that an "*ens*" can be something abstract in the second way as well.

The general doctrine of the abstractness of "*ens*" simply leaves out matter. It neither includes nor excludes being composed with or divided from matter.[48]

---

[47] This latter "*abstractio*," of course, is the same as the "*separatio*" spoken of in *BT*; Thomas never returned to that *BT* vocabulary. This is so even though, according to the vocabulary of the text of Aristotle in the *sed contra* argument of 1.85.1, *all* abstraction is being called "separation." We read: "Sicut res sunt *separabiles* a materia, sic circa intellectum sunt" [as things are separable from matter, so are they in the intellect].

[48] There is no concept of "a being" which includes matter in the *precise target of signification (save through error)*, though all our concepts have a *mode of signifying* which derives from the materiality of the things we primarily know. See *ST* 1.13.3.ad 1 and 1.13.1.ad 2.

## V. TO CONCLUDE

Metaphysics does not exist *as a science* until the first conclusion is demonstrated.[49] Because of the need for habituation in the domain of "particular reason," i.e. the *vis cogitativa*, memorative, and imaginative powers, the drawing of that conclusion quite likely will follow the existence of physics. Thus we read:

> In the apprehensive powers one must consider that the passive factor is twofold: one being the possible intellect [*intellectus possibilis*], the other being the intellect [*intellectus*] which Aristotle calls "passive" [*passivus*], which is particular reason, i.e. the thinking power [*vis cogitativa*] along with the memorative and imaginative [powers]. As regards the first passive factor, there can be an active factor which by one act totally convinces the corresponding passive power: for example, one proposition known by virtue of itself can convince the intellect to assent firmly to the conclusion. A probable proposition does not do this. Accordingly, many acts of reason are required to cause a habit of opinion, even as regards the possible intellect; whereas *it is possible for a scientific habit to be caused by one act of reason, as regards the possible intellect.* Still, *as regards the lower apprehensive powers*, it is necessary that the same acts be repeated often so as to impress something firmly in the memory. Hence, the Phil-

---

[49] Cf. *ST* 1-2.54.4.ad 3:

> ...*he who in some science acquires by demonstration the science of one conclusion has the habit, but imperfectly.* Then when he acquires through another demonstration the science of another conclusion, there is not generated in that person another habit; rather, the habit that was already present is rendered *more perfect*, as extending to more [truths]; in that the conclusions and demonstrations of one science are *ordered*, and *one derives from another*...[...ille qui in aliqua scientia acquirit per demonstrationem scientiam *conclusionis unius, habet quidem habitum, sed imperfecte.* Cum vero acquirit per aliquam demonstrationem scientiam conclusionis alterius, non aggeneratur in eo alius habitus; sed habitus qui prius inerat fit perfectior, utpote ad plura se extendens; eo quod *conclusiones et demonstrationes unius scientiae ordinatae sunt, et una derivatur ex alia.*]

> osopher says in the book *On Memory and Reminiscence* that meditation confirms memory.[50]

Nor is metaphysics *unqualifiedly perfect* until it has provided *all* the conclusions possible with respect to the highest cause, about which it treats in its second part.[51] However, there are no grounds for holding that it cannot exist until one knows of the existence of immaterial substance.

---

[50] Cf. *ST* 1-2.51.3 [my stress]:

> In apprehensivis autem potentiis considerandum est quod duplex est passivum, unum quidem ipse intellectus possibilis; aliud autem intellectus quem vocat Aristoteles passivum, qui est ratio particularis, idest vis cogitativa cum memorativa et imaginativa. Respectu igitur primi passivi, potest esse aliquod activum quod uno actu totaliter vincit potentiam sui passivi, sicut una propositio per se nota convincit intellectum ad assentiendum firmiter conclusioni; quod quidem non facit propositio probabilis. Unde ex multis actibus rationis oportet causari habitum opinativum, etiam ex parte intellectus possibilis, habitum autem scientiae possibile est causari ex uno rationis actu, quantum ad intellectum possibilem. Sed quantum ad inferiores vires apprehensivas, necessarium est eosdem actus pluries reiterari, ut aliquid firmiter memoriae imprimatur. Unde Philosophus, in libro De memoria et reminiscentia, dicit quod meditatio confirmat memoriam.

[51] Cf. the text in n. 49. We should note that when one speaks of metaphysical wisdom, to which our knowledge of God belongs, it cannot in this present life be "perfect" in the sense of being the human being's *possession*; but the little knowledge one can have concerning God is preferable to all other knowledge. Cf. *ST* 1-2.66.5.ad 3.

# INCOMPLETE PERSONS: THOMAS AQUINAS ON SEPARATED SOULS AND THE IDENTITY OF THE HUMAN PERSON

GIUSEPPE BUTERA

## I. INTRODUCTION

In some of her recently published works,[1] Eleonore Stump challenges a fairly common interpretation of Thomas Aquinas on the identity of the human person, an interpretation which she refers to as the constitution view of the human person. According to this interpretation, the identity of the human person cannot be distinguished from his constitution. For this reason, the death of the body is thought to result in the death of the person, since the body is considered one of his constituent metaphysical parts. From this, it follows that a separated soul can no more be identified with the person to whom it once belonged than a part can be identified with a whole. Against this view, Stump has advanced an alternative interpretation according to which persons can survive the death of their bodies and go on living as separated souls. Central to her interpretation is the claim that a thing's identity is not bound up with its metaphysical constitution.

In the first part of the essay (sections II and III), I will argue that Stump's reading of Thomas fails on both exegetical and philosophical

---

[1] Eleonore Stump, *Aquinas* (New York: Routledge, 2003); "Aquinas's Metaphysics: Individuation and Constitution," in *Categories: Historical and Systematic Essays*, ed. Michael Gorman and Jonathan J. Sanford, Studies in Philosophy and History of Philosophy, vol. 41 (Washington, D.C.: the Catholic University of America Press, 2004), 33-44; "Forms and Bodies: The Soul," in Maria Candida Pacheco and Jose Francisco Meirinhos, eds., *Intellect and Imagination in Medieval Philosophy*, vol. 3, Actes du XI Congres Inter-national de Philosophie Medievale de la Societé Internationale pour l'Etude de la Philosophie Medievale (Turnhout: Brepols, 2006), 1379-87; "Resurrec-tion, Reassembly, and Reconstitution: Aquinas on the Soul," in *Die Men-schliche Seele: Brauchen Wir Den Dualismus?*, ed. B. Niederbacher and E. Runggaldier (Frankfurt: Ontos, 2006), 151-72.

grounds. On exegetical grounds, because Thomas explicitly rejects the view she attributes to him; on philosophical grounds, because while constitution is not identity at the level of accidental being, it is identity at the level of substantial being. To lose a hand is one thing; to lose a body something else entirely.

Yet, although I disagree with her reading of Thomas, I do think Stump is right to point out a serious exegetical difficulty with the constitution view, namely, that it makes it very difficult to explain how Thomas could have spoken of the separated souls in terms usually reserved for persons if he did not believe them, in fact, to be persons. It would seem, therefore, that the challenge for those of his interpreters who cannot see their way to giving up the constitution view is to square his metaphysics of the human person, which says that the death of the body marks the death of the person, with his theological belief in the ability of disembodied souls to do the kinds of things persons do.

An attempt to do this will be made in the second part of the essay (section IV), where I will argue that although the separated soul cannot, on Thomas's own terms, be construed as a person, it is more true to say that it is the person to whom it once belonged than to say that it is not. Somewhat against the grain of this conclusion, I will also argue that Thomas assigns much less moral significance to personhood than we moderns do and that this might be the key to understanding why he does not hesitate to use moral categories such as punishment and reward when speaking of separated souls.

## II. STUMP'S REJECTION OF THE CONSTITUTION VIEW

In rejecting the constitution view of the human person, Stump marshals both textual evidence and philosophical arguments to help make her case. The textual evidence consists of a number of passages where Thomas "attributes to disembodied souls properties which he and we take to be most characteristic of human persons."[2] These attributes include the capacity to experience delight[3] and suffering;[4] to

---

[2] Stump, "Aquinas's Metaphysics: Individuation and Constitution," 1383-84.

[3] Thomas Aquinas, *Summa Theologica* (*ST*), trans. by the Fathers of the English Dominican Province (Westminster, Maryland: Christian Classics, 1981), Suppl. III, q. 70, a. 2 ad 5. All quotations from the *Summa Theologiae* are from this translation.

understand and make choices[5]; to appear to the living[6] and respond to their prayers.[7] Taken together, these passages are said to point to a doctrine of personal immortality according to which the human person, not just his soul, "persists after bodily death."[8]

The philosophical portion of Stump's case turns on an analogy. There is no doubt that Thomas believes that it belongs to the constitution of the human person to have two hands. Yet Thomas also believes a person can lose one or both without ceasing to be a person. Hence, constitution is not identity. But if this is so, Stump argues, there is no a priori reason to suppose that a person cannot survive the loss of his body. And if "the remaining constituents can exist on their own and are sufficient for the existence of the substance," then there will be nothing preventing Thomas from supposing "that [a human person, can] survive even the loss of some of [his] metaphysical constituents."[9]

Now, Stump argues that "a substantial form is sufficient for the existence of the supposit whose form it is, and so the existence of a human soul is sufficient for the existence of a human [person]."[10] "Analogously," therefore, although "the metaphysical constituents of a human being normally include matter and substantial form... Aquinas thinks that a human being can exist without being in the normal condition in this way either."[11] Since constitution is not identity, and, Stump argues, what makes someone a person is his substantial form, the death of the body does not spell his doom.

---

[4] Ibid., q. 70, a. 3.

[5] Ibid., q.72, a. 3.

[6] Ibid., q. 69, a. 3.

[7] Ibid., q. 72, a. 2. For Stump's discussion of these passages, see "Forms and Bodies: The Soul," 1383.

[8] Ibid.

[9] Stump, "Resurrection, Reassembly, and Reconstitution: Aquinas on the Soul," 165.

[10] Ibid., 1383. By "supposit" Stump means an individual, concrete existing thing.

[11] Stump, "Forms and Bodies: The Soul," 1382.

It is important to stress that Stump is not trying to reduce the human person to his substantial form. Although she insists that constitution is not identity, it is not metaphysically insignificant, either. Stump goes out of her way to reject any such reduction, arguing instead that a human person is constituted of both body and soul:

> [A] human person is identical to a particular in the species *rational animal.* A particular of that sort is normally, naturally, constituted of an array of bodily parts and is composed of form and matter. Because constitution is not identity for Aquinas, however, a particular can exist with less than the normal, natural complement of constituents. It can, for example, exist when it is constituted only by one of its main metaphysical parts, namely, the soul. And so although a person is not identical to his soul, the existence of the soul is sufficient for the existence of a person.[12]

So, although it belongs to every human person to have a body and a soul, those same persons can continue to exist without their bodies, although to do so, it should be noted, would be to endure a loss of a "main metaphysical part."

## III. PROBLEMS WITH STUMP'S ANTI-CONSTITUTION VIEW

If there is a philosophical problem with Stump's reading of Thomas, what we might call her anti-constitution view of the human person, it is precisely in her attempt to extend a truth about constitution and identity at the level of accidental being to the level of substantial being. Certainly, on Thomas's metaphysics, a substance can endure the loss of at least some of its constituent parts without losing its identity. A hand or a foot, although part of the human person's constitution, is not essential to him. They do not, properly speaking, belong to the essence of the human person, but rather flow from it in the same way risibility and other proper accidents do.[13]

---

[12] Ibid., 1384.

[13] See Thomas Aquinas, *Commentary on Aristotle's* METAPHYSICS, trans. Richard J. Blackwell, Richard J. Spath, and W. Edmund Thirlkel (Notre Dame, Indiana: Dumb Ox Books, 1995), Bk. 6, lect. 3, n. 1219, 418.

But it is difficult to see how a substance could lose a main metaphysical part without ceasing altogether to exist, much less remain "a particular in the species *rational animal.*" Stump would have a point if such parts did not belong to the substance essentially. In that case, a human person could lose his body without ceasing to be a person. But it belongs essentially to the human person to have a body. It is this fact that places him in the genus *animal.* As such, it is no more possible for the disembodied soul to be a person than for two straight lines to form a triangle.

Thomas confirms this line of reasoning in *ST* I, q. 29, a. 1 where he defends Boethius' definition of person as an individual substance of a rational nature. The fifth objection to Boethius's definition is a *reductio ad absurdum.* According to this objection, if a person were in fact an individual substance of a rational nature, then we would have to say that the separated soul is a person. But the separated soul is not a person. Therefore, the objection concludes, Boethius's definition must be wrong. In his reply, rather than taking issue with the objection's denial of personhood to the separated soul, Thomas instead takes the logic of constitution used by Stump and turns it on its head, arguing that just as neither a hand nor any other part of man can be an individual substance, neither can the soul alone—which "is part of the human species"—"be called an individual substance." Because the soul "ever retains its nature of unibility" with the body, Thomas explains, "it cannot be called an individual substance." That is to say, because the soul ever retains its natural ordination to inform a body,[14] the soul separated from the body must be incomplete. Thomas therefore concludes that "neither the definition nor the name of person belongs to [the separated soul]."[15]

At this point, one might wonder what could have prompted Stump to advance an interpretation so apparently at odds with Thomas's explicit teaching on the nature of constitution and identity at the level of substantial being. Two major reasons seem to have been at work in her thinking, one philosophical, the other exegetical. Stump puts the philosophical reason in the form of an objection:

---

[14] For further discussion of this point, see n. 33 below.

[15] Aquinas, *ST*, 1:156.

> The intellectual faculties of the separated soul of Socrates are the intellectual faculties Socrates had during his lifetime. So, for example, the memories that Socrates laid down during his earthly life are the memories of the separated soul of Socrates. And insofar as the will is a rational faculty, the will of the separated soul of Socrates is the same will as the will which Socrates had during his lifetime. Finally, the separated soul also has experiences and passions. If it is in hell, for example, the separated soul experiences pain and has the passion of sorrow; and the mind in the separated soul affected by these passions is the mind of Socrates. But how can these things be true if Socrates has ceased to exist?[16]

The exegetical reason, related to this objection and supportive of it, rests on a number of passages in Thomas's corpus where we find him speaking about the disembodied soul in terms proper to human persons, a fact noted above. Turning first to a consideration of the exegetical reason, we will return to the philosophical one in the next section.

From the fact that Thomas tells us that the separated soul is able to experience delight and sorrow, think, choose, appear to the living and respond to their prayers, Stump concludes that Thomas must have believed that the soul in its disembodied state is a person, since these are the actions of a person, the sorts of actions only persons can perform. Mindful, however, of Thomas's insistence on the existential unity of body and soul, Stump is also careful to say, as we have seen, that human persons are usually constituted of both. She sums up her position by saying that "the claim that the existence of a soul is sufficient for the existence of a person or a human being is compatible with Aquinas's claim that a soul by itself is not a person or a human being."[17] That Stump can say this without contradicting herself is due entirely to her carefully staked out claim that constitution, even at the metaphysical level, is not identity.

---

[16] Stump, "Resurrection, Reassembly, and Reconstruction: Aquinas on Soul," 155.

[17] Stump, "Forms and Bodies: The Soul," 1385.

One of the most explicit disavowals of Stump's anti-constitution view found in Thomas's corpus has the same provenance as the texts she adduces in support of it,[18] namely, the treatise on the resurrection and life everlasting (qq. 69-101), which is in the supplement to the *Tertia Pars* of the *Summa Theologiae*.[19] In q. 75, a. 1 of the treatise, Thomas asks whether there is to be a resurrection of the body. In the second objection, we find the following argument against the bodily resurrection. In Matthew 22:32, Jesus quotes Exodus 3:6, where God says that he is the God of Abraham, Isaac, and Jacob. Now since God is the God of the living and not of the dead, Abraham, Isaac and Jacob must have been alive when Jesus quoted the text, otherwise he would not have quoted it approvingly. And since their bodies had long since died, they must have been without their bodies when Jesus spoke these words, proving that they did not need their bodies to be alive. Therefore, the objection concludes, "there will be no resurrection of bodies but only of souls."[20] The obvious implication for our discussion is that disembodied souls are persons.

Thomas begins his reply by flatly denying that the soul by itself is a person: "Abraham's soul, properly speaking, is not Abraham himself, but a part of him (and not the same as regards the others). Hence life in Abraham's soul does not suffice to make Abraham a living being, or to make the God of Abraham the God of a living man. But there needs to

---

[18] See Stump, "Aquinas's Metaphysics: Individuation and Constitution," 41; "Forms and Bodies," 1383-84.

[19] It is worth noting that the supplement was "composed by [Thomas's] disciples [after his death] on the basis of his commentary on the *Sentences*." Jean-Pierre Torrell, *Saint Thomas Aquinas*, vol. 1, *The Person and His Work*, revised edition, trans. Robert Royal (Washington, D.C.: The Catholic University of America Press, 2005), 147. As such, it represents Thomas's early views. But on this, as on so many other points in his teaching, there is no discernible change between his first treatment of the subject and later ones. As is evident from his treatment of the separated soul in the *Prima Pars* of the *Summa* (q. 29, a. 1), which was written between 1265 and 1268, Thomas continued to believe in the non-personhood of the separated soul long after he wrote his commentary on the *Sentences*.

[20] Aquinas, *ST* Suppl. III, q. 75, a. 1 ob. 2 (5:2862).

be life in the whole composite, i.e., the soul and body."[21] The reason the resurrection is necessary is that bodily death *is* the death of the human person and the resurrection of the body is the only way to restore him to life. That is why Thomas says that "there needs to be life in the whole composite" "to make *Abraham* a living being, or to make the God of Abraham the God of a living *man*."[22] Stump might try to interpret this passage as saying only that it belongs to the constitution of a human person to have a body and a soul, not that a human person's identity is bound up with his constitution.[23] Doing so, however, would render Thomas's reply otiose since it works only if by "Abraham's soul" he means "Abraham's *disembodied* soul," rather than "Abraham's soul in its embodied state."

Another explicit disavowal of Stump's position can be found in *ST* II-II, q. 83, a. 11, part of Thomas's treatise on prayer. In considering whether the saints in heaven pray for us, the fifth objection argues that since St. Peter's soul is not St. Peter, we should not call upon him while his soul is separated from his body. We should instead call upon his soul. But the Church calls upon the person of St. Peter, not his soul. Therefore, the objection concludes, the saints do not pray for us, "at least before the resurrection."[24] In reply, Thomas does not deny the objection's assertion that St. Peter's separated soul is not St. Peter. Rather, he takes it as a given and argues that "it is because the saints while living merited to pray for us, that we invoke them under the names by which they were known in this life, and by which they are better known to us: and also in order to indicate our belief in the resurrection, according to the saying of Exodus 3:6, 'I am the God of Abraham,' etc."[25] Strictly speaking, therefore, our prayers, although addressed to the persons of the saints, are not heard or answered by them but by their souls (which Thomas calls "saints"), which await the resurrection of the body, not just in order that they might be complete,

---

[21] Ibid., q. 75, a. 2 ad 2 (5:2863).

[22] Ibid., emphasis added.

[23] She does just that in "Resurrection, Reassembly, and Reconstitution: Aquinas on the Soul," 169.

[24] Aquinas, *ST* II-II, q. 83, a. 11 (3:1540).

[25] Ibid.

but in order that the persons to whom they once belonged might live again.

## IV. INCOMPLETE PERSONS

### 1. The Doings of Separated Souls

Despite the implausibility of Stump's anti-constitution interpretation, I think she is right to wonder what the disembodied soul—a thing that can delight and sorrow, think and make choices, appear to the living and answer their prayers—could possibly be for Thomas if not a person, and not just any person, but the person whose soul it was in this life. For "if," as she says, "my soul is not *me*... then it seems that *I* do not survive bodily death." Indeed, given that my separated soul will think and will with numerically the same powers I use now, it is hard to see how it will be anything other than me. When I first started to think about this problem, I thought that although Thomas could not answer that it is a *human* person, he could answer that it is a person, nonetheless. But it appears that Thomas's position on the matter will not allow me to say this, unless perhaps "person" could be used in an analogous sense, a possibility Stump does not consider. It is to this possibility that we now turn.

On this interpretation, the disembodied soul would still not be a person, but then neither would it be wholly impersonal. Rather, it would be an incomplete person, as different from a person in the proper sense of the term as an incomplete substance is from a substance. Properly speaking, even as an incomplete person, St. Peter's separated soul would not be the fisherman himself. But neither would it be something wholly unrelated to him as a person. This might be all that is needed to harmonize those passages where Thomas treats the disembodied soul as if it were a person with his clear and unambiguous teaching that, strictly speaking, the separated soul is not a person. Although separated souls cannot be completely identified with the persons to whom they belonged in this life, it is more true to say that St. Peter's separated soul is St. Peter than to say that it is not.

To be at all plausible, this solution will have to be able to explain what it is about the separated soul that compels its categorization as an incomplete person rather than a non-person. One such explanation can be found in Thomas's defense of the doctrine of the resurrection in

Book 4, chapter 81 of the *Summa Contra Gentiles*. Of the objections brought against the resurrection, the third is the most relevant for our discussion. According to this objection, the resurrection is impossible because numerical identity cannot obtain where existential continuity is wanting. But death marks the end of a person's existence, a radical existential discontinuity between what came before and what might come after. So whatever else the person called St. Peter will be at the resurrection, he will not be the man who led the Apostles and was martyred at Rome.[26]

Thomas begins his reply by noting that since the being or act of existence (*esse*) of matter and form must be one, it follows that "matter [can have] no actual being [*esse*] except by form."[27]In most cases, the being of the form is so bound up with matter as to be identical with its "concrete union with matter."[28] Take away the matter of a squirrel, for example, and you take away its form. But this is not true of the rational soul. Its being is not identical with its "concrete union with the body."[29] We know this, Thomas says, because thinking and willing are operations that no bodily organ can perform. But this can be true only if the being of the human soul exceeds the existential bounds of the body. Consequently, since the rational soul's being is not limited to the body, it can survive the death of the body. This goes for the being of the composite, too, which is the being of the person. As Thomas puts it: the being of the rational soul, "*which is that of the composite*, remains in the soul even when the body is dissolved; when the body is restored in the

[26] My example.

[27] Thomas Aquinas, *Summa Contra Gentiles* (*SCG*), Bk. IV, *Salvation*, trans. Charles J. O'Neill (Notre Dame, Indiana: University of Notre Dame Press, 1957), 305, n. 11. All quotations from the *SCG* are from this translation. For the full Latin text of this reply, see n. 30 below.

[28] Ibid.

[29] The Latin from which this phrase is taken is as follows: "Nam esse aliarum formarum non est nisi in concretione ad materiam: non enim excedunt materiam neque in esse, neque in operari." For the full text of Thomas's response, see n. 30 below.

resurrection, it is returned to the same being [*esse*] which persisted in the soul."[30]

From this, it follows that the separated soul is numerically identical *at the level of being* (*esse*) with the person to whom it once belonged. Because the form of the human body is a subsistent form—a living soul that can exist independently of the body—its act of existence does not change when the body dies. Thomas himself concludes as much in the *Summa Theologiae*, which was written a few years after the *Summa Contra Gentiles*.[31] In an article discussing whether the body is necessary for our happiness, he writes:

> But the human soul [unlike the souls of other animals] retains the being [*esse*] of the composite after the destruction of the body: and this because the being of the form is the same as that of its matter, and this is the being [*esse*] of the composite. Now the soul subsists in its own being [*esse*], as stated in the First Part (q. 75, a. 2). It follows, therefore, that *after being separated from the body it has perfect being, and that consequently it can have perfect operation; although it has not the perfect specific nature*."[32]

---

[30] Ibid., 306, n. 11; emphasis added. Because of the importance of this text and the precision of Thomas's language, it is worth quoting the Latin text of his response in full: "Quod vero tertio obiicitur, quod esse non est unum, quia non est continuum: falso in nititur fundamento. Manifestum est enim quod materiae et formae unum est esse: non enim material habet esse in actu nisi per formam. Differt tamen quantum ad hoc anima rationalis ab aliis formis. Nam esse aliarum formarum non est nisi in concretione ad materiam: non enim excedunt materiam neque in esse, neque in operari. Anima vero rationalis, manifestum est quod excedit materiam in operari: habet enim aliquam operationem absque participation organi corporalis, scilicet intelligere. Unde et esse suum non est solum in concretione ad materiam. Esse igitur eius, quod erat compositi, manet in ipsa corpora dissoluto: et reparato corpore in resurrectione, in idem essere ducitur quod remansit in anima" (in *Sancti Thomae de Aquino opera omnia,* vol. 15 [Rome: Leonine Commission, 1930], 253).

[31] See Torrell, Saint Thomas Aquinas, vol. 1, *The Person and His Work*, 332.

[32] Aquinas, *ST* I-II, q. 4, a. 5 ad 2 (2:606); emphasis added. See also *ST* I, q. 76, a. 1 ad 5.

The separated soul continues to be something whose nature is to be united with a body. It never loses its natural desire to inform a body; and not just any body, but the body it used to inform.[33] Therefore, we may say that the separated soul is, in fact, both in terms of its being and form, identical with the person whose soul it was, since it exists by the numerically identical act of existence and is what it is by the numerically identical form. Ultimately, however, the separated soul is not numerically identical with the person himself, at least not at the level of substantial being, because without the body, the human soul by itself is incapable of constituting an individual substance of a rational nature.

Such a being, if not a person, is sufficiently like one to explain how it might be able to do the kinds of things persons do. Though only an incomplete substance, the separated soul exists by the numerically identical act of existence of the human composite of which it was once a part. Moreover, as a subsistent rational form, possessing both will and intellect,[34] the separated soul can delight and suffer, understand and make choices, appear to the living and respond to their prayers.

At this point, someone might object that all of this leaves untouched Stump's question about the identity of Socrates' (and Abraham's and St. Peter's) separated soul and how it could possibly be anything other than Socrates himself given the fact that "the mind of the separated soul of Socrates is the mind of Socrates." In reply, we might consider a logical corollary of the incomplete person hypothesis: the possibility

---

[33] This last point is defended by Thomas in the *Compendium of Theology* (q. 153, 171-72): "Since the soul is united to the body as its form, and since each form has the right matter corresponding to it, the body to which the soul will be reunited must be of the same nature and species as was the body laid down by the soul at death....Furthermore, just as the same specific form ought to have the same specific matter, so the same numerical form ought to have the same numerical matter." All quotations from the *Compendium* are taken from *Aquinas's Shorter Summa,* translated by Cyril Vollert, (Manchester, New Hampshire: Sophia Institute Press, 2002).

[34] "[A]ll the powers of the soul belong to the soul alone as their principle. But some powers belong to the soul alone as their subject; as the intelligence and the will. These powers must remain in the soul, after the destruction of the body": *ST* I, q. 77, a. 8 (1:389).

that full-fledged personhood is unnecessary for subjective conscious experience. In other words, incomplete personhood might be all that is needed to explain how the separated soul of Socrates could have the mind of Socrates, and yet not be Socrates. Although missing its body, the separated soul would still be able to think and will.[35] As a consequence, it would also be possessed of self-knowledge, since it is through knowing its own acts that the mind comes to know itself, and there is no reason to suppose that the separated soul cannot know its own acts.[36]

Now, because Socrates' soul is an incomplete person, the first person pronoun in "I am praying for Meletus' repentance," as well as the concept of person implicit in it, would have to mean something different when thought by Socrates' separated soul than when thought by Socrates himself. Knowing itself to be incomplete in a radically metaphysical way, Socrates' separated soul would also know that such terms as "I", "me," and "person" could apply to itself only in an analogous sense. But apply they would. When Socrates' soul says, "I am praying for Meletus' repentance," it is really saying, "I (i.e., the self-conscious subject of the acts of understanding, willing, etc., performed by me, the incomplete person of Socrates, the separated soul "ordained to the resurrection"[37]) am praying for Meletus' repentance." In this

---

[35] The range of will acts possible to a separated soul is limited by the fundamental orientation of the will at the moment of death. As Thomas concludes at the end of a short argument in *SCG* 4, chap. 95, n. 6: "Therefore, there is not in the separated soul a will changeable from good to evil, although it is changeable from this object of will to that so long as the order to the same ultimate end is preserved" (344).

[36] Thomas argues that in this life the soul comes to a knowledge of itself through its acts. See *ST* I, q. 87, especially a. 1 where, among other things, Thomas says the following: "But as in this life our intellect has material and sensible things for its proper natural object...it understands itself according as it is made actual by the species abstracted from sensible things, through the light of the active intellect, which not only actuates the intelligible things themselves, but also, by their instrumentality, actuates the passive intellect. Therefore the intellect knows itself not by its essence, but by its act" (1:444).

[37] Aquinas, *ST* III, supp. q. 75, a. 1 ad 2 (5:2863).

way, the separated soul could have the mind of Socrates without being the person of Socrates.

## 2. Separated Souls and God's Justice

Even so, there are some things, one would think, that only a full-fledged person could do, things impossible to a separated soul, even granting its existential and formal identity with the person to whom it once belonged and its status as an incomplete person. One of these would be to suffer the punishment or reward merited not by the separated soul itself, but by the person whose soul it once was. Yet this is precisely what Thomas believed. According to the Catholic faith, after death some souls are made to suffer the pains of hell,[38] enjoy the rewards of heaven,[39] or, in preparation for their entrance into heavenly bliss, endure the cleansing fires of purgatory[40] *prior* to the resurrection of the body. But how can this be true when God is just? Or, as Stump puts it: "[I]f the soul of Socrates is not Socrates, then what justice is there in assigning to the separated soul either the reward or the punishment merited by Socrates, who is not the soul?"[41]

---

[38] "[T]he fire [of hell] of its nature is able to have an incorporeal spirit united to it as a thing placed is united to a place; that as the instrument of Divine justice it is enabled to detain it enchained as it were, and in this respect this fire is really hurtful to the spirit, and thus the soul seeing the first as something hurtful to it is tormented by the fire": *ST* Suppl. III, q. 70, a. 3 (5:2830).

[39] "As to the perfect Happiness, which consists in the vision of God, some have maintained that it is not possible to the soul separated from the body; and have said that the souls of saints, when separated from their bodies, do not attain to that Happiness until the Day of Judgment, when they will receive their bodies back again. And this is shown to be false, both by authority and by reason": *ST* I-II, q. 4, a. 5 (2:605).

[40] "It also happens that some men depart this life free from mortal sin but nevertheless stained with venial sin.... In the case of some perfect men sins of this kind are expiated by the fervor of their love. But in others these sins must be atoned for by punishment of some sort; no one is admitted to the possession of eternal life unless he is free from all sin and imperfection": *Compendium of Theology*, q. 182 (208).

[41] Stump, "Resurrection, Reassembly, and Reconstitution: Aquinas on the Soul," 157.

That Thomas sees no difficulty in the suffering of separated souls is apparent from a number of passages found in works spanning his entire writing career. In the supplement to the *Tertia Pars* of the *Summa Theologiae*, which was compiled from his youthful *Commentary on the Sentences of Peter Lombard* after his death, we read that "[t]he purifying of the soul by the punishment of purgatory is nothing else than the expiation of the guilt that hinders it from obtaining glory."[42] A decade later, in the *Compendium of Theology*, Thomas wrote:

> [A]lthough some souls may be admitted to eternal beatitude as soon as they are released from their bodies, others may be held back from this happiness for a time. For it sometimes happens that during their lives people have not done full penance for the sins they have committed, but for which they have been sorry in the end. Since the order of divine justice demands that punishment be undergone for sins, we must hold that souls pay after this life the penalty they have not paid while on Earth.[43]

And, near the end of his life, Thomas reaffirmed this teaching in the *De Malo*, maintaining that "the remission of venial sin in purgatory so far as concerns punishment is effected by purgatory, which man by suffering pays what he owes and thus the debt ceases."[44]

It is important to note that in these passages we find more than an explicit avowal of the belief that the separated souls of the dead can and in some cases do suffer; we find a clear statement of the belief that their suffering is just and in fact somehow also the suffering of the persons whose souls they were in this life. How else could Thomas say that "the remission of venial sin in purgatory so far as concerns punishment is effected by purgatory, which *man* by suffering pays what

---

[42] Aquinas, *ST* Suppl. III, q. 71, a. 6 ad 3 (5:2838).

[43] Aquinas, *Compendium of Theology*, q. 181 (208).

[44] Thomas Aquinas, *On Evil*, q. 7, a. 11 ad 9, translated by John A. Oesterle and Jean T. Oesterle (Notre Dame, Indiana: University of Notre Dame Press, 1995), 303. For more on the dating of these works, see Torrell, *Saint Thomas Aquinas*, vol. 1, *The Person and His Work*, especially Giles Emery's "Brief Catalogue of the Works of Saint Thomas Aquinas," 330-61.

he owes and thus the debt ceases"?[45] Or that "souls pay after this life the penalty *they* have not paid while on Earth"?[46] If Thomas were less insistent that the disembodied soul is not the person who merited to suffer these pains, we might be tempted to conclude, on the strength of these passages alone, that the separated soul simply is the person. But not only will Thomas not allow us to say this, he also apparently sees no reason to do so.

In chapter 91 of Book IV of the *Summa Contra Gentiles*, where we find a defense of the belief that souls "immediately after their separation from the body...will receive punishment or reward," Thomas argues that the body is required neither for their punishment nor for their reward:

> There is, moreover, in the order of fault and merit a harmony with the order of punishment and reward. But merit and fault are fitted to the body only through the soul, since there is essentially no merit or demerit except so far as a thing is voluntary. Therefore, both reward and punishment flow suitably from the soul to the body, but it does not belong to the soul by reason of the body. There is, therefore, no reason in the infliction of punishment or bestowal of reward why the souls should wait for the resumption of their bodies; rather, it seems more fitting that, since the souls had priority in the fault or merit, they have priority also in being punished or rewarded.[47]

We are able to merit punishment or reward because we are endowed with intellect and free will, powers that continue to exist in the separated soul. Because sin begins in these powers, it is only fitting, Thomas maintains, that punishment and reward in the hereafter should begin with the soul, even before it is reunited with the body.

Implicit in this proposal would seem to be the suggestion that what is morally relevant about any human being is not his personhood, but his rationality. Unlike modern notions of personhood, which tend to freight the term with moral significance, all but equating it with moral

---

[45] Ibid; emphasis added.

[46] Ibid; emphasis added.

[47] Aquinas, *SCG*, Bk. IV, c. 91, 335.

agency, the notion of personhood in Thomas's thought appears not to have anything like the same moral heft. It is surely significant that wherever he defends the belief that reward and punishment begin in the next life immediately upon the death of the body, he never considers the objection that it is unfair or vain to punish separated souls for the sins of others.[48] For Thomas, it is enough that a separated soul played an essential and principal part in the person's sins to justify its punishment. The morally relevant subject is the rational soul, not the person.

Granted all that has been said up to this point, however, one might object that it falls short of the mark by proving too much, since it would seem to make the resurrection unnecessary. After all, if the separated soul can suffer the pains of hell, endure the cleansing fires of purgatory, and enjoy the rewards of heaven, what need can there be of the body?

The answer to this question is found in Thomas's reasons for thinking the resurrection necessary. In the first place, he argues for the necessity of the resurrection from the fact that the soul is naturally ordered to inform a body. For, without the resurrection, the separated and never-dying soul would, in the long run, spend virtually all of its interminable existence frustrated, unable to inform a body. But, in a universe created by a wise, benevolent, and provident God, this could not happen. God makes nothing in vain. So although nature itself cannot effect the resurrection, God can and will. For this reason, we may consider the resurrection to have virtually all the inevitability of a natural necessity. Additionally, Thomas argues that the resurrection is also necessary on account of the body's contribution to the soul's perfection, not "as constituting the essence thereof," the way the "soul

---

[48] The only place Thomas comes close to espousing anything like this view is in *ST* Suppl. III, q. 75, a. 2, where he considers whether "the resurrection will be for all without exception." Thomas asserts that "the resurrection is necessary in order that those who rise again may receive punishment or reward according to their merits" (5:2864). From what follows immediately upon this sentence, however, it is most likely that Thomas was not saying that the resurrection is necessary for reward and punishment, but only that reward and punishment cannot be perfected without it.

is necessary for man's perfection," but "as necessary for [the soul's] well-being."[49]

The soul never ceases to be a potentially informing form, by nature ordered to give being and structure to a living body, so that to be reunited with the body is to bring the soul to its natural perfection; it is also to increase the soul's happiness by extending it to the body.[50] What goes for delight goes also for pain. The soul's suffering is increased by the possession of a body, as Thomas makes clear in his description of the suffering of the resurrected damned, who, unlike the saints, will have bodies that are "not subtle and impassible; instead, they will remain in their grossness and capacity for suffering, and, indeed, these defects will be heightened in them."[51]

## V. CONCLUSION

In addition to its ability to explain how the separated soul, even though not a person, can do the sorts of things persons do, the incomplete-person defense of the constitution view of the human person developed in this essay also has the advantage of not reading into Thomas's thought a modern, ethically-freighted conception of personhood. Yes, St. Peter's soul is not St. Peter. And, yes, this is important. But for Thomas it is not nearly as important as the fact that the separated soul in heaven is St. Peter's, and not just his but that part of him that was most truly himself when he was alive.

If Thomas is right, then death must be viewed in a less dismal light than we are accustomed to viewing it in. If the soul is our truest self—the being of our person and our formal cause—and if the loss of the

---

[49] Aquinas, *ST* I-II, q. 4, a. 5 (2:606).

[50] It is not, however, to increase the intensity of the soul's happiness, something Thomas is careful to note. "The desire of the separated soul is entirely at rest, as regards the thing desired; since, to wit, it has that which suffices its appetite. But it is not wholly at rest, as regards the desirer, since it does not possess that good in every way that it would wish to possess it. Consequently, after the body has been resumed, Happiness increases not in intensity, but in extent": *ST* I-II, q. 4, a. 5 ad 5 (2:606). Cf. *De Potentia Dei*, Bk. 2, q. 5, a. 10.

[51] Aquinas, *Compendium of Theology*, q. 176 (203).

body is only a temporary loss, as Thomas argues it must be, then the death of the body cannot be the disaster imagined by so many.

We might be surprised by this conclusion and less than satisfied with it, but I think it is a mark in its favor that it does not render death wholly transparent to reason. By drawing back a little of the thick veil that hides the hereafter from our sight, it suggests a wide and fathomless mystery. Another mark in its favor is its ability to explain how St. Paul could hope for death, as he does in his Letter to the Philippians, without at the same time denigrating the body:

> For to me to live is Christ, and to die is gain. If it is to be life in the flesh, that means fruitful labor for me. Yet which I shall choose I cannot tell. I am hard pressed between the two. My desire is to depart and be with Christ, for that is far better. But to remain in the flesh is more necessary on your account.[52]

In commenting on this passage, Thomas says that it reveals the error of holding that "the souls of the saints are not with Christ immediately after death."[53]As we might expect, Thomas is careful to say that the souls of the saints, not the saints themselves, are with Christ. More importantly, he is careful to explain that St. Paul's desire to die is from the "impulse to love God [, which] moves us to be with God...not absolutely [that is, *not* because we wish to be separated from our bodies], but *to be with Christ*," and this because "*to be with Christ is far better.*"[54] If we love God and are, in the words of another Thomas, "blithe to go to him,"[55] then death will be more devoutly hoped for than feared.

Notice, however, that Thomas does not say that it is better for the soul to be without the body. Neither can he do so without betraying his conviction that every soul is ordained "to the resurrection."[56] If death is indeed something to be devoutly hoped for, then so much more the

---

[52]Aquinas, *Commentary on Philippians*, chap. 1, 66.

[53] Ibid., chap. 1, 70.

[54] Chap. 1, 70.

[55] St. Thomas More, in Robert Bolt's *A Man for All Seasons* (New York: Vintage Books, 1990), 162.

[56] See n. 37 above.

resurrection, not because we cannot be happy without our bodies, but because our happiness and God's justice[57] cannot be complete without them.

[57] See n. 48 above.

# PART II

## Analogies of the Divine

# "The Great Visible God": Socrates, Aristotle, and Thomas Aquinas on the Way from Nature to Nature's God

Christopher S. Morrissey

The Five Ways of Thomas Aquinas (*Summa Theologiae* I, 2, 3) are indebted to a metaphysical doctrine about God that was formulated in a prototypical way by Socrates and then later cast in a distinctive form by Aristotle.[1] The prototypical outline is suggested by Socrates in a conversation reported by Xenophon, which I would like to discuss here first. Next I shall relate this Socratic outline to Thomas Aquinas's metaphysics. Finally, I shall discuss how understanding the approach of Socrates in light of Aristotle is (to my mind) indispensable for appreciating the metaphysics of Thomas, because the Aristotelian clarification pertains to the correlativity of physics with metaphysics: namely, how a visible divine pattern in the universe points to the invisible God.

## I. Socratic Teaching on God

Xenophon testifies in his *Memorabilia* that Socrates, arguing from the manifestly visible order in things, gave a teleological proof for the existence of the divine. In order to rebuke Aristodemus, who was irreligious, Socrates begins with this question:[2]

> [Socrates:] "Suppose that it is impossible to guess the purpose of one creature's existence, and obvious that another's serves a

[1] The central portions of this article were delivered in an earlier version at "The Majesty and Poverty of Metaphysics," The American Maritain Association 2007 Annual Conference, University of Notre Dame, Co-sponsored by The Maritain Center, University of Notre Dame, and Walsh University, October 25-28, 2007.

[2] The following passages are quoted from Xenophon, *Memorabilia* 1.4, in the Loeb translation *Xenophon in Seven Volumes*, vol. 4 (Cambridge, Massachusetts: Harvard University Press; London: William Heinemann, 1979).

> useful end, which, in your judgment, is the work of chance, and which of design?"
>
> [Aristodemus:] "Presumably the creature that serves some useful end is the work of design."

Socrates thus begins, *first*, with the implicit question of *whether a causal order exists.* Note that Aristodemus' answer affirms that a causal order exists. His answer to the question is: *Yes, there is purpose, and there is chance.* In a causal order, some things happen according to their intrinsic or extrinsic purposes, whereas other things happen as a result of the intersection of these independent lines of causality. That is, in a causal order, some things are determined by purpose, whereas others result from chance. To this existential affirmation, Aristodemus has no objection.

Socrates seeks, *second*, to find out *what the essence of the causal order might be.* Is it the handiwork (i.e., the creation) of a divinity?

> [5] [Socrates:] "Do you not think then that he who created man from the beginning had some useful end in view when he endowed him with his several senses, giving eyes to see visible objects, ears to hear sounds? Would odours again be of any use to us had we not been endowed with nostrils? What perception should we have of sweet and bitter and all things pleasant to the palate had we no tongue in our mouth to discriminate between them? [6] Besides these, are there not other contrivances that look like the results of forethought? Thus the eyeballs, being weak, are set behind eyelids, that open like doors when we want to see, and close when we sleep: on the lids grow lashes through which the very winds filter harmlessly: above the eyes is a coping of brows that lets no drop of sweat from the head hurt them. The ears catch all sounds, but are never choked with them. Again, the incisors of all creatures are adapted for cutting, the molars for receiving food from them and grinding it. And again, the mouth, through which the food they want goes in, is set near the eyes and nostrils; but since what goes out is unpleasant, the ducts through which it passes are turned away and removed as far as possible from the organs of sense. With such signs of forethought in these arrangements, can you doubt whether they are the works of chance or design?"

> [Aristodemus:] "No, of course not. [7] When I regard them in this light they do look very like the handiwork of a wise and loving creator."

Aristodemus thus answers the question about the essence of the causal order by agreeing to liken it to the handiwork or creation of a divinity. But note how tentative and qualified his answer is: "when I regard them in this light." He seems unsure of how far this analogy to our own souls ("wise and loving") can be pushed back to establish a firm knowledge of the creator.

Therefore, in reply to this objection of Aristodemus (*Perhaps the essence of the causal order is that it proceeds from something like our soul—wise and loving—but we cannot be sure*) to Socrates' question, Socrates probes further about the essence of the causal order, i.e., whether it is *essentially* the work of a creator:

> [Socrates:] "What of the natural desire to beget children, the mother's desire to rear her babe, the child's strong will to live and strong fear of death?"

> [Aristodemus:] "Undoubtedly these, too, look like the contrivances of one who deliberately willed the existence of living creatures."

Note again how the apparent affirmation of Aristodemus is highly qualified. (*Yes, they "look like" acts of intentional intelligence.*) Socrates notices the qualification ("look like") and so he probes further, testing for Aristodemus' lack of humility:

> [8] [Socrates:] "Do you think you have any wisdom yourself?"

> [Aristodemus:] "Oh! Ask me a question and judge from my answer."

> [Socrates:] "And do you suppose that wisdom is nowhere else to be found, although you know that you have a mere speck of all the earth in your body and a mere drop of all the water, and that of all the other mighty elements you received, I suppose, just a scrap towards the fashioning of your body? But as for mind, which alone, it seems, is without mass, do you think that you snapped it up by a lucky accident, and that the orderly ranks of

> all these huge masses, infinite in number, are due, forsooth, to a sort of absurdity?"
>
> [9] [Aristodemus:] "Yes; for I don't see the master hand, whereas I see the makers of things in this world."

Now, at last, Aristodemus' true opinion about the essence of the causal order has come out. Socrates has learned that Aristodemus in fact objects to the essence of the causal order being considered by analogy as the handiwork of a "wise and loving creator." Aristodemus, a pretentious sophisticate, considers the analogy to be too anthropomorphic. He now professes materialistic positivism, saying that although he can see human artists at work, he has never seen God.

Socrates therefore further unfolds the analogy of our souls, to a *third* point, about an essential *property* of the causal order, so as to provide an answer to Aristodemus' second objection ("anthropomorphism" regarding the creator, which Aristodemus has added to his first objection of "uncertainty" regarding what creation "looks like"):

> [Socrates:] "Neither do you see your own soul, which has the mastery of the body; so that, as far as that goes, you may say that you do nothing by design, but everything by chance."

With this, Socrates has now articulated a property that flows from the essence of the causal order, namely, that not all causes in a causal order have to be material.

Aristodemus realizes that he now has no honest argument or better analogy that can support his previously declared positivism. There is no necessary reason why, in principle, immaterial or unseen causes must be denied as possibly having visible effects. And so Aristodemus now abandons his materialism. But to this *property* of the causal order that Socrates has just articulated (i.e., that there is no reason for it to exclude *immaterial* causes, because not all causes need be material) Aristodemus proceeds to make a *third* objection:

> [Xenophon:] Here Aristodemus exclaimed: [10] [Aristodemus:] "Really, Socrates, I don't despise the godhead. But I think it is too great to need my service."

To this new objection—that even if the creator is indeed something like our souls, he must be even more unlike them, and will therefore transcend our attempts to grasp him—Socrates replies by unfolding the analogy to our souls still further:

> [Socrates:] "Then the greater the power that deigns to serve you, the more honour it demands of you."
>
> [11] [Aristodemus:] "I assure you, that if I believed that the gods pay any heed to man, I would not neglect them."

Aristodemus still considers the analogy to be too anthropomorphic, but since he is unable to refute it, he now pivots to argue, not for God's non-existence, but rather for God's unknowable and uncaring super-existence.

Next, Socrates replies to Aristodemus' objection (i.e., that we must deny that God is personal in a human sense, because he must be more *impersonal* than he is personal) now by arguing that God is rather personal in a pre-eminent sense, and therefore *most truly personal.* Socrates thus establishes a *fourth* point about *the cause* of the property (not all causes are material) that flows from the essence of the causal order (which is essentially ordered by a wise and loving divinity); namely, that the *cause* of the property of any immaterial causes within the causal order must be *most truly personal* because of its care for man (*Memorabilia* 1.11–14):

> "Do you... yet think that the gods take no care of you? What are they to do, to make you believe that they are heedful of you?"

Socrates concludes, from the pre-eminence (compared to material causality) of *immaterial* causality, that the immaterial source of the causal order is not only *personal* (a property established on analogy to our souls), but that divinity is, not unknowable and uncaring, but rather possessing the best and most personal qualities of being *wise and loving*, since it is the invisible personal knowledge and care of the divinity that is visibly manifest—in spite of all chance events—in the various purposes of the visible causal order.

But still Aristodemus is skeptical, and he demands direct commerce with the unseen divinity, rather than to accept the indirect inferences of merely mental reasoning:

> [15] [Aristodemus:] "I will believe when they send counsellors, as you declare they do, saying, 'Do this, avoid that.' "

Socrates then concludes with an attempt to show Aristodemus how unreasonable his skepticism is. At the very least, conventional piety towards divinity is more reasonable than Aristodemus' intellectual qualms, because at least conventional religion does not deny, like Aristodemus, the eminently reasonable analogy from our souls that divinity must be personal, in an eminently wise and loving way (*Memorabilia* 1.15–19).

I would conjecture that Aristotle inherited this fourfold Socratic pattern of argumentation and made it his own. As I have outlined above, the Socratic line of argumentation in Xenophon arguably shows a nascent Aristotelian procedure; namely, the method of proceeding from (1) *existence* to (2) the *essence* of what exists, to (3) a *property* flowing from that essence, to (4) the *causes* of that property.

In Socrates' prototypical articulation of this pattern, we saw him affirm (1) that a *causal order*, comprised of both purpose and chance, *exists*; (2) that the *essence* of this order is that it is *created* by an immaterial divinity who is analogous to a wise and loving soul; (3) that this essentially created order, insofar as it manifests key *properties* indebted to *immaterial causes*, points definitively to that immaterial divine source of creation; and (4) that the only proportionate cause of such intentional immaterial properties is the invisible *personal agency* of their likewise immaterial, spiritual source.

Like Socrates, Aristotle sought to argue for the reality of the unseen Deity, basing his *physical* proof on the *visible* order of God's effects. This proof proceeds from the *physics* of the causal order. I would argue that the same procedure characterizes Aquinas's First Way. Further, like Socrates, Aristotle also made use of the analogy from the *invisible* soul to make a *teleological* proof for the existence of the divine. This proof proceeds from the *metaphysics* of the causal order. I would argue that the same procedure characterizes Aquinas's Fifth Way.

The correlative relationship between the two proofs, physical and metaphysical, is what I think ultimately structures the later Thomistic analysis. In retrospect, I believe this Thomistic analysis also sheds light on the fourfold pattern of argument characteristic of both Socrates and Aristotle.

## II. THOMISTIC TEACHING ON THE WAYS TO GOD

The teleological proof for the existence of God is most crisply summarized in the Fifth Way of Thomas Aquinas to demonstrate God's existence. The Fifth Way is arguably a compressed version of the argument that we just saw Socrates making to Aristodemus. In order to understand the probative force it holds for both Socrates and Aquinas, I think Aristotle's conception of teleology supplies the requisite clarifications.

Aristotle's understanding of teleology is controversial. Despite the controversy, I would maintain that all five of Thomas' famous Ways are characteristically Aristotelian. My position contrasts with *Aristotle on Teleology*,[3] in which Monte Ransome Johnson denies that there is a 'teleological' proof for the existence of God in Aristotle. In particular, Johnson argues that the fragmentary evidence from Aristotle's *On Philosophy* (*Peri Philosophias*) cannot be read as evidence that Aristotle conceives of a 'teleological' argument for the existence of God.

In the section of this essay that will follow the current one, I wish to propose a re-reading of three fragments from *On Philosophy* that Johnson discusses, and then add one from the *Protrepticus*. This fragmentary evidence from Aristotle, I argue, can help us understand how Aristotle conceives of a 'teleological' argument for the existence of God that is correlative to the physical approach from nature to nature's God. Once we properly distinguish physical from metaphysical proofs in Aristotle, I think we may see how the metaphysical 'teleological' proof must not be set in false opposition to the physical proof from motion, because the two are in fact correlative.

But before I pursue this point by discussing my chosen four fragments, let me first address the controversy not from the controverted standpoint of Aristotle, but from the later, more articulated, standpoint of Aquinas. That way, I may give a preliminary refutation in principle of the false dichotomy that I believe informs Johnson's reading of the fragments.

---

[3] Monte Ransome Johnson, *Aristotle on Teleology* (Oxford Oxford University Press, 2005). See also the reviews at <http://ndpr.nd.edu/review.cfm?id=6883> and <http://ccat.sas.upenn.edu/bmcr/2006/2006-08-37.html>.

Johnson characterizes the Aristotelian position as proceeding from a physical argument for the necessity of a First Mover rather than from a 'teleological' natural theology proof. In one way, this is definitely true of Aristotle; the former procedure is physics, the latter metaphysics. Aristotle definitely has a focus on physics. (I would even go further and affirm, with Benedict Ashley, O.P., and with that strand of the Thomistic commentatorial tradition that he represents, that metaphysics is not known to exist unless physics proves the existence of its subject matter).

Yet, *pace* Johnson, I believe Aristotle also distinguishes the correlative relationship between the physical and the metaphysical aspects involved in the discussion of the existence of God. As Benedict Ashley has put it to me, in *Physics* VIII Aristotle proves that the First Mover must be the first efficient cause of motion in our universe, but *Metaphysics* XII proves from final causality that the First Mover must be the cause of motion in any universe; in other words, the former is a physical proof *from creatures*, the latter a metaphysical one *from the nature of the Creator*.[4]

Ashley and I thus would argue that the physical proof must come first in the order of knowledge (*prima quoad nos*), otherwise we can have no assurance that such a discipline as metaphysics even exists with its own distinctive subject matter (viz., being as being, whether material or immaterial). Once it is demonstrated (in *Physics* VIII) that only the Pure Act of the First Mover can explain the actual activation of change in *our* material universe, then metaphysics (in *Metaphysics* XII) can consider the final causality involved in the Prime Mover's relation to *any* universe.

God is the first efficient cause of the being of all beings. Correlatively, this being of all beings exists for a good purpose, the final cause of the universe. Hence we may in a preliminary way refute Johnson's position in general, for his fundamental philosophical orientation is unclear: not only on the distinction between the physical

---

[4] I verified this verbal formulation with Fr. Ashley at the 2007 American Maritain Association conference; the italics indicate his qualifications as he emphasized them to me.

and the metaphysical, but also on their correlativity. Of the physical proof, Ashley maintains:

> ...the demonstration of the existence of a first immaterial cause given in *Physics* VIII...cannot be metaphysical, but is presupposed to metaphysics, that is, First Philosophy.[5]
>
> No step in this argument requires a metaphysical notion of Being as *ens commune*, but only the analysis of *ens mobile* proper to natural science. If the argument were proper to metaphysics, it would be circular, since metaphysics presupposes the argument's conclusion, namely, that immaterial being exists.[6]

For this very reason, Thomas adopts the proof from motion as the "most evident" of his famous Five Ways.

Yet Ashley propounds a thesis about the scarcely appreciated correlativity in the Five Ways: viz., that *Thomas' first three Ways are physical, whereas the Fourth and Fifth are best seen as metaphysical.* Ashley writes:

> The second way from *efficient agency* and the third from *necessity* are variations on this first way. Once we understand the first way based on the observed effect that is motion, the second way argues from the *agents* or moved movers that cause the motion. Furthermore, if we consider the efficient causality of these agents, we see that the action of the first immaterial cause is *necessary* if they are to act, since the fact that they as moved movers are in act is merely *contingent*; and this is the third way. Thus the first three of the five ways are based on three effects, all related to efficient causality: (1) the effect of *motion*, (2) the effect of *agency* of the moved movers, and (3) the *necessity* of the first cause for these contingent agents to act and produce the observed motion.... The other two of the five ways... namely, those through formal and final causality...[pertain] more properly not to natural science but to First Philosophy.[7]

---

[5] Benedict Ashley, O.P., *The Way toward Wisdom* (Notre Dame, Indiana: University of Notre Dame Press, 2006), 95-96.

[6] Ibid., 96.

[7] Ibid., 100-01.

I myself would wish to refine this reading of Thomas's Five Ways.[8] I would argue that the Second Way indeed proceeds from efficient causality, but that the Third proceeds from the standpoint of material causality, the Fourth from formal causality, and the Fifth from final causality. I think that this seems to better fit the main point of Ashley's clarifications:

> Aristotle, after proving in natural science the existence of a God of motion and its immateriality and hence the need and validity of a Metascience broader in scope than natural science itself, left a deeper consideration of this problem to Metascience. Aquinas completed Aristotle's discussion by his famous *Quinque Viae* or Five Ways of proving God's existence. Of these Five Ways the first is rated by Aquinas as "the first and more evident (*manifestior*) because it is taken from motion," the type of change most evident to our senses and proper to natural science [ST I, 2, 3]. This implies that the other four ways somehow epis-emologically presuppose the first, not as if they are its cor-ollaries, but because it precedes them in the order of the intuitive evidence of the middle terms that are their premises.
>
> Thus the *Physics* first intuits the existence of motion from sensible observation and then by analysis of motion arrives at the notion of the four causes. The second and third way, presupposing the proof from motion, derive their middle terms from *efficient* causality: the second from the series of efficient causes that produce motion, the third from the possibility or necessity of the effects of efficient causality. The fourth way, however, no longer argues from efficient causality but from *formal* causality (degrees of perfection) and the fifth way from *final* causality. Final causality, however, is nothing but the predetermination of the efficient cause to produce the perfect actualization of the formal cause.[9]

Although there are many different views on the unity (or lack of unity) of the Five Ways, I would argue that the First Way is physical but all the rest are metaphysical. Perhaps this also helps explain why we

---

[8] *ST* I, 2, 3.

[9] Ashley, *The Way toward Wisdom*, 421.

find in Thomas no more than *five* Ways. Aquinas makes no claim that there are only five, but compare Ashley's remarks:

> No sixth argument from *material* causality is possible since God is the Unmoved Mover, that is Pure Act, while a material cause must be in potency. Yet in all five proofs the notion of being as not only actual but as changing and thus also potential enters into the demonstration, and this concept of potential being is derived from material causality. Aquinas in a rare tone of contempt berates a certain David of Dinant for thinking that God is "prime matter" [*Contra Gentiles*, I, q. 17, n. 139]. Yet this absurdity is found rather frequently in monistic thinkers, who in their struggle to explain the phenomenal world in relation to the Absolute, speak of it "emerging" or "flowing" or "diffusing" from the Absolute and "returning" to it on the analogy of prime matter receiving various forms which it eventually loses.[10]

But yet the Third Way does, in its own fashion, involve material causality. That is, the Third Way proceeds from the *inadequacy* of material causality alone, arguing that contingency alone, i.e., material causality alone, without relative degrees of the more and more necessary, is irrational, because this is unable to account for the correlative relation of material causality to formal causality (based on the correlativity of matter to form) in any changing universe.[11] And Ashley's main point still remains true:

> Our knowledge of God also excludes any possibility that he could be an *intrinsic* material cause of his effects since he is utterly free of potentiality. Nor, since he is Pure and Necessary Act, can he be the *intrinsic* formal cause or act of anything that is contingent and thus somehow potential. Thus the language sometimes used in monistic worldviews that speaks of the Absolute as the "ground of all beings," as if the Absolute were the matter out of which phenomenal things are made, or as the "soul of the universe," as if the Absolute were a form in matter, can

[10] Ibid.

[11] Cf. Christopher S. Morrissey, "Aquinas's Third Way as a Reply to Stephen Hawking's Cosmological Hypothesis," *Études maritainiennes-Maritain Studies* XXVII (2011): 99–121.

> only be understood as metaphors and not proper analogies. Yet the Stoics and other more spiritual monists have called God the Logos, or Energy, or Force, or Soul that animates the material cosmos.[12] For Plotinus too the World Soul was the Third God. But an intrinsic formal cause is correlative to the matter that it informs, and if God were such he would depend for his existence on matter and would not be its free Creator.[13]

Recall that I have already suggested above that the Fifth Way resembles the Socratic teleological argument. Many thinkers express reservations about both formulations; and I think they are right to do so, because, on my view (which I am now revealing, as the main thesis behind this paper), Aquinas's Ways Two through Five acquire their metaphysically demonstrative force only after a first consideration of the physical proof that they in fact presuppose (viz., the First Way), and I maintain this view because of my interpretation of Aristotle (which differs from that of scholars like Johnson). Thus, my "Aristotelian" understanding of the correlativity between physics and metaphysics would allow one to glimpse the strength of the original "Fifth Way" argument that in Socrates had not yet been established as truly demonstrative. In brief, I would argue that Ways Two through Five, as metaphysical, are correlative to the First Way, which is alone purely physical, although it does conclude with a demonstration of the metaphysical order of being.[14]

Concerning how the metaphysical proofs (the Second through Fifth Ways) are correlative to the physical proof (the First Way), Ashley's remarks are most helpful in clarifying how to understand this correlativity; namely, that we must understand it from the standpoint of the interrelatedness of the four causes:

> Just as matter and form are correlative so that they complement each other, so efficient causality, if it has regular, productive effects that maintain the natural order, is correlative

---

[12] Ashley notes: "The use of "Word" (*Logos*) in the Gospel of John, chap. 1 is not intended to speak of God in the Stoic sense of a World Soul, but in a Trinitarian sense of a Divine Person" (*The Way toward Wisdom*, 524, n. 44).

[13] Ashley, *The Way toward Wisdom*, 422.

[14] Ibid., 97.

> to final causality; and all natural science explanations through law-like efficient causality must also be through final causality, that is, they must be teleological (or "teleonomic")... since nothing occurs in natural processes except through efficient causes that are predetermined to produce effects that have the regularity of a predictable probability.[15]
>
> The natural unit has (1) some organization or order (formal cause) and (2) at the same time has potentiality (material "cause") for becoming other than it is. (3) This potentiality is actualized from outside by another natural unit (efficient cause), and this actualization is either destructive of the unit, or actualizes it in its own line of stability and actuality, and hence is (4) teleological (final "cause").[16]

Given this general philosophical framework that recognizes the correlative aspects within intrinsic causality (matter and form) and extrinsic causality (agent and end), we can now proceed to classify three of Johnson's fragments from Aristotle's *On Philosophy*, according to how they speak of causality, whether physically or metaphysically.

## III. ARISTOTELIAN TEACHING ON GOD

First, consider the fragment from Cicero, *De natura deorum* (II xxxvii 95), which shows Aristotle arguing for how different levels of *physical* actuality are intuitively grasped by the mind. The thought experiment is an inversion of Plato's allegory of the cave. But notice that Aristotle's cave passage is not an allegory. It is a statement about degrees of actuality; some are actually more intelligible in their degree of reality than others.

Contra Plato, Aristotle maintains that the most intelligible is not the mathematical, as if it were more actual than the sensible; the Forms are not the higher reality. For Plato, the escape from the cave, from convention to nature (from *nomos* to *phusis*), while starting with what is naturally perceived by the senses, allegedly ends by attaining a higher,

---

[15] Ibid., 324.

[16] Benedict Ashley, "Change and Process", in John N. Deely and Raymond J. Nogar, eds., *The Problem of Evolution* (New York: Appleton-Century-Crofts, 1973), 267-78, quoted from 294.

non-sensory intelligibility. But, for Aristotle, the sensible is not placed in opposition to the intelligible. In his thought experiment, the escape from the cave is likewise from convention to nature, but, unlike Plato, he stresses the need to escape from the mind-dependent to the mind-independent.

Hence the mathematical or the intelligible, insofar as they keep one stuck in one's head with beings of reason (*entia rationis*), will always be of a lesser degree of actuality than real beings (*entia realia*), since real beings are, after all, the mind-independently real from which the mind-dependent is abstracted. This truth is intuitively and immediately grasped by the mind, and it is well illustrated by Aristotle's thought experiment:

> Suppose there were men who had always lived underground, in good and well-lighted dwellings, adorned with statues and pictures, and furnished with everything in which those who are thought happy abound. Suppose, however, that they had never gone above ground, but had learned by report and hearsay that there was a divine spirit and power. Suppose that then, at some time, the jaws of the earth opened, and they were able to escape and make their way from those hidden dwellings into these regions which we inhabit. When they suddenly saw earth and seas and skies, when they learned the grandeur of clouds and the power of winds, when they saw the sun and realized not only its grandeur and beauty but also its power, by which it fills the sky with light and makes the day; when, again, night darkened the lands and they saw the whole sky picked out and adorned with stars, and the varying light of the moon as it waxes and wanes, and the risings and settings of all these bodies, and their courses settled and immutable to all eternity; when they saw those things, most certainly would they have judged both that there are gods and that these great works are the works of gods.[17]

Johnson thinks Aristotle in this fragment is describing the false inferences of others. Even if this were so, the deeper point to be

---

[17] Cicero, *De natura deorum* II xxxvii, 95; trans. Jonathan Barnes, "Fragments from Aristotle's Dialogues", in *The Complete Works of Aristotle* (Princeton, New Jersey: Princeton University Press, 1984), 2392.

grasped is one that Aristotle would in fact share with these alleged others, just as he shares it with Socrates: namely, that it is by considering the different degrees of actuality found in beings, whether mind-dependent or mind-independent, that the mind is intuitively led to grasp the physical truth that, if we observe *manifest differences of degree in actuality,* then this must bear witness to a causal order (whereby the higher manifestly imparts actuality to the lower; e.g., a plant generates seeds). Any metaphysical "argument from design" will always rest upon this first principle of physics, which is arrived at intuitively from observations of material causality in actual operation (e.g., in actuality, the parents always give birth to the children, and never vice versa, etc.). It may be only a story, but its metaphysical lesson seems clear; namely, that "there are more things in heaven and earth ... than are dreamt of in your philosophy," because actual effects will always demand proportionate causes as their explanation.

Yet, although supremely rational, the intuitive awareness (both here in Aristotle's story and also in Socrates' teleological argument) of the physical principle of causality that structures the manifest order of actuality in the world has not yet moved beyond attaining intuitive awareness of a polytheistic plurality of higher causes. We may note that Socrates' proof to Aristodemus of the care of the Deity also remained on this level, not moving higher than a polytheism in its argument.

But consider a fragment from Sextus Empiricus (*Ad math.* IX.20-23), which reports on Aristotle discussing how to proceed analogically from the causal hierarchy of ordered actualities (in their *multiplicity*) to that hierarchy's ultimate *unitary* cause. It reasons from many actual effects to one First Cause:

> Aristotle used to say that men's concept of god sprang from two sources–the experiences of the soul and the phenomena of the heavens. From the experiences of the soul, because of its inspiration and prophetic power in dreams. For, he says, when the soul gets by itself in sleep, it then assumes its nature and foresees and foretells the future. The soul is also in such a condition when it is severed from the body at death. At all events, he accepts even Homer as having observed this; for he has represented Patroclus, in the moment of his death, as foretelling the death of Hector, and Hector as foretelling the end of Achilles. It was from such events, he says, that men came to

> suspect the existence of something divine, of something in itself akin to the soul and of all things most knowledgeable.
>
> And from the heavenly bodies too: seeing by day the revolution of the sun and by night the well-ordered movement of the other stars, they came to think that there was a god who is the cause of such movement and order.[18]

I conjecture that for Aristotle the two sources are connected, because, based on our experience of ourselves, with our soul being experienced as a unity with a higher actuality than everything else observable, a unity possessing a greater actuality that acts as the cause of various experienced effects, we can postulate something akin to this unitary soul as likewise being behind the visible effects of the universe.

Moreover, I think a fragment from Philo shows that Aristotle, upon attaining this essential insight of the soul analogy applied to the physical approach to God, does not then conceive of God onto-theologically, i.e., as a 'physical' cause with a somewhat 'physical' nature (along the lines of a Demiurge). Instead, the transition to metaphysics occurs by recognizing that *God cannot be a part of the material universe.*[19] For the universe is only "the great visible God," according to Aristotle (who thereby engages with the heights of speculation adumbrated in Plato's *Timaeus*). That is, for Aristotle, the universe is the great *material* sign of the unseen, *immaterial* First Cause, because the *actuality* of being is the "uncreated and imperishable" effect housed within any humble material being, which thereby points to that being's "uncreated and imperishable" eternal cause:

> Aristotle was surely speaking piously and devoutly when he insisted that the universe is uncreated and imperishable, and when he charged with serious blasphemy those people who maintained ...that the great visible God, Who contains in truth

---

[18] Rose frag. 10, trans. by A.-H. Chroust in *Aristotle: New Light on His Life and on Some of His Lost Works* (London: Routledge & K. Paul, 1973).

[19] On this point, there is an excellent summary in diagram form at Robert Sokolowski, *Eucharistic Presence* (Washington, DC: the Catholic University of America Press, 1994), 42-48.

> the sun and the moon and the remaining pantheon of the planets and fixed stars, is no better than the work of man's hands ...[20]

To be sure, it is in light of Aquinas's metaphysical doctrine that I would maintain that Aristotle's emphasis on the *nature of the universe* here is meant to emphasize something about the *nature of God*: God is in no way something material; he has no admixture of potency. Even if the material universe is "uncreated and imperishable," this is still trumped by the immaterial "uncreated and imperishable" Source of actuality who invisibly gives, and sustains, the *existence* of "the great visible God." *The universe itself* thus supplies the First Way to the great invisible God. Therefore this phrase—"the great visible God"—ought to be seen as a kind of poetic shorthand for Aristotle's proof from motion. I realize this interpretation is controversial (and leaves me open to charges of anachronism), but I would maintain it on the basis that I only wish to read Aristotle in the same spirit that Aquinas did.

Admittedly, none of these fragments, strictly speaking, offer a *metaphysical* teleological proof for God. But I argue that they do offer the necessary insights into the *physical* realm that I think are implicitly part of such a proof, once the transition from the material to the immaterial is made via the proof from motion. It is this very proof from motion that I believe they are suggesting, with their various accounts of the path from nature to nature's God.

How, then, is such an approach from nature to nature's God a path of thought from creatures, one ultimately correlative with the properly metaphysical demonstration of God's nature as what primarily causes the teleological ordering of "the great visible God"? Consider this fourth passage, a passage from Aristotle's *Protrepticus* that shows how the mind wisely attains metaphysical knowledge of the existence of God (by means of understanding, as far as is rationally possible, the nature of the God who is the unitary, immaterial source of the ordered actuality in all beings).[21] In this remarkable *Protrepticus* passage, Aristotle says that any human thought thinking about the diverse actions of *secondary causality* in the universe implicitly presupposes the actuality of God (Thought Thinking Itself) and that the explicit

---

[20] Chroust, p. 462, n. 213. [Ross 13, R2 14, R3 12, W 13], Leg Alleg 3.32.97-99.

[21] Aristotle, *Protrepticus* (from Iamblichus), B27 = 35.5-14 = dP 66.1-9 = A25.

recognition of this is human wisdom's highest achievement. Human wisdom's highest achievement is coming to the explicit realization of the *primary causality* that human thought's activity must actually presuppose in all its acts:

> ...the conception of an actually existing, wise principle and ruler of all: it is *this* that would have to underlie all cognition as its ground; it is *this* that both would dwell together with contemplative wisdom, and it would be proper for it to do so.[22]

Aristotle's suggestion seems to be that the one creating First Cause can only be *personal* because that is what a person thinking about Pure Act will realize: that Pure Act is the Thought Thinking Itself that all wise thought thinks. The purpose of all our activity is to attain what "will best promote the contemplation of God" (*Eudemian Ethics* VIII 1249b14-21). Thus, for Aristotle, physics has an indispensable correlative role to metaphysics' teleological "natural theology" about nature's God, because the physical approach first secures the intellectual insights we need to attain a fully rational contemplation of God as Pure Act. Then, at its peak, such thinking becomes truly metaphysical, i.e., self-reflexively aware of its cognitive kinship with the divine.

## IV. THE CORRELATIVITY OF PHYSICS WITH METAPHYSICS

Because the metaphysical contemplation of God has rational value only if it stays in touch with the physical and does not contradict it, I have argued here about how for us the knowledge of Pure Act as the highest *final cause* must be correlative with our *self-reflexive* knowledge of creatures, i.e., as beings existing within the asymmetrical system of potency and act, an asymmetrical system which becomes most manifest when we observe examples of efficient causality (e.g., everything moved is moved by another, etc.).

Yet many thinkers erect obstacles to the delicate balance of both physics and metaphysics required by such an Aristotelian-Thomistic natural theology. For example, Johnson himself criticizes Chroust's

---

[22] My translation from the Greek in Iamblichus. Cf. M. R. Johnson with D. S. Hutchinson, "Authenticating Aristotle's *Protrepticus*," *Oxford Studies in Ancient Philosophy* XXIX (2005): 193-294.

reading of the fragments, siding with Ross against Brentano on the matter of Aristotle's theology, artificially setting efficient causality at odds with God's final causality. But in the spirit of Jacques Maritain, who to my mind has already detailed the reasons why Johnson should be regarded as having picked the losing side in that debate,[23] we should simply note here that there is no need to force an artificial decision and to choose one proof over the other, setting the physical against the metaphysical. In his exegesis, Johnson thinks it necessary to choose the physical over the metaphysical, abandoning the nuances possible in reading Aristotle that commentators like Aquinas and Maritain have seen and that I have tried here to recapitulate by distinguishing the physical and metaphysical thought which I have discerned in my four fragments chosen from Aristotle.

But it is interesting to note that Johnson's interpretation of Aristotle—to emphasize the physical procedure in Aristotle at the expense of the metaphysical—is atypical. Typically, scholars choose the *metaphysical* over the physical in their exegesis of Aristotle, as when it is denied that Aristotle's God is an efficient cause of anything, but rather only a final cause. As Maritain has observed:

> Aristotle is often credited with certain errors made by his disciples or commentators, especially about ...causality. But a careful study of the text proves that...[he did not] teach that God is not the efficient cause of the world and moves it only as the end, or good, which it desires. (The passage in the *Metaph.*, xii, 7, means simply that God moves as final cause or object of love the [angelic] intelligence which moves the first heaven; he does not affirm that God can act only as final cause and has not made things. On the contrary, in *Metaph.* ii, 1, 993 b 28, he says that the heavenly bodies are dependent on the first cause, not only for their motion, but for their very being. *Cf. Metaph.* vi, 1, 1026 b 17.) *Cf.* also the passage from Alexander of Aphrodisias...in which

[23] See his "Marginal Notes on Aristotle," in Jacques Maritain, *Bergsonian Philosophy and Thomism* (Notre Dame, Indiana: University of Notre Dame Press, 2007), 349-77, esp. 360.

> God's efficient causality in Aristotle's system is admirably brought out.[24]

Maritain refers here at the end to the passage in which Alexander says that Aristotle "leads us from the things which are themselves on the lowest plane, but most familiar to us, up to the Father, who has made all things, to God the most sublime, and proves that as the founder [i.e., the one who works on metals] is the cause of the unity of the globe and the brass [meridian in an armillary sphere], so the Divine Power, author of unity and maker of all things, is for all beings the cause of their being what they are."[25]

I have argued that the *locus classicus* for this demonstration from nature to nature's God—which ultimately contemplates what we can know of God's divine nature simply by reasoning about it—is found in a conversation with Socrates reported by Xenophon. It then acquires probative force with Aristotle's articulation of the correlative physical considerations. In Aquinas's Five Ways, we see it preserved as the way of wisdom, that ancient Greek way from *the great visible God* (from physical nature) to the metaphysical reality of *God in himself*, a way that has remained, and shall always remain, part of Christian patrimony.[26]

---

[24] Jacques Maritain, *Introduction to Philosophy* (Lanham, Maryland: Rowman & Littlefield, 2005), 54, n.2.

[25] *Commentary on the Metaphysics* at 1045a36, quoted in Maritain, *Introduction*, 53.

[26] Cf. Wayne Hankey, *God in Himself: Aquinas' Doctrine of God as Expounded in the* Summa Theologiae, Oxford Theological Monographs (Oxford: Oxford University Press, 1987), reprinted in 2000, in the series Oxford Scholarly Classics.

# From the Relative to the Absolute: Louis de Raeymaeker's "Metaphysical Proof" for the Existence of God

William P. Haggerty

## I

In a recent article, Professor John F.X. Knasas mourns the passing of neo-Thomism in contemporary Catholic intellectual circles.[1] According to Knasas, late 20$^{th}$ century Thomism was a battleground between two competing schools of thought. Until the Second Vatican Council, neo-Thomism flourished. Represented chiefly in the writings of Étienne Gilson and Jacques Maritain, the neo-Thomist position featured a characteristically *a posteriori* approach to knowledge: beginning with the apprehension of actual beings given in sensation, neo-Thomists sought to articulate a sound metaphysics with the help of transcendental concepts "that span the breadth of the real, from creature to creator."[2] All such neo-Thomists accepted the same epistemological presuppositions, though they generally fall into two camps: "existential" neo-Thomists who define *esse* in terms of "existential act"; and "Aristotelian" neo-Thomists who tend to define "being" as "formal act." After Vatican II, a new brand of Thomism emerged, dominating the schools and winning particular favor among Catholic theologians. Following the groundbreaking work of the Belgian Jesuit, Joseph Marechal, Transcendental Thomism rejected the *a posteriori* approach of neo-Thomism, opting instead for an *a priori* understanding of human knowledge. Transcendental Thomists maintain that "human knowing" is ultimately the "knower's own intellectual dynamism to Infinite Being," a dynamism which is "innate, or inborn to the intellect."[3] Though it might be argued that

[1] John F. X. Knasas, "Whither the Neo-Thomist Revival?," *Logos: A Journal of Catholic Thought and Culture* Vol. 3 (Fall 2000), 121-49.

[2] Ibid., 127

[3] Ibid., 129

Transcendental Thomism has its origin in the classical works of Augustine and Bonaventure, Knasas believes that the movement is largely a critical response to the Kantian philosophical perspective in late modernity.

Transcendental Thomism has proven remarkably successful in replacing neo-Thomism in Catholic universities, though Knasas sees its victory as a philosophical—and epistemological—"disaster," because it opens the door to skepticism and relativism.[4] One does not have to agree in every detail with his critique in order to recognize the need for a reconsideration of neo-Thomism. In light of this, it is all the more disappointing that, when listing the exponents of neo-Thomism, Knasas neglects to mention the contributions of a great 20th century philosopher whose Thomist credentials were almost as impressive as Gilson's or Maritain's. Associated for many years with the Higher Institute of Philosophy at Louvain, Fr. Louis De Raeymaeker played a significant part in the recovery of Thomistic philosophy. In his seminal work, *The Philosophy of Being: A Synthesis of Metaphysics*, he constructed a profound defense of "existential" neo-Thomism, while responding to the unique intellectual challenges of modernity. If Knasas is correct, and there is a need for a "neo-Thomist revival," perhaps it would be useful—especially in light of the current debate about the status of Thomistic metaphysics—to reconsider De Raeymaeker's work. Towards this end, I would like to examine his argument for the existence of God. While impressed with the Five Ways, De Raeymaeker also developed within his writings a "metaphysical proof" that draws upon some of the central themes in Thomistic metaphysics. In the following remarks, I will first explore the argument, setting it within the context of his overall treatment of the question of being, then briefly show how the proof supplies an unparalleled approach to God, and finally identify its sources in the writings of St.Thomas.

## II

The "metaphysical proof" is principally devoted toward solving the problem of being. Hence, before proceeding to the argument proper, I would like to examine De Raeymaeker's treatment of this question. Since his analysis presumes some acquaintance with Thomistic

---

[4] Ibid., 136

metaphysics, I shall also touch upon his account of the structure of finite being.

According to De Raeymaeker, the metaphysical question is a variation on the classical problem of the one and the many. This problem comes into view after a direct encounter with being, for "being never reveals itself without a question mark."[5] The "point of departure" for this encounter is found in a sustained reflection upon the movement of "consciousness" in experience.[6] In its first moment, consciousness is an "experience of self," a "coming into contact" with the "living ego." Such awareness is always a recognition of the self as "being," and it involves an "ontological perception" that is direct and undeniable.[7] At the same moment, the ego is also made aware of that which exists outside of it, of a "world" of objects that forms a "non-ego." In this confrontation, it immediately encounters the non-ego as "surrounding it," as placing an "insurmountable limit" upon its activity:

> A limit unites just as it separates adjacent regions; it is the place where distinct sectors meet each other. Thus the ego and the non-ego are related one to the other. The limited ego does not exist without its limits, nor does it exist without the non-ego which limits it. It is by its own nature an ego in the world, an ego surrounded by non-egos.[8]

Through further reflection upon its own activity, the ego gradually recognizes its "real and radical distinction" from the non-ego.[9] In the exercise of its freedom, it comes to know itself as an "autonomous" being; it is not simply a part of the world. This awareness of its liberty,

---

[5] Louis De Raeymaeker, *The Philosophy of Being: A Synthesis of Metaphysics*, trans. Edmund H. Ziegelmeyer, S. J. (St. Louis: B. Herder Book Co., 1954), 32.

[6] Ibid., 32. By beginning his study of metaphysics with an "act of attentive reflection" on the experience of "consciousness," De Raeymaeker reveals his interest in, and mastery of, the early 20th century phenomenological movement.

[7] Ibid., 13.

[8] Ibid., 16.

[9] Ibid., 17.

however, goes hand in hand with an appreciation of the unavoidable limitations forced upon it by the world. The ego knows that it is neither "responsible" for the world itself nor for its own "origin," which mysteriously "lies outside" of its will.[10] In its confrontation with the non-ego, furthermore, it inevitably discovers other conscious beings who indicate by their external behavior a "personal interior life" similar to its own. It is especially by means of this contact that the ego establishes the "truth that there are many beings."[11]

This experience is at heart an "affirmation of being" because, in recognizing its opposition to the other, the ego not only affirms its own existence but the existence of the non-ego as well.[12] Now, every affirmation of being reveals the metaphysical problem because every such affirmation uncovers conflicting notes in the data itself. Indeed, two radically "incompatible" properties define the being and activity of every reality—i.e., "the absolute element of its value of being and the relativity of its mode of individual being."[13] It is important to understand what De Raeymaeker means here. First, in any grasp of the real, one encounters being as an "incontestable fact" that the intellect must affirm and cannot deny upon penalty of contradiction. It is surely an incontrovertible truth, for example, that whenever something exists, and for however long it exists, it is impossible to say that it does not exist. To say that something exists *now*, at this particular point in time, is to affirm a truth that obtains not only for the *now*, but "for all times." The statement has a value that is "unconditional," absolute, that transcends this particular moment in the temporal order. The property of necessity which is discovered in such existential judgments is grounded upon the "unshakeable solidity" of the reality itself. And this same solidity, this "absolutely definitive consistency," characterizes being as a whole: each and every reality, whatever its ontological status, expresses a value of being that is absolute.[14] De Raeymaeker writes:

---

[10] Ibid., 21.

[11] Ibid., 22.

[12] Ibid., 23.

[13] Ibid., 31.

[14] Ibid., 24.

> Being exists; and by its own peculiar power, its "*virtus essendi,*" it excludes radically and without condition or any restriction all that would be opposed to it and that would tend to justify a different affirmation.... Being rests upon its own unshakeable and irresistible force...[15]

What does it mean to consider being as "absolute"? First and foremost, it means that being cannot be restricted or qualified in any fashion: it neither rests upon "any extrinsic condition" nor possesses any "relation to some term outside" of it, because, outside of being, there is only nothing.[16] As absolute, being is completely independent and occupies a "unique domain" that is "self-sufficient" and self-explanatory. Since it includes everything and is opposed to nothing, being is "the whole of everything" and "penetrates" to the core of every reality with an "absolute validity."[17] Unlimited and unopposed, it enfolds everything in a fundamental unity. Its absolute character is grasped with particular force in our idea of being, which, in its transcendental breadth, forms "the foundation" for "all intellection."[18]

But, while being as "absolute" contains everything, it is also shot through with relativity. As we have seen, the ego becomes aware of itself and its limitations only in relation to the non-ego. While

---

[15] Ibid.

[16] Ibid., 25.

[17] Ibid., 27.

[18] Ibid., 28 It should be noted that the analogical idea of being, while conveying the character of the absolute, also contains within it the relative or particular modes of being as well. De Raeymaeker suggests that the idea of being differs from universal (specific or generic) abstract concepts inasmuch as it is "not limited to signifying one aspect of the reality" (36). By restricting or qualifying a particular reality through abstraction, a specific or generic concept provides only an imperfect or incomplete account of the being; its univocal precision is a sign of its abstraction from (or separation from) the full richness of the reality. In its transcendental reach, however, the idea of being touches upon "that which is beyond all abstraction," the concrete individual; as such, it resembles a sort of "intuitive apprehension." The knowledge grasped in this idea is also "obscure," but its imperfection is due to its holding or hiding within it "the confusion of the particular modes which it implies" (37).

subsisting in its own right, the ego does not stand alone; there is something "outside of it," opposed but related to it. There are many beings, "autonomous" subjects which exist in "different times" and at different places, and which possess "different modes and forms."[19] In order to capture the precise character of being's relativity, De Raeymaeker introduces the notion of participation: every finite being truly participates in the value of being, but it does so according to its own proper "mode," in its own individual manner. The doctrine of participation implies two central features about finite being. First, participation means that particular being is not the whole of being, since—by reason of its very individuality—it necessarily refers to the existence of other beings in the same line of perfection. Grounded together in the absolute value, particular beings form a unique *complexus*, a fundamental order, since there is no "source of participation...more profound" than being itself.[20] As part of this order, each being must be conceived in terms of its relation to the other parts within the whole and to the whole itself. De Raeymaeker is so impressed with the relative character of particular being that he writes of its being "welded" or "riveted" to the order.[21]

Yet participation also entails the real autonomy of the participant. In emphasizing the fundamental unity of being, De Raeymaeker insists that the bond that holds the finite terms together is one that is characteristic of an "order." An order is a unity in multiplicity, a "real multiplicity reduced to unity." The *complexus* of beings is not a mere "arrangement of parts," but an order of autonomous participants.[22] The participant as such takes part in being, has a "share" in being, but this by no means suggests that it "forms a part of being"; it is a completely finished subject, a whole within the whole. Though it is limited, its limitation does not imply any "ontological incompletion" on its part, but rather that its peculiar mode of being, its individuality, is distinct from the others, and thereby does not embrace the others, let alone

---

[19] Ibid., 26.

[20] Ibid., 31.

[21] Ibid., 287.

[22] Ibid., 29.

exhaust the full "perfection of the order."[23] Consequently, the "relativity" characteristic of the participant in being cannot be equated with the relations found among the multiple parts or finite modes that go to make up an individual subsistent being. De Raeymaeker is clear about this: each particular being is a distinct *suppositum*. While fully contained in the order, it maintains its autonomy; and, in possessing its own proper *esse*, it subsists and "bears witness" to the value of the absolute.

The precise outlines of the problem of being are clear. Participation in being, relativity on the level of the absolute, is a given. But how is this order possible? How can being, an unlimited unity, suffer limitation and multiplicity? For that matter, how can finite being, mired in relativity, nevertheless subsist and express the value of the absolute? To account for the order, De Raeymaeker suggests that an adequate solution must "preserve" both the unity in being and the actual "subsistence of its multiple elements."[24] For this reason, a radical pluralism that sacrifices unity for the sake of subsistence would be as unacceptable as a metaphysical monism that guarantees unity by eliminating the genuine autonomy of finite beings.

This problem requires an exhaustive analysis of the structure of particular being. In line with the Thomistic tradition, De Raeymaeker offers a full treatment of this question.[25] He first explores the internal complexity of particular beings in the doctrine of the real composition of essence and existence. The complete account of any being includes a

---

[23] Ibid., 30.

[24] Ibid., 32.

[25] Later in his treatment, De Raeymaeker fills out the structure of finite being. To explain participation on the level of specific perfection, he argues for the form-matter composition within the essence of material beings. And, to account for the active becoming characteristic of all finite beings, he introduces the substance-accident composition. Together with essence and existence, these principles are inserted into a comprehensive act/potency schema: each pair of correlatives includes a principle of act that supplies the perfection "uniting" the terms within the order, and a principle of potency that represents the individual mode by which the being participates in, or possesses, the perfection.

"double affirmation": the being *is*; and the being is *this being*.[26] Inasmuch as it subsists, particular being possesses a value that is absolute, which it shares with other beings. Yet inasmuch as it exists in its own proper mode, insofar as it is *this being*, and not some other, it must possess a reason for the individuality that helps distinguish it from other beings in the same line of perfection. Thus, particular being forms a kind of *complexus*, composed as it is of two distinct, but inseparable, principles: the real "principle of being," the "root of subsistence," which is responsible for the value of being, and the real principle of the mode of being, which is in turn responsible for the individuality and the limitation found in being.[27] Whereas the principle of being provides the ground of autonomy for particular being, the mode of being "completely individualizes" it so that particular being finds itself belonging to, or included within, an order of beings. De Raeymaeker emphasizes that these principles, which are identified in the Thomistic tradition as essence (quiddity or nature) and existence (*esse*), possess the character of "transcendental relations." Transcendental relations are neither real beings nor parts of being, but ontologically correlative principles that must never be considered apart from "the relation which bind them together."[28] As pure correlatives, each term functions wholly in connection with its corresponding co-principle; the principles of essence and existence thus "communicate" their character to each other so as to constitute the unity and being of finite reality.[29] De Raeymaeker's analysis, while clarifying the ontological status of particular being, also serves to deepen the "mystery of participation." "Belonging to an order" necessarily implies the presence of complexity within particular being; in other words, external relativity demands an internal relativity, an inner structure of metaphysical co-principles, which constitutes the "ontological reason" for participation. At its core, finite being is nothing but a "cluster of relations," and its relativity is so com-

[26] Ibid., 99

[27] Ibid., 332.

[28] Ibid., 105.

[29] Ibid., 104.

prehensive that even the principle of being, the value of the absolute, emerges as a mere correlative.[30]

With this background, let us proceed to the formal argument. The study of being shows that particular beings form a *complexus*, an order of beings "absolutely unique."[31] In every order, the many are linked so as to form a unity, a whole. Hence, to give an account of any order, one must first identify the "principle of unity" that supplies the ultimate reason for the order. Now, unlike all other orders, the order of beings is "absolute," fundamental; this means that the members that constitute the whole are contained in it by reason of their "entire reality," their "*being-in-itself*."[32] In other words, the "*being in itself*" of particular beings cannot be something considered apart from their relation to the order. Rather, it is identical to their inclusion in the order itself.

The doctrine of participation makes this clear. Particular being is a distinct *suppositum* which participates in the value of being in an "individual" and "incommunicable" way.[33] By means of this participation, it subsists, it expresses the value of the absolute; yet, by way of this same participation, it subsists in a wholly individual fashion, it is only one among many possible beings. It thus enters into a profound "synthesis" with every other particular being, and belongs so completely to the *complexus* that it can never be "isolated" or abstracted from it in any manner.[34] Moreover, its inclusion in the order is not by means of some "accessory" relation that is added on to what it already possesses; it belongs simply by reason of "what it is," by reason of its very "*being in itself*." Particular being is a correlative, and since a relation cannot be understood without reference to its *terminus*, an adequate explanation of particular being must necessarily include an explanation of the full *complexus* of beings.[35] To account for the "least

---

[30] Ibid., 336

[31] Ibid., 282.

[32] In the following analysis, I will also quote from a later, condensed version of De Raeymaeker's proof, "The Metaphysical Problem of Causality," published in *Philosophy Today* Vol. 1 (1957), 219-30.

[33] De Raeymaeker, *The Philosophy of Being*, 283.

[34] Ibid., 283.

[35] De Raeymaeker, "The Metaphysical Problem of Causality," 227.

reality," De Raeymaeker notes, one must furnish an explanation for the whole of reality.

Now, the question is whether particular being by itself can offer such an account. De Raeymaeker immediately spots a problem. As a mere part within the whole, no particular being can possibly furnish an explanation of another particular being. This follows from its "incommunicable individuality." As distinct *supposita*, particular beings are by definition "opposed" to each other in the same line of perfection. Made "distinct by reason of their own limits," they are outside of each other; each possesses what the other lacks.[36] As proof of their "mutual exteriority," De Raeymaeker cites the "free actions" of the human person.[37] The ego's decisions are irrevocably the responsibility of the ego and the ego alone. Just as one person cannot be held responsible for the decisions of another, so no particular being can hope to account for the existence or activity of another particular being. And, if this is the case, it can hardly supply a reason "for all the realities contained in the order."[38] Moreover, since the reason that accounts for the order and the reason that explains particular being is one and the same, in failing to provide an answer for the whole, the particular being cannot sufficiently explain "its own reality." It lacks an "absolute foundation."

Nor would it suffice to point to the "coexistence of finite beings in the universe" as if their mere collective presence in being were enough to account for the order.[39] De Raeymaeker insists that an answer cannot be found in the "unlimited ensemble" of finite beings: because they are opposed to each other by reason of their individuality, their very diversity as individuals cannot explain their "unity" in being, for diversity as such cannot produce unity. Besides, this would be like suggesting, he notes, that the principle of the order could be discovered "partially in each particular being," so that, by means of simple addition, one could arrive at a sufficient reason. Yet such an explanation, containing "as many parts as there are beings," would lack

---

[36] Ibid.

[37] De Raeymaeker, *The Philosophy of Being*, 285.

[38] De Raeymaeker, "The Metaphysical Problem of Causality," 227.

[39] De Raeymaeker, *The Philosophy of Being*, 283.

unity, and thus could not serve as a principle of the whole.[40] De Raeymaeker's conclusion is inescapable: the sufficient reason for the order, the "adequate explanation" of the whole, cannot be discovered in any particular being, or in any collection of finite beings, or even in the "unlimited ensemble" of finite beings.

At this stage of the argument, two things are abundantly clear: the order of beings needs a foundation, and the reason that provides this foundation must be extrinsic to the order itself. As we have seen, a particular being, by the very act of belonging to an order, is defined by its relativity, its limitation in being. This ontological status necessarily prevents it from providing an adequate explanation for its own existence, or for its place within the order. Now, if the same holds true for each and every particular being, it follows that the reason which ultimately accounts for the order as a whole cannot be a particular or finite being itself. In other words, if it is to function as the unparticipated "source of all participation" in being, this "fundamental cause" must be free from the internal and external relativity that marks particular being in its existence and action. The "unique creative cause," the "absolute basis" of all particular beings, cannot be found within, or exist relative to, the order of being; it must be unlimited or non-finite being, "pure subsistent being," "being without restriction"—"God, the Creator, the Cause, absolutely free."[41]

De Raeymaeker suggests that this same conclusion can be reached by way of an analysis of the internal structure of any particular being. As we have seen, particular being forms a kind of *complexus* on its own; it is a "cluster of relations," a structure of correlative principles. Now the unity of this structure, the "harmony" of the correlatives, cannot be accounted for by the particular being alone. Let us take the case of the real composition of essence and existence. The principles of being and the mode of being are "distinct and irreducible" transcendental correlatives. "Transcendental relations" are radically "distinct" from each other and thus irreducibly opposed; as such, they cannot "form a unity" of themselves.[42] Yet these principles operate exclusively as

---

[40] De Raeymaeker, "The Metaphysical Problem of Causality," 228.

[41] De Raeymaeker, *The Philosophy of Being*, 286.

[42] Ibid., 255.

correlatives; each term cannot be conceived outside of its relation with its distinct co-principle. Since, as correlatives, they necessarily form the structure that constitutes the unity and reality of finite being, but, as distinct principles, they cannot account for this unity, it follows that particular being requires an extrinsic cause, a composer, responsible for its foundation. And if the internal structure of existence and essence provides the "ontological reason" for the particular being's external relativity, it is not so surprising that particular being fails to explain this "reason," since it cannot account for the order as a whole.[43] From either angle—whether one looks to its internal structure or to its external relations—particular being requires a cause.

It is only with the affirmation of the creative Cause that the problem of being can be solved. As De Raeymaeker has argued, to explain the order of beings, an adequate solution must preserve the fundamental unity found in being while allowing for the actual subsistence of the many. The proof, which is really a reflection upon the meaning of participation, shows why particular being cannot meet these demands. Participation requires both subsistence and relativity, and these two aspects constitute a fundamental tension in being that cannot be resolved on the level of particular being itself. The argument makes this clear. Whereas particular being's utter relativity dictates that it cannot stand alone in reality, its autonomy prevents it from becoming subsumed into the whole as a finite part. The creative Cause can provide for both of these needs. Because all finite beings participate in the infinite being of God, they all are grounded in the same perfection, express the "same absolute value of being," and "flow from the same source."[44] It is thus not remarkable that they are found welded to the same order. Their radical unity in being, their "unshakeable consistency," is ultimately due to the Absolute source which binds them together in "its all powerful fecundity."[45] The thorough-going relativity that characterizes the members of the order is a consequence of their complete dependence upon the Absolute. And, while their participation in "pure subsistent being" provides for their unity, it also

---

[43] Ibid., 256.

[44] Ibid., 287.

[45] Ibid., 287.

accounts for their autonomy. As De Raeymaeker points out, the "radical subordination" of the finite to the Infinite is nothing other than a dynamic partaking of the "absolute independence of the active and creative God."[46] Finite being, a pure "gift of the Absolute," cannot help but express the value of its unlimited source.

III

I believe De Raeymaeker's proof is stronger than other, better known, arguments because it avoids certain difficulties traditionally associated with these proofs. First, it concludes directly to a creative Cause that is infinite and unique. The proof concerns the problem of being. Being is absolute, all-inclusive, which means that the order of beings embraces all orders and values. Whether the proof is successful or not, at least it does not have the typical shortcomings of arguments that begin from a more restricted order within being. The history of philosophy testifies to the struggles of theists who have constructed proofs for God's existence by starting from some limited feature within the material order. I have no wish to discredit cosmological or teleological arguments here; they remain vital and serious contributions to philosophical theology. However, even when these arguments establish the existence of a First Cause, there is still much philosophical work that remains before one is able to reach the infinite, creative source of being.

De Raeymaeker's proof avoids this problem. The argument cuts to the chase, as it were, and gets "to the bottom of the problem." In attempting to ground the all-embracing order of being, it leaves nothing out of consideration. Particular beings are dependent on a cause by reason of their very limitation. To account for the entire order of finite beings, the creative Cause must be free of such limitation—it must be unlimited, Infinite Being. Were it restricted in any fashion, were it "infected" with relativity, it would belong to the order and thus could not supply the reason for the order.[47] Nor is there any need to

---

[46] Ibid., 326.

[47] In speaking of the infinite Cause here, we must note that De Raeymaeker understands the "infinite" as the negation of the "finite." Now, the meaning of the "finite" corresponds to the notion of "belonging to an order," and the parallel concepts of the "multiple" and the "relative" (69). That which is

introduce additional steps in the argument to establish the unicity of this cause. Because it provides the foundation for the "absolutely unique" order of beings, the creative Cause itself must be absolutely one and unique. This point goes to the heart of the proof: particular beings reveal an absolute solidity in being that their diversity can never

---

"finite" is said to be limited by, or exist "relative" to, all the other members within the same order. Given this, the "infinite" can be understood in connection with the order as a whole: an order is "infinite" because it is not limited by, or opposed to, anything existing outside itself (at least with respect to the relative perfection of the order); as such, it is "absolute" and "unique." As an example, we can speak of each physical body within the universe as being limited by other bodies—that is, each body exists relative to the other physical units within the order itself. Yet we must admit that the entire *complexus* or collection of physical bodies which comprises the physical universe as a whole is "infinite," because, by containing all physical bodies, it is not limited by, or opposed to, any physical body outside of it.

Now the "ensemble of finite beings," according to De Raeymaeker, appears to be the absolute order which includes all other orders. The question as to whether such an "ensemble" contains an "inexhaustible multitude" of finite elements within it—a problem that uncovers another meaning of the concept of the "infinite"—while philosophically interesting in itself, does not immediately concern us here. The real question for De Raeymaeker is whether this "unlimited order of beings" is the "absolute infinite." If the order cannot sufficiently account for itself, as he argues, it is in need of a principle or source which is causally responsible for its existence. In considering this possibility, De Raeymaeker points out that such a principle necessarily transcends the order:

> ...the fundamental principle of unity would not limit this order in the sense attributed up to now to the word 'limit,' for it would not constitute a realm adjacent to it. In other words, such a principle could not limit the ensemble of finite beings in the way in which one finite being limits another finite being; otherwise, it would also be a limited being itself, and it would be in its place only in the interior of the order of beings. All this would be tantamount to distinguishing two infinites: first of all, the ensemble of limited beings, whose infinity (while being perfectly unlimited, not bounded by an adjacent domain) is declared relative, since it is related to a real principle distinct from this ensemble; and in the second place, this last principle itself, in no limited and finite sense, whose infinity, without relation to anything, is consequently perfectly absolute (73-74).

explain. This radical unity must have its reason in a source whose uniqueness is unassailable and whose inner unity is the model of "utter simplicity."

Secondly, the proof is preferable to arguments that attempt to show the impossibility of an infinite regress of finite causes. Within the *complexus* of being, one discovers a series of ordered causes. Each term within the series functions as a caused cause: while really working to produce its effect, it depends in turn on a prior cause for its own operation. Some theists contend that if it can be determined that the series of ordered causes is limited in number and enjoys a first term, then it can be shown that this first term must have its source in a creative Cause wholly distinct from the series itself. On the other hand, if the series is without beginning, or infinite in number, there would be no reason to posit an absolute cause since every term in a beginningless series "would find in a preceding finite cause its explanatory reason."[48]

De Raeymaeker not only considers such arguments open to serious difficulties, but, given the conclusions of the "metaphysical proof," quite unnecessary. As he has suggested, finite being, inasmuch as it belongs to an order, is wholly dependent upon the action of a creative Cause. Since a finite cause cannot sufficiently explain its own existence,

---

[48] Ibid., 287. According to De Raeymaeker, Thomas is not attempting to establish the impossibility of an infinite series in the First, Second, or Third Way. In a note on the Second Way, he comments (297): "It seems certain to us that St. Thomas does not seek the "first" Cause by passing through a series of causes, of which this cause would be the first term. First of all, he hesitates to declare himself capable of proving that the infinite series is impossible. Then, he defends the view that the creative action of God produces finite beings directly, without the intervention of a subordinate cause (*Summa Theol.*, I, q. 45, a.5), so that the divine causal influx is not transmitted by intermediary causes but it is exerted immediately on every creature." What, then, is the point of Thomas' attack on the infinite regress? De Raeymaeker's position here seems close to the one taken recently by John F. Wippel. Wippel argues that Thomas is not concerned with "refuting the very possibility of a beginningless series of essentially ordered caused causes, but with showing that such a series is meaningless and has no explanatory power unless one also admits that there is an uncaused cause." *The Metaphysical Thought of Thomas Aquinas* (Washington, D. C.: the Catholic University of America Press, 2000), 461.

it cannot offer an "adequate reason" for its "whole effect" or even "for a part of (its) effect."[49] Now, all particular beings are in the same boat and possess the same ontological status; they exist relative to an "absolute principle." And, if the whole series of finite causes is insufficient, it matters little whether that series in question is finite or infinite in number. By multiplying finite causes to infinity, one only ends up with an infinity of insufficiency—or, as De Raeymaeker claims, "zero multiplied as much as you wish, still equals zero."[50]

Finally, the argument offers a definitive response to metaphysical monism. To be sure, every Thomist will reject a monistic position, but De Raeymaeker seems especially concerned with this problem because of his sensitivity to the radical unity in being. This concern comes across in his high regard for Hegel and German Idealism. In the Hegelian system, finite being is so completely "open" to "the other" that its ontological status is reduced to that of a part or mode within the "one, unique being."[51] Now, De Raeymaeker considers monism (and pantheism) objectionable not only because it eliminates the real autonomy of finite being, but because, by making the finite a part of the Infinite, it renders our conception of the Absolute incoherent, a "receptacle of contradictions."[52] The metaphysical dualism of creature and Creator, which De Raeymaeker's proof defends, avoids these difficulties by protecting the absolute character of the creative Cause while preserving the actual subsistence of finite being. We have seen how this works. The proof concludes to the total independence of the Absolute. The creative Cause can never be confused with its effects: particular beings might be "absolutely relative," but God is by no means "relatively absolute." And, in promoting the profound distinction between creature and Creator, the proof preserves the autonomy of particular being. Since the relative can never be identified with the Absolute, finite being cannot be conceived as a mere part or mode of the Infinite; its relation of radical subordination to the

[49] Ibid., 288.

[50] Ibid.

[51] Ibid., 76.

[52] Ibid., 186.

Absolute, which its status as creature implies, requires its very real subsistence in being.

IV

What is the textual inspiration for De Raeymaeker's argument? While the movement from the relative to the Absolute has its foundation in the Thomistic metaphysical teaching as a whole, the argument itself is chiefly an exposition, and defense, of the principle that "whatever exists by participation is dependent on a cause." De Raeymaeker's focus on participation certainly helps explain his unqualified support of the Fourth Way, a proof often associated with this doctrine. In his interpretation, the *Quarta Via* bears a striking resemblance to the "metaphysical proof." This argument is crucial to Thomas' position precisely because it is based upon participation, (the) "most fundamental reason of the close union of all finite reality with infinite and absolute Being."[53] Whereas all Five Ways focus on some "indication of limitation" within finite being, the Fourth Way goes to the heart of the matter—it begins with "limitation, as such." Considered within the proof as a degree of being, and thereby "limited in all it comprises," particular being exhibits a "deep-seated relativity" that must find its sufficient reason in a "Being...which is not a degree, since being the source, it is complete, perfect."[54]

The trouble is that the *Quarta Via*, and participation arguments in general, have not fared especially well in recent scholarship. We may take as an example the judgment rendered by De Raeymaeker's contemporary at Louvain, Fernand Van Steenberghen. In his study *Hidden God*, Canon Van Steenberghen is nothing if not critical of the *Quarta Via*.[55] All of the arguments present difficulties: they are either incomplete (First, Second and Fifth Ways) or deficient in structure (Third Way). But Van Steenberghen takes particular aim at the Fourth Way. The argument is flawed principally because of its connection to Platonism. Van Steenberghen contends that a scholastic fondness for

---

[53] Ibid., 299.

[54] Ibid., 298.

[55] Fernand Van Steenberghen, *Hidden God: How Do We Know That God Exists?*, trans. Theodore Crowley, O.F.M. (Saint Louis: B. Herder Book Co., 1966).

dialectic sometimes lured Thomas into committing the cardinal sin of the Platonist—that of conflating the real and the conceptual orders. The Fourth Way is evidence of this. There is no doubt that, within the conceptual order, one can speak of the "logical participation" of "generic and specific concepts" in the transcendental idea of being.[56] These concepts are the limiting "differences" that work to draw out the analogical richness of this idea, and thus they are always predicated in relation to their conceptual "maximum." However, within the real order, the degrees of perfection show merely that being is "shared among finite beings."[57] The question remains whether there exists a maximum in the real order. Under the spell of neo-Platonism, Thomas simply identifies the two orders. Without justification, he posits the existence of an Infinite Being, a maximum *ens*, upon which the "more and the less" depend. Implicit in the argument is the doctrine of participation, the teaching that "finite beings are participants in an Infinite Being."[58] But this teaching is merely assumed by St. Thomas; it is not demonstrated. And, since it is not immediately evident that the perfection of being can exist beyond the order of finite beings, Van Steenberghen argues one cannot say whether the "more and the less" in the real order necessarily refer to a maximum. Thus, participation cannot serve as a premise or a step on the path toward God; in fact, it cannot—and should not—be introduced into the metaphysical mix until one has first demonstrated the actual existence of an Infinite Being. And this goal is not achieved by the *Quarta Via*.

Nor is Van Steenberghen's judgment any less critical with respect to arguments that explicitly use participation. In a later work, he finds similar problems with Thomas' argument from the *Lectura* on St. John's Gospel. The proof in the *Lectura* rests upon the principle that "everything which is such by participation is reduced to something which is such of its essence." Since all things "which exist participate in being," and are thus "beings by participation," Thomas concludes that there must exist something "which would be *esse* itself through its essence in that its essence would be its *esse*," the "cause of all being,

---

[56] Ibid., 151.

[57] Ibid., 152.

[58] Ibid., 152.

from whom all things which exist participate in being."[59] Though this argument represents a significant improvement over the Fourth Way, inasmuch as it expressly draws on participation, Van Steenberghen claims that it contains the same flaw—it begs the question. He concludes:

> ...by affirming that all the beings of this world are "beings by participation," St Thomas assumes what he must demonstrate. At the point of departure, one can speak of *logical participation* (all beings participate in the transcendental idea of being) and establish that being is a perfection really *shared* by all the beings. But one can speak of *real participation* only after having established the existence of the Infinite Being, *Esse subsistens*.[60]

What about De Raeymaeker? Does his devotion to the doctrine of participation compel him to use arguments his colleague rejects? In examining his work, it is best to keep in mind two important points. First, despite occasional references to such texts and an endorsement of the *Quarta Via*, De Raeymaker does not directly model his proof upon any of these arguments. Secondly, unlike Van Steenberghen, who offers an historical-textual examination, De Raeymaeker is writing an "ontology of Thomist inspiration," what W. Norris Clarke might call a "creative retrieval" of St. Thomas. Thus, he borrows from his master only what he needs in order to complete his argument.

---

[59] *Lectura super evangelium Johannis*, in *S. Thomae Aquinatis opera omnia*. vol. 6, ed. R. Busa, (Stuttgart-Bad Cannstatt, 1980), 227: "Quidam autem venerunt in cognitionem dei ex dignitate ipsius dei: etisti fuerunt platonici. Consideraverunt enim quod omne illud quod est secundem participationem, reducitur ad aliquid quod sit illud per suam essentiam, sicut ad primum et ad summum; sicut omnia ignita per participationem reducuntur a dignem, qui est per essentiam suam talis. Cum ergo omnia quae sunt, participant esse, et sint per participationem entia, necesse est esse aliquid in cacumine omnium rerum, quod sit ipsum esse per suam essentiam, id est quod sua essentia sit suum esse: et hoc est deus, qui est sufficientissima, et dignissima, et perfectissima causa totius esse, a quo omnia quae sunt, participant esse." (All translations of Aquinas are by the author.)

[60] Fernand Van Steenberghen, *Le problème de l'existence de Dieu dans les écrits de s. Thomas d'Aquin* (Louvain-la-Neuve, 1980), 280. The English translation is by the author.

What do we find in *The Philosophy of Being*? At a crucial point in his proof, De Raeymaker provides textual support for his claim that multiplicity cannot "constitute" a reason for unity. He cites four passages from St. Thomas. The first three (*De Potentia* 7, a. 1; *Summa Contra Gentiles* II, 41; and *Summa Contra Gentiles* I, 18) employ some version of the formula, "diverse things, inasmuch as they are diverse, are not united" (*diversa autem, in quantum huiusmodi, non faciunt unum*). The final passage, taken from the *Prima Pars* of the *Summa Theologiae*, q. 44, a. 1, refers to an argument in which Thomas cites Plato's claim that "before all multiplicity we must posit unity" (*ante omnium multitudinem ponere unitatem*). This is an interesting, eclectic set of passages, but I suggest that, if we examine these texts closely, they will show how De Raeymaker's proof draws upon some central themes in Thomistic metaphysics.

The first and third citations belong together, since both texts reason from the efficiently caused character of composite being to the absolute simplicity of God. Let us take the first text from *De Potentia* 7, a. 1. Composition implies diversity of parts in the thing composed. Now since "diverse things as such are not united," Thomas argues, the distinct principles of a composite need some extrinsic cause to join them together. Furthermore, since every composite being exists solely on the basis of the union of its parts, it must depend upon a "prior agent" as well. But Thomas observes that God is "the First Being, from whom all things exist"; as such, He is uncaused and cannot be composite, but must be altogether simple.[61]

De Raeymaeker's reference to this passage might seem curious at first. While Thomas does employ the principle found in his proof, he applies it here to the inner composition of finite being, and not to the order of being as a whole. Yet, as we have seen, De Raeymaeker later

---

[61] *Quaestiones Disputatae De potentia Dei* in *S. Thomae Aquinatis opera omnia*. vol. 8 (Parma: Fiaccadori, 1856; reprinted New York: Musurgia 1949), 147: "Secunda ratio est, quia cum compositio non sit nisi ex diversis, ipsa diversa indigent aliquot agente ad hoc quod uniantur. Non enim diversa, inquantum huiusmodi, unita sunt. Omne autem compositum habet esse, secundum quod ea ex quibus componitur, uniuntur. Oportet ergo quod omne compositum dependeat ab aliquot priore agente. Primum ergo ens, quod Deus est, a quo sunt omnia, non potest esse compositum."

insists that the caused character of particular being can be established through an analysis of its internal structure. The external relativity characteristic of the finite order necessarily implies an inner relativity at the core of each being.

The second reference, drawn from the *Summa Contra Gentiles* II, 41, belongs to a larger treatise (Chapters 39-45) concerning the question of the origin of the distinction of things in which Thomas eventually concludes (Chapter 45) that such "diversity" must have its reason in the "intention of God Himself." Chapter 41 is restricted more narrowly to showing that this distinction cannot be due to a diversity of agents. Thomas argues in the following manner: Ordered effects cannot proceed from diverse causes that are not ordered, because the diverse, inasmuch as they are diverse, cannot form a unity. Now distinct things in creation are discovered to be "ordered to each other," and not by chance, so that in the majority of cases "one is moved by another." It is thus impossible, Thomas concludes, that the distinction of things thus ordered would be on account of a "diversity of agents lacking order." Since unity cannot arise from diversity, the order that one finds in creation must at least be caused by ordered agents. But Thomas has just argued that if there were a diversity of ordered agents, these agents would ultimately find their principle in "some one cause" by which they are united. Such an agent would thus be "the first and sole cause of the distinction of things."[62]

Of the four passages De Raeymaeker cites, this argument most closely resembles his own account. Both proofs proceed directly from an ordered diversity in being to a unitary cause of the order. Moreover, the dialectical tension found here between unity and diversity corresponds to the opposition between relativity and subsistence seen in *The Philosophy of Being*. Although its philosophical background needs to be developed (and, in particular, its association with the doctrine of

---

[62] *Summa Contra Gentiles* (Turin: Marietti, 1922), 128: "A diversis causis non ordinatis non procedunt effectus ordinati, nisi forte per accidens; diversa autem, in quantum huiusmodi, non faciunt unum. Res autem distinctae inveniuntur habere ordinem ad invicem non casualiter, quum ut in pluribus unum ab alio moveatur. Impossibile est igitur quod distinctio rerum sic ordinatarum sit propter diversitatem agentium non ordinatorum."

participation), the argument supplies a principal textual inspiration for the "metaphysical proof."

The final passage, taken from the *Prima Pars* of the *Summa Theologiae*, cites the Platonic claim that "before all multiplicity we must posit unity." Question 44 concerns "the procession of creatures from God," and its first article asks "whether it is necessary that every being be created by God." Thomas suggests that whenever a perfection is "found in anything by participation," this perfection "must be caused in it" by something that possesses the perfection "essentially." Now he recalls his earlier demonstrations that God has been shown to be "*esse* itself subsisting through itself," and that "subsisting being" must be one. Granting these claims, it follows that all beings other than God "participate in *esse*," since "they would not be their own being"; that is, they do not possess the perfection of being essentially. Thus, inasmuch as all creatures are made diverse by their "diverse participation of being," they must proceed from "one First Being."[63]

This argument should sound familiar. With some changes, Thomas adopted its basic structure in more formal proofs—notably in the argument found in the *Lectura* on St. John's Gospel. Unfortunately, it suffers from the same defect that ruins the *Lectura* argument in that its guiding principle (that whatever exists by participation requires a cause) lacks a sound justification. Yet, while De Raeymaeker cites this passage because of its clear appeal to participation and its strong affirmation of his conclusion, it differs in structure and style from his own proof. He does not assume from the start that participation in

---

[63] *Summa Theologiae, Prima Pars*, ed. P. Caramello (Turin-Rome, 1948), 224: Si enim aliquid invenitur in aliquo per participationem, necesse est quod causetur in ipso ab eo cui essentialiter convenit; sicut ferrum fit ignitum ab igne. Ostensum est autem supra, cum de divina simplicitate ageretur; quod Deus est ipsum esse per se subsistens. Et iterum ostensum est quod esse subsistens non potest esse nisi unum: sicut si albedo esset subsistens, non posset esse nisi una, cum albedines multiplicentur secundum recipientia. Relinquitur ergo quod omnia alia a Deo non sint suum esse, sed participant esse. Necesse est igitur omnia quae diversificantur secundum diversam participationem essendi, ut sint perfectius vel minus perfecte, causari ab uno primo ente, quod perfectissime est. Unde et Plato dixit quod necesse est ante omnium multitudinem ponere unitatem."

being implies a first cause, nor does he "jump too quickly" to the Infinite Being as St. Thomas apparently does.

Now, when we consider all four passages together, we can see that they do more than provide a guided tour through De Raeymaeker's Thomistic sources; they also retrace the movement of his argument in *The Philosophy of Being*. He starts with a reflection on the meaning of participation, attempting to draw out the full implications of this doctrine through an examination of the structure of finite being. The first three passages sketch a portrait of particular being in all of its radical dependence. Participation means external relativity (*Summa Contra Gentiles* II, 41); but external relativity in turn implies internal relativity, an inner structure of relations at the core of every particular being (*De Potentia* 7, a. 1; *Summa Contra Gentiles* I, 18). And whether one considers the diverse finite terms bound together in the order of being, or the irreducibly distinct co-principles that compose the reality of particular being, we are dealing with a *complexus* whose unity must be explained. It is at this stage that De Raeymaeker can turn to the argument from the *Summa Theologiae*, for, having uncovered the "deep-seated relativity" in being, he is now in a position to conclude with Thomas that "whatever exists by participation is dependent on a cause."

In the end, Van Steenberghen may be correct in his assessment of the Thomistic arguments from participation. The *Quarta Via* and the *Lectura* proofs take too much for granted. By employing the notion of participation, whether implicitly or explicitly, these arguments assume that the mere presence of degrees of "more and less" in being points immediately to a unitary cause responsible for the shared perfection. But De Raeymaeker does not make the same mistake. The "mystery of participation" is for him the fundamental problem in metaphysics, and it requires a thorough analysis of both the internal and external structure of finite being. Thus, far from begging the question, De Raeymaeker's solution to this problem offers a complete explanation for the reasons why every participant in being requires a cause. In working this out, he calls upon all the elements of Thomistic metaphysics at his disposal. While his references may not always meet the exacting demands of textual scholarship, his argument remains sound.[64]

---

[64] Nonetheless, I think there is another Thomistic argument that more closely parallels De Raeymaeker's in its style and structure. It does not contain an explicit reference to participation, but the doctrine seems present therein. This is the well-known proof from plurality, from the "many to the one," and its classic formulation is found in *De Potentia*, q. 3, a. 5. The proof in Article 5, just like the passage in Question 44 of the *Summa Theologiae*, is principally devoted to showing that all things are created by God, though it can stand independently as an argument for God's existence. It runs thus:

> Oportet enim, si aliquid unum communiter in pluribus invenitur, quod ab aliqua una causa in illis causetur; non enim potest esse quod illud commune utrique ex seipso conveniat, cum utrumque, secumdum quod ipsum est, ab altero distinguatur; et diversitas causarum diversos effectus producit. Cum ergo esse inveniatur omnibus rebus commune, quae secundum illud quod sunt, ad invicem distinctae sunt, oportet quod de necessitate eis non ex seipsis, sed ab aliqua una causa esse attribuatur. Et ista videtur ratio Platonis, qui voluit quod ante omnem multitudinem esse aliqua unitas, non solum in numeris, sed etiam in rerum naturis": *Quaestiones Disputatae De potentia Dei* in *S. Thomae Aquinatis opera Omnia*, Vol. 8 (Parma: Fiaccadori, 1856; reprinted New York: Musurgia, 1949), 33.
>
> (It is necessary that, if something common is found in many, that something must be caused in them by some one cause. For it is not possible that this common feature belongs to each one by reason of itself, since each according to what it is by itself, is distinguished from the others, and diversity of causes produces diversity of effects. Therefore, since being is found common to all things, which according to what they are are distinct from one another, it is necessary for being to be attributed to them not by themselves, but from some one cause. This seems to be the reasoning of Plato who claimed that before all multiplicity there must be some unity not only in numbers but in the nature of things.)

We have here, stated in somewhat different terms, the basic elements of De Raeymaeker's argument. Despite their very real diversity as subsistent subjects, particular beings share a fundamental likeness in being. The principle of their agreement, the source of their ontological similarity, cannot be placed at the door of particular beings themselves—either singly or collectively—because, considered as distinct individuals, they differ from

And De Raeymaeker's approach has a solid basis in the work of St. Thomas. Van Steenberghen goes too far in suggesting that one must forgo any reference to the doctrine of participation in constructing a formal proof for God's existence. He writes as if participation can mean only two things for Thomas: the "logical" participation of generic and specific concepts in the idea of being, or the "ontological" participation of all finite beings in *esse subsistens*, Infinite Being. Yet Thomas offers a much more comprehensive (and nuanced) treatment of this problem in his work. As John F. Wippel has recently shown, Thomas does refer to "ontological" and "logical" participation, but he also writes of finite being's "participation in *esse commune*."[65] When considering this form of participation, Thomas means only that finite being partakes of the "perfection signified by the term *esse*," that each being according to what it is possesses its own proper "*esse*" or *actus essendi*. This is no doubt the role par-ticipation plays in *The Philosophy of Being*, and it is a perfectly respectable philosophical approach to God. As De Raeymaeker has shown, on the basis of a critical examination of participation, one must eventually raise the question of causality. In considering this approach, Wippel notes:

> One may move from one's discovery of individual beings as participating in *esse commune* to the caused character of such beings, and then on to the existence of the unparticipated source (*esse subsistens*). Once this is established, one can then speak of them as actually participating in *esse subsistens* as well.[66]

I believe that this is the approach Louis De Raeymaeker adopts in his brilliant "retrieval" of Thomistic metaphysics. The "metaphysical proof" remains an argument grounded upon St. Thomas' teaching on participation.

---

each other, and diversity or multiplicity as such cannot produce similarity or unity. To explain this "common feature," a cause is required, and given that the perfection in question is being, the absolute and most "profound" value, this cause must be the unique and total creative source of the entire order.

[65] Wippel, *The Metaphysical Thought of Thomas Aquinas*, 117.

[66] Ibid., 117.

# MARITAIN ON THE NATURAL DESIRE TO SEE GOD: REFLECTIONS APPRECIATIVE AND CRITICAL

MICHAEL D. TORRE

Having stayed for some time in Salamanca, I could not but be familiar with the famous words of Br. Luis de Leon. Having been unjustly imprisoned for over five years by the Inquisition, and then fully exonerated, he returned to his teaching post. Upon first ascending the lectern, he surveyed his expectant audience and serenely began: "as I was saying yesterday..."[1] My beginning cannot be as splendid or as immortal; still, I here continue an argument made to this Association. I have argued that Maritain, contrary to his own self-understanding, was more of a lay theologian than a philosopher.[2] I will not re-argue that thesis here, but will again only remind us of the vast number of works he wrote dealing with truths that derive from faith: the whole second part of *The Degrees of Knowledge* is a case in point. And so, too, is the matter I will take up here: the natural desire of any intellectual creature to see God. For this matter, Maritain repeatedly argued, could only be understood fully, or adequately, from truths of faith.

It is not surprising that he made such a claim. For this desire is the "lynchpin" or "point of contact" between the orders of nature and grace and is the basis for Thomas's careful, detailed, and concerted effort to establish their proper relation in the *Summa Contra Gentiles*. And here I come to my first critical reflection on Maritain: he never bothers to examine that work in any depth. This is even more surprising given that the matter Thomas expressly seeks to understand in it—namely the relation between the truths of faith that are *accessible*

---

[1] See "Leon, Fray Luis de" in the *Enciclopedia de la Religión Católica* (Barcelona: Dalmau y Jover, 1953), T. IV, 1231-32.

[2] See "To Philosophize *For* the Faith: Jacques Maritain's Intellectual Vocation," in *The Vocation of the Catholic Philosopher: From Jacques Maritain to John Paul II*, ed. John P. Hittinger (Washington, D.C.: American Maritain Association, 2011), 110-31.

to reason and those that *transcend* it—was so close to the project of Maritain's whole life. And yet one will look in vain throughout Maritain's entire *oeuvre* for any substantive discussion of *The Summa Contra Gentiles*. As we shall see, because of this lacuna, I believe he fails to grasp fully what Thomas's own doctrine is on this important matter.

It is also somewhat surprising that he apparently did not know the work of Fr. Guy de Broglie, S.J., which re-awakened theologians to what Thomas held in that work and that began the arduous and involved discussion on the relation between nature and grace that has so intensely occupied Catholic theologians ever since.[3] And yet one will look in vain in Maritain's work, or even in his correspondence with Charles Journet, for a discussion of de Broglie's findings. In truth, Maritain never wrote in depth on the natural desire for God or dedicated an article to it alone. So, perhaps it is not too surprising that Lawrence Feingold never once referred to Maritain in his doctoral dissertation, which fairly exhaustively examined the natural desire not only in Thomas, but also in his interpreters: ancient to contemporary.[4]

And yet, upon closer examination, one will find that Maritain was preoccupied with the natural desire to see God throughout his career. He speaks of it first in his *Réflexions Sur l'Intelligence et Sur Sa Vie Propre*: thus, in a work dating to 1923. He takes it up again some ten years later, in *The Degrees of Knowledge*. Then there is the whole section, called "Nature and Grace," which bears on it in his article on "The Immanent Dialectic of the First Act of Freedom," in *The Range of Reason*, dating from 1945. And he touches upon it again in a successive series of works: *An Introduction to the Basic Problems of Moral Philosophy* (from 1949), *La loi naturelle ou la loi non écrit* (from 1950), *Approaches to God* (from 1953)—a work that contains a whole chapter entitled "The Desire to See God"—*The Sin of the Angel* (from 1955) and *The Philosophy of History* (from 1957). In fact, he was interested in it to the very end of his life, as two articles in *Untrammeled Approaches* attest: a remark in "Along Unbeaten Pathways" and a note added in 1972 to "Beginning with a Reverie."

[3] See Guy de Broglie, "De la place du surnaturel dans la philosophie de saint Thomas," *Recherches de Science Religieuse*, XIV (1924): 192-240 and 481-96.

[4] Lawrence Feingold, *The Natural Desire To See God According to St. Thomas Aquinas and His Interpreters* (Rome: St. Apollinare Studi, 2001).

Maritain thus dealt with this issue *continually* throughout his long life, even if he always did so all-too-briefly. His ideas on the issue are both interesting and complex; furthermore, in places they undergo a significant evolution.

Let me indicate at the outset, however, how his ideas do *not* change. From beginning to end, he distinguishes the *natural* desire to see God from the love of *charity* that is founded on God's sanctifying grace and that is *supernatural*; and he is clear that we are only rendered in some manner truly "proportioned" to the end of seeing God (i.e. to *glory*) through the latter: through *grace*, not nature.[5] In the same way, he is always clear that *what* we desire (that is, to see God) entirely *transcends* nature and cannot be accomplished by any power of nature. His worry with Blondel, who first provokes him to examine the matter, is that he does not *distinguish* carefully enough between nature and grace, between metaphysics and faith: there is a "formal discontinuity"[6] between them. Thus, "a *natural mystical contemplation* [of God would be]...a contradiction in terms."[7]

Nevertheless, from the beginning to the end of his career, Maritain is also intent upon avoiding a *separation* between nature and grace.[8] He was always fond of Aquinas's *dictum* that grace does not destroy nature, but perfects it, and he always regarded such a separation as the besetting sin of Renaissance, anthropomorphic, humanism. Here is how he puts this attitude in *Integral Humanism*: "man and human life are ordered simultaneously to two different *absolutely ultimate ends*, a properly natural *ultimate* end, which is perfect prosperity here on earth, and a supernatural *ultimate* end, which is perfect beatitude in heaven. Thus, by a sagacious division of labor which the gospel had not foreseen, the Christian will be able to serve two masters at once, God

---

[5] "Sanctifying grace is...the root principle of the operation which is the Beatific Vision and *demands as its due* to see God as He sees Himself": Maritain, *The Degrees of Knowledge* (New York: Scribners, 1959), 255.

[6] Maritain, *Réflexions Sur L'Intelligence et Sa Vie Propre* (Paris: Nouvelle Libraire Nationale, 1924), in vol. III, 93-161, 155 and 157.

[7] Ibid., 135.

[8] Ibid., 157.

for heaven and Mammon for the earth."[9] If one is to hold both to the gospel teaching and to the unity of the human person, this division must be firmly rejected. He accordingly even refuses to *name* a supposed condition of human happiness *absent* the gift of grace as a natural "*beatitude*," reserving the latter term *only* for supernatural glory and referring to this other, supposed, condition as a "natural *felicity*": a happiness "in motion" that is never fully satisfied, that never reaches a final term, "resting place," or "saturation."[10] And thus, also, when he asks himself, in *The Degrees of Knowledge*, whether "we should "suppress every *organic* relation between them [metaphysics and mystical experience, nature and grace]," he responds: "Certainly not. There are *vital* relations between them."[11] At stake in his entire investigation of our natural desire, then, is how best to articulate this vital and organic relation, while respecting the formal distance between nature and grace. Rightly defining our natural desire, then, is an example *par excellence* of "distinguishing to unite."

Not surprisingly, Maritain places the chapter in *The Degrees of Knowledge* that examines it ("Mystical Experience and Philosophy,") *between* metaphysics and the supernatural wisdom of the Holy Spirit. And, since he dedicates it to his theological mentor, Fr. Garrigou-Lagrange, O.P., it also comes as no surprise that his first position on this matter (both there and in his earlier *Réflexions Sur L'Intelligence*) should follow his view, which itself was a "classic" Dominican position on this matter, at least since the Renaissance. He argues, then, that even the *possibility* of being truly happy, in the Beatific Vision, is "a mystery of faith *as incomprehensible as* the Incarnation of the Word;"[12] without Revelation, not only do we not know *how* this might be achieved, but we don't even know *if* it could be.[13] That our nature *can* be fulfilled or achieved by grace, *it alone* can make us "know and feel."[14] Indeed, to

---

[9] Maritain, *Integral Humanism* (New York: Scribners, 1968), 22.

[10] Maritain, *Réflexions*, 52.

[11] Maritain, *Degrees*, 283; my italics.

[12] Maritain, *Réflexions*, 151-52: my italics, and my translation (here and in all citations of this work).

[13] See Maritain, *Degrees*, 284, n. 1; my italics.

[14] Maritain, *Réflexions*, 154.

"love God as our friend and as communicating His properly divine life, and to want to see God by His essence and in His deity, *as something realizable*, is a *folly* as regards the powers of our nature alone."[15] True, *faith* teaches us that we are *made for* this happiness; but, as late as 1949, he will still hold that this truth "goes beyond philosophy and could even be *offensive* to it....Such a *possibility* seems more than paradoxical in the light of what we know of the ordinary situation of men and women, and...even seems *contrary* to everything that experience teaches us about human possibilities."[16] Maritain first approaches the natural desire, then, having placed a strong emphasis on the *distance* between nature and grace.

In the light of this distance, what in fact *is* this "natural desire to see God"? It is a desire born of knowing that God exists; that is to say, it is an *elicited* desire. Because we know that God exists, as the first cause of being (a truth we can reach in philosophy), we have a natural desire to know this cause fully. But this desire both is and is known to be *inefficacious*, because we can see that it desires something *beyond our power*. For the same reason, we can say that it is a *conditional* desire: "*if* this were possible, ah, what happiness!"[17] Although our knowledge that God exists engenders a *spontaneous* and *instinctive* desire, upon reflection we can see that its object is *impossible*.[18] It is, then, a mere *wish*, like wanting to fly, a desire that leads to no further volitional acts, because known to be impossible: "metaphysics naturally engenders in the soul a certain *velleity* it is unable to satisfy, a *confused and indeterminate desire* for a higher knowledge."[19] One could even speak of a natural *aspiration* to see God, for "it is a general law that the lower—without for that reason quitting its own nature and its specific bound—always tends to the higher and seeks to make contact with it."[20] Yet this

---

[15] Ibid., 154.

[16] Maritain, *An Introduction to the Basic Problems of Moral Philosophy* (New York: Magi, 1990), 118; my italics.

[17] Maritain, *Réflexions*, 152.

[18] Maritain, *Degrees*, 285, n. 1; my italics.

[19] Ibid., 284; Maritain's italics.

[20] Ibid.

aspiration remains no more than an "inefficacious yearning"[21] for a good recognized as beyond our nature. He clarifies this further in an appendix to *The Degrees of Knowledge*: "the created intellect has as its formal and specifying object only being and tends naturally to God only from this angle. That is why its natural desire to know the First Cause in its essence remains, insofar as it is natural, both conditional and inefficacious."[22]

Were our nature left to itself, then, in a supposed state of "pure nature," it would have possessed a certain "*melancholy*," since it would have been unable to attain a final, perfect, happiness. He goes so far as to say that "metaphysical melancholy is *natural to our species*, thus natural to our happiness itself, insofar as it is human [alone]."[23] Later, he will mention other of our natural "nostalgias," such as to be free but impeccable.[24] Such "impotent desires"[25] to surpass nature need not be fulfilled; and so, in a state of pure nature, man's "natural desire would have been frustrated without any violation of the *principle of finality* which protests against the possibility of an unconditional desire of nature being in vain."[26] He thinks Thomas says nothing different in the *Summa* (I, 12, 1), because he there "proceeds as a theologian, by *presupposing* the *possibility* of man's attaining *perfect* or absolute beatitude [of which] faith alone assures us."[27]

Yet, if nature is not proportioned to glory or final beatitude save by grace, it is still in itself *proportionable* to this; for every intellectual nature is capable of seeing God[28]; it is capable, then, of being raised to a new state by grace, and thus proportioned to glory. This is just what it means to say that it possesses an *obediental potency* for these.[29] Maritain

---

21 Ibid., 286.

22 Ibid., 455 (Appendix IV).

23 Maritain, *Réflexions*, 153; my italics.

24 Maritain, *The Sin of the Angel*, 96.

25 Maritain, *Degrees*, 285.

26 Ibid, 285, n. 1; Maritain's italics.

27 Ibid.; Maritain's italics.

28 Maritain, *Réflexions*, 154, n. 48; Maritain's italics.

29 Ibid.; my italics.

emphasizes this fact of our nature: "if our understanding, inasmuch as it is human, is directly ordered to being as it is concretized in sensible things, still, *as intellect [as nous] it remains ordered to being in its fullness.*"[30] Likewise, this capacity is consonant with our *natural* or *innate* desire to love God more than oneself, as the common good of the universe; for this reason, our nature is *perfected* by grace.[31] In our *fallen* state, *this* natural love of God remains *inefficacious* or impossible to fulfill, given its weakness; but, in a supposed state of pure and unfallen nature, it would have been effective, and would have ordered us to love God above all things: not as our friend or with supernatural charity, but as the "supreme and subsistent Good" of the universe.[32]

Several later works complete this point. In *La loi naturel ou la loi non écrit*, he argues that the precept to love God and neighbor that undergirds the natural law would, in that supposed state, have been a precept of a *natural* love for each.[33] (For fallen man, that is no longer possible, so *now* the law can only be fulfilled by possessing charity, which means that, at base, the natural law—now revealed in the Decalogue—conceals "a supernatural substance."[34]) In his last year, he even argues that this natural love of God is *in fact* the destiny of infants dying in original sin: they attain the heights of what nature alone can achieve and love God above all things (and their neighbor as their equal).[35] And, in *The Sin of the Angel*, he had argued that the angels would have had an analogous condition and destiny, supposing they had been created in a state of nature and remained in it.[36] Maritain thus remains consistent with much of his first doctrine throughout his life.

---

[30] Maritain, *Degrees*, 248; my italics.

[31] Ibid.; my italics.

[32] Maritain, *Degrees*, 271.

[33] Maritain, *La loi naturel ou al loi non écrit*, 234.

[34] Ibid., 235.

[35] Maritain, "Beginning With A Reverie," from *Untrammeled Approaches*, trans. Bernard Doering, Preface by Ernst R. Korn (Heinz R. Schmitz) (Notre Dame, Indiana: University of Notre Dame Press, 1997), 24. He must thus allow that the natural love of God above all that original sin had rendered *inefficacious* is, by God's grace, *overcome* in them.

[36] Maritain, *The Sin of the Angel*, 34.

Nevertheless, he ends by making an important change to his position. A beginning is made in *The Basic Problems of Moral Philosophy*, and its point is maintained thereafter, in *La loi naturel ou la loi non écrit*, *Approaches to God*, *The Sin of the Angel*, *The Philosophy of History*, and *Untrammeled Approaches*. In all these works, Maritain acknowledges the *present depth* of our strictly natural desire to see God, a fact that strikes him now more forcibly. He renames it a "trans-natural" desire; that is, we naturally desire a goal that transcends our nature.[37] In *Basic Problems*, he notes that "everywhere you see the aspiration to a superhuman condition, and all this bears witness to the existence of a desire for an absolute happiness which would make us like gods."[38] And, in *Untrammeled Approaches*, he declares that this "aspiration towards what is *naturally impossible*...is as *essential* to us as our skin;" should "we try to wrench from our hearts this aspiration" (which is "at the heart of all the great religions of humanity"), we "will bring about the degeneration of our nature, and in so doing the very idea of our nature."[39] He there characterizes this understanding of man as "more Pascalian than Aristotelian;" and he says "it presents us with an image of man that is at once grandiose and pathetic"[40] (rather than merely the latter): it symbolizes the "grandeur and misery" of our condition.

Furthermore, Maritain offers us an *explanation* of its present strength: it is due to the fact that human nature was "immediately and conclusively *infinitized*" by grace and the "supernatural desire issuing from faith:"[41] an event that occurred in our first elevation to the supernatural order. For faith not only activates supernatural desires; it also "*fixes* our natural desire (now made unconditional [in faith]) for

---

[37] The outline of Maritain's position is already clear in "The Thomist idea of Freedom," Chapter V of *Scholasticism and Politics* (New York, Macmillan, 1940; Freeport, New York: Books for Libraries Press, 1972 reprint), 94-113: "...there exists in us, as reasonable animals, a natural desire, which is not exactly of ourselves but of a transcendental element within us, to pass beyond the human condition" (106). (The essay is from 1937, and thus well before the publication of De Lubac's *Surnaturel* in 1946.)

[38] Maritain, *Basic Problems*, 115.

[39] Maritain, "Along Unbeaten Pathways," in *Untrammeled Approaches*, 411.

[40] Ibid.

[41] Maritain, *Basic Problems*, 116 and 117.

the transnatural object: to know the God of reason, the God we know by His effects, in His essence. If faith departs...the effect which depends on the efficient action produced by faith—the fixation of the transnatural desire for beatitude, and of the transcendental desire to see the First Cause—remains in nature."[42] And, in *The Philosophy of History*, he insists that "it is very important that we admit this superelevation *in the very order of nature.* If we don't admit it, we are led willy nilly to a kind of SEPARATION between nature and grace, to a kind of naturalism—nature will have its own course separately from any contact with grace."[43] We see Maritain here seeking to "narrow the distance" between nature and grace, while respecting their formal difference; for the strength of the desire he argues is in fact now at work remains *substantively natural*, even though this is due to the influence of grace.

This new emphasis on the strength of our natural desire is consonant with a crucial shift he makes in his understanding of it, in *Approaches to God*. For he there develops an idea already mentioned in *The Degrees of Knowledge*, namely that "our intellect is *ordered* to *being in its fullness* [my emphasis]." Here is how he now describes this: our elicited desire to see God as the effect of known causes "*follows* [my emphasis] from the very nature of that quest of being which *essentially characterizes the intellect.*"[44] Again, what he now terms our "trans-natural" desire reaches "for the infinite, *because* [my emphasis] *the intellect thirsts for being.*"[45] Thus, while the elicited desire remains inefficacious, still "according as it *emanates from nature*, it is a *natural and necessary desire*. It is *not* a simple velleity, a superadded desire, a desire of superogation."[46] Not only does Maritain here *retract* a

---

[42] Ibid. (The idea is problematic. The desire in question is intellectual, and each person receives his intellectual soul directly from God. It is difficult to see how the gift of faith could have changed our *body* such that future infusions of our souls would have their intellectual desire altered from what it would otherwise have been.)

[43] Maritain, *The Philosophy of History*, 130, n. 10; Maritain's italics and my capitals.

[44] Maritain, *Approaches to God*, 97; Maritain's italics and my bold.

[45] Ibid.; Maritain's italics and my bold.

[46] Ibid.; my italics.

characterization he had made in *The Degrees*, but he goes on *also* to retract his interpretation of the *Summa*, I, 12, 1: "Because this desire which asks for what is impossible to nature is a desire of nature *in its profoundest depths*, St. Thomas Aquinas asserts that it cannot issue in an absolute impossibility. It is in no wise necessary that it *be* satisfied, since it asks for what is impossible for nature. But it is necessary that by some means (which is not nature) it be *able* to be satisfied, since it necessarily emanates from nature."[47] This is how Maritain, now rather differently, understands the "obediential potency": we *must* "*be able to know* God in His essence through a gift which transcends the possibility of our natural forces."[48]

There is always a worry here that one will end in having nature ground some particular truth of faith or gift of grace: an end he

---

[47] Ibid. (Here is a key text from Aquinas on the *dictum* that *a natural desire cannot be in vain*: "If we should proceed to infinity in our desire for ends so that one end should always be desired on account of another to infinity, we will never arrive at the point where a man may attain the ends desired. But a man desires fruitlessly what he cannot get; consequently, the end he desires would be useless and vain. But this desire is natural, for it was said above [9] that the good is what all things naturally desire. Hence it follows that a natural desire would be useless and vain. But this is impossible. The reason is that a natural desire is nothing else but an inclination belonging to things by the disposition of the First Mover, and this cannot be frustrated. Therefore, it is impossible that we should proceed to an infinity of ends" [*Commentary on Aristotle's Nicomachean Ethics* (Notre Dame: Henry Regnery, 1964; Dumb Ox Books, 1993), 8]. The reason a natural desire cannot be in vain, then, is because God's intention [which it is] cannot be in vain. Clearly a natural desire not being "in vain" does not entail that it is *actually* attained in every instance, only that it be *possible* to be attained. It would take another full study to explicate Thomas's idea here fully. Suffice it to say that the impossibility is rooted in God, and [I would argue] specifically in God's *wisdom*: just as a wise architect does not lay a foundation for an unbuildable building, so God does not make a nature with a natural inclination that is vain and useless.This idea is not original. [See Stanislas Dockx, O.P., "Du désir naturel de voir l'essence divine selon saint Thomas d'Aquin,"*Archives de Philosophie*, 1964: 49-96.] Maritain himself never attempts to explicate Aquinas's *dictum*, just as he barely discusses scholarly debate on the natural desire to see God.)

[48] Ibid.

obviously wishes to avoid, since this makes nonsense of both. No doubt that accounted for his original interpretation of I, 12, 1. He addresses that worry with the following distinction: "The argumentation of St. Thomas in the question of 12, a. 1 of the *Prima Pars* establishes rationally the *possibility*, I do not say of the *supernatural order* such as the *faith presents it* [my emphasis] to us and as it implies the *specifically Christian* [my emphasis] notion of grace, but *an order superior to nature*, the notion of which remains *still indeterminate* [my emphasis], except in this, that through the *divine generosity* [my emphasis] man can therein be rendered capable of knowing God in His essence."[49] Nevertheless, human reason (in recognizing that this desire is rooted in our nature and that it cannot be fulfilled by it) comes to see that, for any possible answer to *how* it might be fulfilled (and therefore how one might be perfectly happy), philosophy cannot guide us. Philosophy must end, then, with this question: "*Shall we* go beyond philosophy in order to get our answer?"[50] This is indeed to narrow the distance between nature and grace and avoid their separation; for now reason, rightly pursued on its own terms, shows that nature and philosophy cannot answer the question nature poses to us concerning our final destiny and ultimate happiness. We see that by nature we desire something that transcends nature, and thus we see that *nature* can only be fulfilled through a divine *faith* that is true.

Although Maritain does not make much of his later shifts (as we saw, he continues to affirm many elements of his first position), nevertheless we should not underestimate the importance of the change he is making. He had earlier argued that the Beatific Vision was as "*incomprehensible as the Incarnation*." That is here being *retracted;* for the possibility of the former is being affirmed, whereas the *way* it will be so (namely through the Incarnation) remains a matter known only to faith. Likewise, earlier he had claimed that the Beatific Vision is a "*folly*" or perhaps even an "*offense*" to philosophy; it is now being

---

[49] Ibid.; Maritain's italics and my bold.

[50] Ibid., 100. (Note that Maritain here only argues philosophy sees its limitation, and its need to be transcended. *Faith and theology* do transcend it, and supply human reason with an answer to its question. One *could* defend *this* argument, then, *without* defending his further yet similar idea of a "moral *philosophy* adequately considered.")

regarded as no such thing, but a real possibility. Earlier, he had argued that were it *not possible* to fulfill our natural desire, this would not "offend against the principle of finality"; now, by contrast, he straightforwardly holds that, were that the case, our nature would indeed have been made in vain. Most importantly, he had earlier confined the natural desire to no more than an inefficacious wish to know beyond our natural powers; now, however, he argues that this inefficacious desire is itself rooted in something more profound that is innate to us: the natural end or order of the intellect to being. He might have said "the natural order of the intellect to *know* the *truth* about being," in which case he would have clearly stated what he implies, namely that every intellectual creature has an innate inclination to its perfection, and thus (implicitly) to know (i.e. see) God. Impliedly, his last position on this matter very importantly alters his entire outlook.

I will be much briefer in my evaluation of Maritain's thought on this matter. It is hard not to appreciate the carefulness with which he always approaches this question, combined with his characteristic verve that brings "scholastic distinctions" to life. It is especially admirable that he should struggle so hard and so long to "get the nuances right" and that he should be willing to retract his earlier views, when he thought he saw more deeply. Furthermore, it is good to see him coming back in the end to some of the positions Thomas clearly teaches.[51] Thus, he places the Beatific Vision in Book III of the *Summa Contra Gentiles*, as a truth *accessible to reason*, but the Incarnation in Book

---

[51]As to why Maritain is at first satisfied with his previous interpretation of Thomas (a question my essay prompts and prompted), my own guess as to reasons are these: (1) he never seems to have made a study of the *Summa Contra Gentiles*; (2) there is no evidence that he was aware of the growing debate over its meaning until considerably later in his career; (3) he was initiated into his Thomism by Dominicans, and ever felt himself indebted to the major Dominican commentators, to whose tradition he felt he himself belonged, and was thus ready to follow the lead of a man such as Garrigou-Lagrange on this matter, at least at the beginning of his career; (4) also, he did not see himself as a professional theologian and thus was more ready to defer to the latter's judgment on what he saw as basically a theological controversy; (5) finally, he had felt Blondel had unduly "blurred" the distinction between philosophy and faith, and he was thus disposed to insist on their formal separation: a distance he ends by lessening.

IV, as a truth that *transcends* it. Likewise, he straightforwardly says in the *Summa Theologiae* that it is a truth of *reason* as well as faith, and that nature would be made in vain were it not possible. Furthermore, his entire analysis of the natural desire in the *Summa Contra Gentiles* is manifestly dealing, at root, with an innate inclination for truth of *any* created intellect (one that, as a natural inclination, *every* intellectual creature possesses, whether or not that person knows the necessity of a First Cause). In all of these ways, I believe Maritain's final position rightly turns us in the direction of Thomas's express positions.[52]

It is important to note, however, that none of Thomas's texts lend themselves to being used as Maritain does in defending the state of pure nature. This is patent, for example, in the question whether man was created in a state of grace (I, 109, 6): the alternatives Thomas examines there are between being created immediately in grace or then being raised to it, before original sin. Likewise, in the question before that of whether the angels were so created (I, 62, 2 ad 3), he had distinguished three ways we turn to God: perfectly, in glory; imperfectly, in sanctifying grace; or by the operation of God turning us, where he uses the same text from *Lamentations* he will later use when affirming man's need to be converted by God to prepare for sanctifying grace (I-II, 109, 6). Thus, assuming the angels were not created in sanctifying grace, the alternative is *not* that they be created in a state of pure nature, but rather in a state of nature aided by God's operation turning them to Him, which operation Maritain holds (and rightly, I believe) requires *actual* grace. Nor does Thomas assert that infants in Limbo possess a natural love of God above all things, for the simple reason that original sin makes that inefficacious and they are in that

---

[52]As to what led to his shift (another question my essay rightly prompts), I am unclear about this myself and would like to have a better "feel" for it than I do. Certainly, he knew of the De Lubac controversy, and was not entirely ill-disposed to the Jesuit theologian (as René Mougel has pointed out: see his "La position de Jacques Maritain à l'égard de *Surnaturel*," *Revue Thomiste* 101 [2001]: 73-98). He remained sympathetic to his Dominican "opponents," but without being a "hard-liner" (as his later teaching on the impossibility of the angel's impeccability indicates). I think perhaps he was aware of the growing tide of secularism that was rising and recognized the importance of stressing the significance of man's *natural religiosity*, and, hence the importance of insisting on his *profound* and *natural* desire to see God; but I am unsure.

state. Nor can his teaching on the precept of charity be used as Maritain attempts. He rightly sees that, for Thomas, the gospel loves of God and of neighbor are "the first general principles of the *natural law*" (I-II, 100, 1, 3 ad 1); and that Thomas holds that *these principles* (i.e. acts of *charity*, not any purely natural love) "are self-evident to human reason, either through reason or faith." To the objection that then one cannot fulfill the precepts of the natural law without grace, Thomas simply responds: "man *cannot* fulfill all the precepts of the law unless he fulfill the precept of charity, which is impossible without charity. Consequently, it is *not possible*, as Pelagius maintained, for man to fulfill the law without grace" (I-II, 10, ad 3). Thomas is here speaking of the Decalogue, which, as Maritain sees, *reiterates* the natural law (I-II, 100, 1 and 3). There is no evidence at all that a supposed natural love absent charity could somehow "substitute" for this (in the state of "pure nature").

Note that Thomas, just in discussing this question of the need for charity (and thus sanctifying grace) argues that this does not enjoin something *impossible* absolutely, since "man can *dispose* himself to possess charity, and when he possesses it, he can use it" (I-II, 10). True, he could not dispose himself without the aid of actual grace. However, we should remember that, while Thomas holds that we are indeed held to do "many things which we cannot do without the aid of healing grace, such as to love God and our neighbor, and likewise to believe articles of faith" (II-II, 2, 5), nevertheless the *only reason* he assigns for some *possibly* not being given such healing grace is *sin*: "from whomever it is withheld it is justly withheld, as a punishment of a previous, or at least original sin." If, then, the *natural* law requires charity, which Thomas expressly claims that it does, there is no reason, on Thomas's terms, to imagine that a gracious aid will be *withheld* to anyone who is created *without* sin: at a minimum, they would receive the actual grace by which one created without sanctifying grace could *dispose* himself to receive it. There is, then, no need for Maritain to propose his imagined substitute of loving the honest good, and loving God (and neighbor) with a *natural* love, rather than charity.

Finally, and most to the point, it is unfortunate that Maritain never remarks the fact that Thomas clearly, unequivocally, and constantly criticizes Aristotle regarding his notion of imperfect beatitude.[53] As early as the *Sentences* (IV *Sentences*, d. 49, q. 1, a. 1, qu. 4, sol. IV), he says that Aristotle holds that "perfect beatitude is not possible to man" and that we should order all our activity to attaining only imperfect, earthly, happiness. Note that this would seem to make sense to anyone who argued we should seek goods only within our power. However, Thomas argues, "this position is not *reasonable*." And the reason it is not is because, wherever there is an *essentially* rational or intellectual creature (rather than brutes), it must be possible *at some time* to reach perfect, and not just imperfect, beatitude; for "otherwise the natural intellectual appetite which is in man would be frustrated." Since perfect beatitude is not possible in this life, "we concede simply that the perfect beatitude of man is after this life." Note well, Aristotle's position is held to be wrong not because it opposes faith, but because it is *unreasonable*. He makes the identical argument in his commentary on the key passages from the first book of Aristotle's *Ethics*. As noted (see my #46), he also explains there why a natural desire cannot be vain: "the reason is that a natural desire is nothing else but an *inclination* belonging to things by the *disposition of the First Mover*, and this cannot be frustrated." He also argues that Aristotle's imperfect happiness does "not seem to measure up in all respects to the conditions for happiness" that he had laid down: namely that it be *perfect* and *complete* or self-sufficient; and he draws the same conclusion: "*since* a *natural* desire is not in vain, we can correctly *judge* that perfect beatitude is reserved for men after this life" (202). The same position is argued repeatedly and at length in the *Summa Contra Gentiles*, where he concludes with these moving words: "there is abundant evidence of how even the brilliant minds of these men suffered from the *narrowness of their viewpoint*. From which narrow attitudes we shall be freed if we grant, in accord with the foregoing *proofs* that we can reach true felicity after this life" (III, 48). The same doctrine shows up in the *Summa Theologiae* (I, 12, 1), the *Compendium of Theology* (2, 8), and the *Commentary on John* (I, Lect. 11, #212): in short, Thomas teaches this doctrine from first to last. In the *De Malo* (V, 1, ad 1) he even says that man is "*ordained by nature* to happiness as to an ultimate end, which

---

[53] It would of course be unfair to signal out Maritain for criticism here: many others also failed to remark on Thomas's texts referred to in this paragraph, especially the decisive one from *IV Sentences*.

happiness consists in the *vision of God*" and thus that "our nature *would* have been made in vain," had it been defeated by original sin, which is why God chose to remedy it, by becoming incarnate in Christ Jesus and offering us His grace.[54]

Now, I have already noted that Maritain does finally come towards Thomas's thinking, inasmuch as he finally acknowledges that we can see that the Beatific Vision is *possible*, on the basis of our inherent intellectual inclination and the principle that it is impossible that such a desire be frustrated, or be in vain. And yet I believe one can show that Thomas's thought is more radical even than that. While I will not argue this here, I believe one can show that his position is that our deepest natural desire not only *can* be fulfilled, but that it *will* be fulfilled, *unless it is impeded by sin* (either original or actual). Such a claim would obviously require even more than another essay. But I think that, had Maritain better studied Thomas's arguments against Aristotle and also his teaching in the *Summa Contra Gentiles*, he would have seen that Thomas's entire point of view differed considerably from the one with which he began. When it came to the vexed question of God's permission of evil and the sufficiency of His aid to avoid it, Maritain

---

[54] Aquinas could have found an antecedent to his last argument in Augustine: "Here we come across the slanderous question that is so often asked by those who are ready to blame their sins on anything but themselves: 'If it was Adam and Eve who sinned, what did we poor wretches do? How do we deserve to be born in the blindness of ignorance and the torture of difficulty? Why do we first err in ignorance of what we ought to do, and then, when the precepts of justice begin to be open to us and we will to do them, we are powerless, held back by some sort of necessity of carnal desire?' My response is brief: let them be silent and stop murmuring against God. *Perhaps their complaint would be justified if there were no Victor over error and inordinate desire.* But in fact there is one who is present everywhere and speaks in many ways through creation that serve him as Lord. He calls out to those who have turned their backs on him and instructs those who believe in him. He comforts the hopeful, encourages the diligent, helps the struggling, and hears the prayers of those who cry out to him (*On Free Choice of the Will* [Indianapolis: Hackett, 1993], 107). The complaint that "perhaps would be justified" is very close to what Thomas has asserted: people would be "justified" to complain that a *natural desire* (to act justly) had been *rendered vain* by a Fall without remedy; however, that the remedy chosen is the *Incarnation* is a truth of *faith.*

noted that "deeper renewals" were sought regarding it and that "finally a great variety of opinions surged up among the Dominican theologians, which is the sign of a certain uneasiness."[55] He urged that the "school position" needed to be "rethought," not just "altered slightly." The same kind of theological situation also existed concerning the doctrine of our natural desire to see God. Although there is a great deal to honor and appreciate in Maritain's thinking on this subject, I think both Thomas and the truth will be better served by a more radical reflection, one that seeks to penetrate Thomas's profound doctrine to its depths.

---

[55] Maritain, *God and the Permission of Evil* (Milwaukee: Bruce, 1966), 20.

# THE MAJESTY OF INTERSUBJECTIVITY: MARITAIN AND MARCEL *CONTRA* CARTESIAN SUBJECTIVITY

JOHN MARSON DUNAWAY

## I. INTRODUCTION

As a non-philosopher, I would not claim to have fully understood *The Degrees of Knowledge*. It is a truly difficult book that requires a great deal of intellectual spade work. And yet, an important facet of Maritain's genius is his ability to speak the language of people in many academic fields, as well as to poets and artists. So, as a student of language and literature and a person of faith, I have found his epistemological masterpiece to be unusually valuable for sorting out questions that bear upon the interrelation of various domains of intellectual inquiry: art and morality, science and religion, and empirical science vs. philosophy of nature. Published over threequarters of a century ago, it remains an invaluable resource in distinguishing the degrees of knowledge in order to understand how they may ultimately be united in human consciousness.

Jacques Maritain considered René Descartes one of the most deleterious of philosophers and a key figure in all that has gone wrong in Western thought since the seventeenth century. He singled him out along with Martin Luther and Jean-Jacques Rousseau in the 1927 book that traced some of the more significant modern philosophical errors (*Three Reformers*). No wonder then that, when he published his response to Jean-Paul Sartre (*Existence and the Existent*, in 1947), he swiftly homed in on Sartre's clear embrace of Cartesian subjectivity. As you will soon see, this paper could easily have been entitled "The Majesty of Intersubjectivity and The Poverty of Sartrian Existentialism." In these remarks, I wish to explore the post-World War II confrontation of existentialism and Thomism in an effort to focus our attention on the crucial role that intersubjectivity must play in any viable ontology.

*Existentialism Is a Humanism*[1] is the transcript of a public lecture given in Paris by Jean-Paul Sartre on 29 October 1945 at the invitation of the Club Maintenant and published (with only minor revisions) as a book by the Editions Nagel the following year. The author of *Being and Nothingness* had been accused of grim pessimism and a lack of human solidarity by both communists and Catholics. Thus, he was seeking to present his particular version of existentialism in a constructively humanistic light.

Jacques Maritain, for his part, was eager to respond to Sartre's philosophy with a more ontologically complete picture of human existence, one that would reveal the poverty of Sartrian thought and compete successfully for the minds of young Frenchmen, who were looking for a sound philosophical foundation for reconstructing their cultural identity in the wake of the long, hard years of the German Occupation. So, just one year after Sartre's little popularizing book appeared in print, Maritain published his *Existence and the Existent* (1947). It is probably safe to say that this "short treatise" (his original title in French) represents a direct response to Jean-Paul Sartre's public defense of atheistic existentialism.

A third major text that I shall be using in this analysis can be considered another pointed response to Sartre, and one that harmonizes admirably well with Maritain's thought. Gabriel Marcel's two volumes on *The Mystery of Being* were the Gifford Lectures in Aberdeen, Scotland, in 1949 and 1950. The first volume is entitled *Reflection and Mystery* (Chicago: Regnery, 1950) and the second *Faith and Reality* (South Bend, Indiana: Gateway, 1951). So, within the space of the five years immediately following WWII, three of France's most important philosophers were engaged in a very public dispute over the nature of being, and I believe the role that intersubjectivity played in that confrontation is worth revisiting. In this brief essay, then, I combine Maritain's Thomist metaphysics with Marcel's notion of intersubjectivity in an effort to demonstrate how they correct Sartre's Cartesian subjectivism. I quote here from the English translations of Maritain's *Distinguish to Unite, or The Degrees of Knowledge* (1932) and the two volumes of Marcel's *The Mystery of Being* (1950), but for Sartre's

---

[1] Jean-Paul Sartre, *L'Existentialisme est un Humanisme* (Paris: Editions Nagel, 1946).

*L'Existentialisme est un Humanisme* and Maritain's *Existence and the Existent*, I provide my own translations of the original.

## II. SARTRE'S CARTESIAN SUBJECTIVISM

In the very beginning of his text, Sartre acknowledges that his own version of existentialism takes its departure precisely from pure subjectivity, that is, the Cartesian *cogito*, or "the moment in which man apprehends himself in his solitude."[2] "There can be no other truth at the point of departure than this one: *I think, therefore I am*, that is the absolute truth of the conscience apprehending itself."[3] The very foundation of Sartre's philosophy—the proposition that existence precedes essence—means everything must begin with subjectivity. Hence, for him, there is no human nature, no natural law, and there are no moral or ethical norms that guide us in our choices. "Man is nothing else than what he makes himself."[4] This radical freedom that Sartre embraces in his Cartesian subjectivity is a direct consequence of his taking Ivan Karamazov literally. "The point of departure of Existentialism [is that] everything indeed is permitted if God doesn't exist, and consequently man is abandoned."[5] The communist critics to whom Sartre wished to respond had seen clearly that such an approach, imprisoning the Existentialist within Cartesian subjectivity, would necessarily entail a profound philosophical solipsism out of which it would be impossible to achieve genuine solidarity.

Maritain says: "It's one thing to know that God is a transcendent and sovereign Self, but it's an altogether different matter to enter oneself, with all one's baggage and one's own existence and flesh and bones, into a vital relationship where created subjectivity is confronted with this transcendent subjectivity and waits for one's salvation from it, in

---

[2] Ibid., 11: "Le moment où l'homme s'atteint dans sa solitude."

[3] Ibid., 64: "Il ne peut pas y avoir de vérité autre, au point de départ, que celle-ci: *je pense donc je suis*, c'est là la vérité absolue de la conscience s'atteignant elle-même."

[4] Ibid., 22: "L'homme n'est rien d'autre que ce qu'il se fait."

[5] Ibid., 36: "C'est là le point de départ de l'existentialisme. En effet, tout est permis si Dieu n'existe pas, et par conséquent l'homme est délaissé."

trembling and love. That belongs to the realm of religion."[6] Maritain's rejection of the Cartesian subjectivity in Sartrian existentialism is grounded in this deep conviction that humans are able to relate to one another as subjectivities (rather than objectifying each other) and that the reason for that ability is the ultimate Subjectivity of the Divine. Because we are known by God as subjectivities, we are immersed in an existence whose profoundest meaning is created by the network of relating subjectivities that Gabriel Marcel calls "intersubjectivity." Though Maritain does not use the word, he obviously agrees wholeheartedly with Marcel.

Sartre, with Descartes, can only be aware of his own existence through his awareness of his ongoing thinking process. He is a perfect subjectivity. But the only way he can know the subjectivities around him is by objectifying them, thus rendering them effectually lifeless. Each individual Cartesian or Sartrian subjectivity understands itself, then, as the center around which reality revolves. And Sartre has eliminated the possibility of the Divine Subjectivity, even as objectified. For this reason, when he says "Hell is other people," he means that he is aware that they are objectifying him in just the same way he is objectifying them, making them functions of his own subjectivity.

## III. MARITAIN'S METAPHYSICS AND CONNATURALITY

Maritain draws from St. Thomas his understanding of how each individual knows oneself. This self-knowledge is obscure, shadowy, non-scientific, experiential, and incommunicable. It is the intuition of being, such as Maritain describes it in *A Preface to Metaphysics*, as well as *Existence and the Existent*. "Subjectivity as subjectivity is unconceptualizable, it is an unknowable abyss—unknowable through notions, concepts, or representation, through any kind of science, introspection, psychology, or philosophy. How could it be otherwise, since all reality known conceptually, by notions or representations, is known as an

---

[6] Jacques Maritain, *Court traité de l'existence et de l'existant* (Paris: Paul Hartmann, 1947), 120: "C'est quelque chose de savoir que Dieu est un Soi transcendant et souverain, mais c'est une tout autre affaire d'entrer soi-même, avec tout son baggage et sa proper existence et sa chair et ses os, dans la relation vitale où la subjectivité créée est confrontée à cette subjectivité transcendante, et attend d'elle son salut, et tremble et aime. C'est l'affaire de la religion."

object, not a subject?"[7] Thus, Sartre's knowledge both of himself and of others is a form of objectification.

Maritain had already demonstrated this insight in "The Majesty and Poverty of Metaphysics," the opening chapter of *The Degrees of Knowledge*. There he asserts that the poverty of "incurably nominalist" philosophers is that "while having a taste for the real indeed, they nevertheless have no sense of being."[8] The majesty of metaphysics lies in its ability, by means of abstract conceptualization, to arrive at notions that he says are analogous to humans' knowledge of the Divine. Its poverty lies in its inability directly to name the Divine name, since "metaphysics makes God known to us only by analogy."[9] Thus it is that "the most perfect fruit of the intellectual life still leaves man unsatisfied."[10] In fact, it awakens a desire for union with God in the direct experiential way that is opened by intersubjectivity, which Maritain mostly refers to as charity or sometimes "*l'amour fou*," mystical mad love. "Here below, intellect can enter the realm that lies beyond all method only by a renunciation-of-knowing in which God's Spirit, by making use of the connaturality of charity and the effects produced in affection by the Divine Union, grants the soul a loving experience of that very being which no notion approximates or can approximate."[11]

One of the more central tenets of Gabriel Marcel's argument in both volumes of *The Mystery of Being* is that Sartre's pure subjectivity is a perspective from which he can never adequately account for being. He proclaims that a genuinely robust metaphysic must be anti-Cartesian. The only perspective from which to apprehend being in its rich, mysterious fullness is a relational one. It is precisely in the relatedness to other subjectivities that our subjectivity can hope to apprehend its full meaning. In what I consider a stroke of aphoristic genius, Marcel puts it this way: "It is a metaphysic of *we are* as opposed to a metaphysic

---

[7] Ibid., 115.

[8] Jacques Maritain, *Distinguish to Unite, or The Degrees of Knowledge*, trans. Gerald B. Phelan (New York: Scribner's, 1959), 1.

[9] Ibid., 6.

[10] Ibid.

[11] Ibid., 14.

of *I think*."[12] Marcel's analysis of Sartre is a devastating exposé of the latter's inadequacy to define being. He notes that Sartre "is himself obliged to take the other only as a threat to my liberty...or as a possible source of seduction."[13] When Sartre wrote his famous line in *No Exit* ("Hell is other people"), he revealed "his impossible position; ...he can have no understanding of *philia* or *agape*. In the end it is only on the one hand the domain of *eros*...or, on the other...that of a community of work."[14] And the community of work, he goes on to say, is only solidarity as viewed from the outside.

Maritain sheds light on the problem of the metaphysic of *I think* by recalling Pascal's thinking reed rather than Descartes' thinking subjectivity. He finds a 20$^{th}$-century version of Pascal's famous metaphor in a quote from Somerset Maugham's *The Summing Up*: "To myself I am the most important person in the world; though I do not forget that, not even taking into consideration so grand a conception as the Absolute, but from the standpoint of common sense, I am of no consequence whatever. It would have made small difference to the universe if I had never existed."[15] Maritain says such a consciousness causes us to vacillate between the two Pascalian infinites of our miserable inconsequentiality on the one hand and our astounding nobility on the other and that the only way to resolve the antimony is to escape this solipsism by transferring the center of the universe from ourselves to God.

## IV. MARCEL'S INTERSUBJECTIVITY

Just specifically what does Marcel mean, then, by intersubjectivity? And is it really in complete harmony with Maritain's metaphysics? First of all, Sartre holds that I am nothing more than my acts, my life. Man, he asserts, "only exists insofar as he realizes himself, thus he is nothing

---

[12] Marcel, *The Mystery of Being*, vol. II: *Faith and Reality*, tr. René Hague (South Bend, Indiana: Gateway, 1951), 9.

[13] Ibid.

[14] Ibid.

[15] Somerset Maugham, *The Summing Up* (Garden City, New York: Doubleday, Doran & Co, 1938), quoted in *Existence*, 123.

else than the sum total of his acts, nothing other than his life."[16] Marcel insists that "I ought to say both that I am my life and that I am not my life; the apparent contradiction tends to vanish away if we understand that I am weighing the actual life I have been leading in the balance of the potential life I carry within me, the life that I aspire to lead, the life that I would have to lead if I wanted to become fully myself; it is into this life of potentiality and aspiration that I penetrate when I turn inwards....It is in the name of a [personal] vocation...that I may be led to condemn a life which is the very life which, up to the present, I have actually been leading."[17] Hence, while agreeing with Sartre in emphasizing the moral responsibility for owning up to one's actions and how they engage the rest of humanity—which, by the way, is clearly the most valuable contribution that Sartrian existentialism has made—Marcel also avoids the idealist trap that made Sartre's philosophical system a dead-end.

A further example of the way Marcel gives the lie to Sartre's bald assertion that a human being is nothing other than his or her life is his consideration of the apparent narratability of an individual's life. "My life presents itself to reflection as something whose essential nature is that it can be related as a story,"[18] he observes. To narrate, however, is necessarily to summarize, and "the summarizing of the parts of a tale is in a certain sense obviously an opposite kind of operation from the unfolding of the tale as a whole. ...We have the naive idea of the story as reproducing life—we talk, for instance, of some story as a 'slice of life' or praise its 'documentary' exactness—but anything like a reproduction of life, in the strict sense, is just what a story cannot provide."[19] It's hardly surprising to note that Gabriel Marcel here evokes Proust's quixotic project "in search of lost time (*à la recherche du temps perdu*)." For, in Proust's effort to recapture the past, he himself eventually realizes that he is actually ending up with something new, rather than reconstructing what is hidden in his involuntary memory.

---

[16] Sartre, *Existentialism*, 55.

[17] Marcel, *The Mystery of Being*, vol I: *Reflection and Mystery* (Chicago: Regnery, 1950), 137.

[18] Ibid., 154.

[19] Ibid., 155.

The real story in Proust's great novel is the forging of a new self for the author. The past, he discovers, cannot be reconstructed nor narrated with any degree of accuracy or completeness. The narration itself comes to have the supreme significance for him.

Gabriel Marcel's meditation on being is able to preserve the ineffable mystery of ontology that Sartre had buried under his Cartesian subjectivist perspective. In the course of Marcel's quest to uncover the true nature of being, he broods for pages and chapters over the question of identity. Who am I? he wonders. Am I my body? A beautifully revealing reflection on the question produces the insight that "I am my body only in so far as I am a being that has feelings."[20] From there he proceeds to explore feeling as a mode of participation. Now Marcel's notion of participation is closely akin to Maritain's philosophy. Participation in an enterprise, he suggests, is a matter of feeling more than thought. "This will to participate is itself metaphysically possible only on the basis of a kind of human consensus (and a consensus, of course, is literally merely a thing felt, rather than something thought)."[21] He speaks of the peasant's deep attachment to the land, comparing it to the artist's deep contemplation of the landscape she is painting. Both, he suggests, are forms of participation, and they point toward the "intimate relationship that exists between participation and the creative spirit."[22] One is immediately reminded of Maritain's notion of connatural knowledge. Even empirical knowledge, according to the Thomist, is immaterial, in that the known is made present within the knower and the knower becomes by participation, in some measure, the known. Maritain cites an example of this affective union in the artist who enters into a profound communion with the subject of his or her painting. But with Marcel's "metaphysics of *We are*," Maritain would no doubt already see a nascent affective union with God unattainable by reason alone. The soul in a state of grace becomes a "partaker of the divine nature" (II Peter 1:4) and grows into an experiential knowledge of the Divine. Such a mode of knowing is wedded to the creativity of the human spirit in its various ways of living out the connectedness of intersubjectivity. Here we are entering

[20] Ibid., 101.

[21] Ibid., 115.

[22] Ibid., 117.

what Maritain calls the *suprarational* degrees of knowledge, inhabited by theology and mystical wisdom.

In "The Majesty and Poverty of Metaphysics," Maritain evokes in soaringly lyrical terms the analogous roles of the metaphysician and the poet (a description, by the way, that echoes the parallel callings of Jacques as philosopher and his wife Raïssa as poet).[23] "The metaphysician breathes an atmosphere of abstraction which is death for the artist. Imagination, the discontinuous, the unverifiable, in which the metaphysician perishes, is life itself to the artist. While both absorb rays that come down from creative Night, the artist finds nourishment in a bound intelligibility which is as multiform as God's reflections upon earth, the metaphysician finds it in a naked intelligibility that is as determined as the proper being of things. They are playing seesaw, each in turn rising up to the sky. Spectators make fun of their game; they sit upon solid ground."[24] Marcel would probably have said that Sartre was one such spectator, neither a true metaphysician nor a true poet. For Marcel, the analogy is between not only the metaphysician and the artist but also the contemplative mystic, and elsewhere Maritain too brings these three functions into intimate relationship. Contemplation, says Marcel, "must be considered as a mode of participation, and even as one of participation's most intimate modes. But, on the other hand, a true artist, a Vermeer, a Corot, a Hokusai, is also a contemplative—he is anything but a superficial spectator and nothing if not a deep participant."[25] The awareness of the ultimate Subjectivity as God, then, is the means of escape from Sartre's Cartesian trap. "I am known by God," declares Maritain, and "God does not need to objectify me in order to know me."[26] Objectification betrays the subject, thus creating the agonizing Sartrian definition of hell as other people. Intersubjective relations, made possible by God's first knowing us as subjectivities, are grounded in the divine nature of self-giving love. "To

---

[23] It would not be exaggeration to say that they both were called to mystical contemplation.

[24] Maritain, *Degrees*, 2.

[25] Marcel, *Reflection*, 123.

[26] Maritain, *Existence*, 127: "Je suis connu de Dieu. ...Il n'a pas besoin de m'objectiver pour me connaître."

say that the union of love makes of the beings whom we love another ourselves for us is to say that it makes them for us another subjectivity, another subjectivity of our own. Insofar as we truly love them, that is to say, not for ourselves but for themselves...we know them in their very subjectivity, at least to a certain degree."[27]

| The Human Knower | The Mode of Knowing | The Knowledge Attained |
|---|---|---|
| **A) artist/poet/ mystic** | intersubjectivity/agape/caritas | Connatural Knowledge of the Divine [or dimly intuiting the Divine] |
| **B) metaphysician** | abstract/conceptual notions directed outward | Analogies of the Divine |
| **C) Cartesian thinker** | abstract/conceptual notions directed inward | "L'enfer c'est les autres" or, I am objectified by others, or I am alone in my subjectivity |

**Diagram of relationships**

[27] Ibid., 139: "Dire que l'union d'amour fait de l'être que nous aimons un autre nous-mêmes pour nous, c'est dire qu'elle le fait pour nous une autre subjectivité, une autre subjectivité nôtre. Dans la mesure où nous l'aimons vraiment, c'est à dire non pour nous, mais pour lui...nous le connaissons dans sa subjectivité même, du moins dans une certaine mesure."

By now it seems to me that we can accurately say that Gabriel Marcel's notion of intersubjectivity is one that works harmoniously in Maritain's Thomist metaphysics. When we put Maritain's *Existence and the Existent* together with Marcel's *The Mystery of Being*, we have a strongly complementary corrective to Cartesian subjectivity, a rich metaphysics of *We are*, which contrasts clearly with Sartre's metaphysics of *I think*. Ultimately, this study has suggested to me that intersubjectivity, rather than actually being included in metaphysics, probably should be characterized as adding to and completing it. Like connaturality, it is most at home in poetic or mystical experience. I thought I would try to draw a kind of schematic or diagram, the way Maritain sometimes did, to express these relationships.

My conclusion from this graph: It takes both A & B to counter C. Gabriel Marcel was both; Maritain, with Raïssa, amounted to both. Sartre, in his efforts to avoid being objectified by the other, remained imprisoned in his own subjectivity. Jacques Maritain showed us how to escape that prison through the analogies of the Divine that are accessible to the metaphysician who seeks beyond his own subjectivity. Gabriel Marcel—along with poets like Raïssa and contemplatives like her husband—opens us to the intersubjectivity that enables us to commune, both with God and with other humans, in a rich connaturality.

In *Existence and the Existent*, Maritain concludes his chapter on "Subjectivity as Subjectivity" with a meditation on the grand fulfillment of subjective connatural knowledge in the beatific vision. "When we arrive at the terminus where we as subjects shall see ourselves in God and in divine eternity, all the moments of our past life will be known to us in the immediacy of the instant in which they were lived, and all our acts (even the bad ones, now not only pardoned but no longer leaving any trace or shadow) as emanating presently in the freshness of subjectivity, this time transluminous itself. And in the virtue of the vision in which our intelligence possesses the *Ipsum esse subsistens,* we shall know not only ourselves and all our life in a sovereignly existential way, but also the other creatures, whom in God we shall finally know as subjects, in the unveiled depths of their being."[28] It is a passage reminiscent of Revelation 2:17, where Jesus says, "To him that overcometh will I give to eat of the hidden manna, and will give him a white stone, and in the stone a new name written, which no man knoweth saving he that receiveth it."

[28] Ibid., 132: "Mais quand parvenu au terme le sujet se voit en Dieu et dans l'éternité divine, tous les moments de sa vie passée lui sont connus dans l'actualité et la présentialité de l'instant où ils ont été vécus, et tous ses actes (même les mauvais, maintenant non seulement pardonnés, mais ne laissant plus ni tache ni ombre) comme émanant présentement de la fraîcheur de la subjectivité, cette fois translumineuse elle-même. Et dans la vertu de la vision où son intelligence possède l'*Ipsum esse subsistens*, il ne connaît pas seulement lui-même et toute sa vie d'une manière souverainement existentielle, mais aussi les autres creatures, qu'en Dieu il connaît enfin comme sujets, dans les profondeurs dévoilées de leur être."

# PART III
## Maritain's Philosophy of Being

# DIFFICULT ACROBATICS: "GRAVITATING HEAD FIRST TO THE MIDST OF THE STARS"

## JOHN G. TRAPANI, JR.

Jacques Maritain's essay, "the Majesty and Poverty of Metaphysics," appears in book form as the opening chapter of his major opus, *The Degrees of Knowledge*. This book appeared in French in 1932, and in English, in 1935. The essay itself, however, originally appeared in 1925 as *Chroniques No. 1* in the "*Le Roseau d'Or*" series. The early date of this essay situates it at a special time in Maritain's life and, when we consider it within this historical context, it takes on a special meaning that transcends its publication history.

Right from the beginning of their conversion and baptism[1] in 1905-06, Jacques and his wife, Raïssa, focused on deepening and growing in their faith. From their early years forward, their days were highly structured and devoted to a balance of study and prayer.[2] Although Raïssa led Jacques to his salutary discovery of the wisdom of St. Thomas Aquinas in 1909, we read this earlier entry in Maritain's diary (later published as *Notebooks*) from 1908, one that contains a powerful indication of the future relation between Jacques' deep commitment to his Catholic faith and his work as a philosopher: "I resolved to abandon all 'personal inquiry' in philosophy, all desire to know *by myself*, being sure to know everything essential and everything necessary by the Word of God, and trusting for the rest on the blessed night of faith."[3] Maritain's desire for spiritual growth led him to begin in 1922 the monthly meetings of the Thomist Circles. These monthly study and prayer gatherings continued at his home in Meudon for the next fifteen years. Even a cursory glance at the topics of these retreats and

---

[1] Jacques and Raïssa were baptized on June 11, 1906.

[2] Cf. Jacques Maritain, *Notebooks* (Albany, New York: Magi Books, Inc., 1984), 42–43. The book is a translation by Joseph W. Evans of Maritain's *Carnet de Notes* (Paris: Desclée de Brouwer, 1965).

[3] Ibid., 46 (emphasis added).

discussions[4] reveals a life of prayer and holiness centered in Christ and His Mystical Body, the Church. Thus, when we situate the original 1925 composition date of "The Majesty and Poverty of Metaphysics" within the historical context of Maritain's personal life, the true substance of this essay becomes more pronounced: even as Maritain pursued a life-long project of making clear what the human mind rationally *can* say of the divine, he also acknowledged at the same time that unaided human endeavors alone are never truly adequate to comprehend and articulate the ultimate transcendent mystery of God. Moreover, by this time, Maritain was also personally convinced that human intelligence...and human action...were both in need of the indispensable assistance that comes from divine grace.

On the surface, the basics of "The Majesty and Poverty of Metaphysics" are these: the majesty of metaphysics is its "human wisdom;" its poverty is that it remains, when all is said and done, an entirely human science. It does not...and cannot...name God by His own name, the name revealed to the prophets, the name possible to utter, but impossible, on account of the limits of human intelligence, to grasp. Furthermore, considering the fact that metaphysics is human wisdom, the term "wisdom" itself may be somewhat confounding, since we use this word to refer to many different kinds of wisdom: practical wisdom, theoretical or speculative wisdom, theological wisdom, and infused or mystical wisdom.

Beyond this surface reading, however, there is a still deeper richness to Maritain's essay. Poor indeed would we be if an unaided metaphysics that is the fruit of our own intellectual labor were all that there is. At best, we might be philosophically titillated, yet the longings of our intellectual nature would remain unsatisfied. For this reason, Maritain distinguishes between a metaphysics developed by someone who lacks "a divine gift" of intuition from a metaphysics that has been developed by someone who is animated by one. The former, he says, runs the risk of falling victim to nominalism, where the term "being" becomes a mere abstraction without substantive reality.[5] In this way, it runs the

---

[4] Cf. Ibid., 148–74.

[5] Jacques Maritain, "The Majesty and Poverty of Metaphysics," *The Degrees of Knowledge* (Notre Dame, Indiana: University of Notre Dame Press, 1995), 1.

risk of becoming the metaphysics of those for whom philosophy is little more than a "Glass Bead Game," a reference to an invention of, and the subtitle of a book (*Magister Ludi*) by the Pulitzer-prize winning German novelist, Herman Hesse. In a metaphysics such as this, philosophers would move concepts around like chess pieces as they play an intellectual game—it is a clever and masterful form of logical gymnasttics but, in the end, it has no real meaning or significance for lived-existence. Like Hesse's protagonist, Magister Ludi, such philosophers, too, risk drowning in the icy lake-waters of actual existence because conjured or fabricated intellectual abstractions are seldom adequate for satisfying the intellect's natural desire for understanding the truths of real life.

On the other hand, there are those who do receive the divine gift of what Maritain calls "the intuition of being." Gifted in this way, Maritain observes that they thus are called upon to perform "difficult acrobatics"[6]—they are at once supremely blessed...and yet, even in the face of this gift, they remain burdened by the natural limitations of human intelligence. How are we to understand this gift and the metaphysical demands it creates?

In itself, and for those who have this gift, it turns out to be both a blessing *and* a curse. The blessing is the gift itself and the glimpse of the divine that this intuition reveals. By contrast, the curse consists in the inability to articulate adequately what the gift reveals or, perhaps worse, it consists in the inability to fully understand and/or appreciate the significance of this gift itself or what it reveals.

In order to help his readers to get beyond these limitations, Maritain resorts to a contrast between the natural grace bestowed upon the *true* metaphysician and that bestowed upon the *true* poet: the metaphysician and the poet complement one another, he tells us, as they alternately play "seesaw, each in turn rising up to the sky...." Their respective intuitions are like a "flash of a *spiritual light* in which a glimpse of God is revealed to" them and they both absorb "rays that come down from creative *Night*."[7] *Spiritual light*? This is the majesty of the gift, a glimpse of God revealed. But why, we might ask, does

---

[6] Ibid., 2.

[7] Ibid. (emphasis added).

Maritain refer to the rays of that spiritual light as coming down from creative *night*? Is it that, here again, we meet the poverty that comes from the limits of both our purely human intelligence, on the one hand, and our inability to articulate and express adequately what glimpses we do receive, on the other hand? Even though these metaphysical and poetic intuitions complement one another, from an entirely human perspective, human knowledge—even that infused with the intuition of being and the revelations of poetic intuition—is, by itself alone, still never truly sufficient or adequate to grasp and express the true majesty and ultimate incomprehensibility of the divine.

Throughout his discussion, Maritain contends that the nurture of human life in modern times has severely limited our ability to grasp these insights; indeed, "we can no longer think" in terms of the truth of being. Maritain even goes so far as to acknowledge that "true, timeless metaphysics no longer suits the modern intellect." And yet, the timeless truths concerning the spiritual-intellectual dimension of human nature help us to understand Maritain's mind more completely, and they provide the foundation for his reply to these objections: "the intellect has not changed its nature," he says; rather, "it has acquired habits"...and some very bad habits at that! Fortunately, he goes on, "habits can be corrected." And so, while the poet may be more sensitive to shifting fashions, the metaphysician must cling "desperately" to the immutable truths of reality in order to remind the age in which he or she lives of the difference between those matters that are changeable and a function of human creativity, as opposed to those things that are unchangeable because they are a part of the fixed, intelligible structure of reality. This undertaking is neither easy nor is it optional. Once bitten by the metaphysical intuition of being, and armed with the logical structures and arguments of a sound epistemology rooted in the truths of a realist ontology, we are obligated to embark upon a renewed "course of action."[8]

And yet, for Maritain, "there is no tilling of the soil in heaven."[9] Metaphysics in itself is useless in the service of the needs and demands of the practical affairs of human life, where many see the advances of

---

[8] Cf. Ibid., 2–3.

[9] Ibid., 4.

the empirical sciences as reigning supreme. These advances in the sciences, manifest in their technological applications, make our lives more comfortable, more pleasant, and more effortless. But the benefits of this progress, if considered alone, still leave the human spirit hungry and parched. What we need, Maritain reminds us, are not simply the truths of science that serve our natural desire for a comfortable life; rather, what we need is a "truth we may serve. For that truth is the food of the spirit. And, by the better part of ourselves, we are spirit."[10] Maritain makes clear that it is these so-called "useless truths" of metaphysics that give back to us our "balance and motion;" they enable us "to gravitate, head first, to the midst of the stars." Indeed, it is metaphysics that reveals to us "authentic values and their hierarchy," and they in turn provide us with the foundation of the ethical principles needed for the "renewed course of action." For this reason, and echoing the famous distinction of Aristotle, metaphysics, while least necessary, is indeed most important. Without speaking the Holy Name of God revealed through the prophets, metaphysics at its summit can lead us to a "knowledge of the invisible world of divine perfections spelled out from their created reflections." Thus, metaphysics is "the door to the leisure of that great speculative activity in which intellect alone can breathe, set, as it is, on the very peak of causes."[11]

With all of this having been said, the fact remains that, without divine agency and divine assistance, our natural longings and desires remain unfulfilled. Specifically, there are two desires of our spiritual human nature: the intellect longs for ultimate Truth and the fullness of Being, while our intellectual appetite, the will, longs for Goodness Itself, a longing that culminates in the joy or *gaudium* that comes from the possession of the One who is Truth and Goodness Itself. In this regard, Maritain's ideas are in perfect accord with Aquinas' answer to the question whether, in this life, it is better to know God or to love Him. Ultimately and in itself it is better to know God, Aquinas says, since it is this fullness of knowledge that our human intellectual nature naturally desires, to see God face to face in the Beatific Vision; however, in this life, where our knowledge is limited, incomplete, and in danger

---

[10] Ibid.

[11] Ibid., 4–5.

of error, Aquinas cautions that it is better to love God than to know Him.

Maritain echoes this point when he says that, in and of itself, the life of the intellect "is not enough for us. It needs a complement,"[12] especially since the intellectual union given through the intentionality of knowledge (i.e., the union between the knower and the known) is so imperfect. For Maritain, this complement comes about through a union of a different sort, namely, the union between the lover and the beloved. At its highest natural level, the union that results from the human love for God accomplishes, on this very earth, what the intellect in this life cannot: "Love thus arising, impels the soul to a union in the real order, a union which intellect, left all to itself, cannot achieve...."[13]

But there is more. There is the good news that comes from that very Wisdom that transcends metaphysics and indeed surpasses all understanding, and that good news is this: we are able to love God because He has first loved us. This fact itself surpasses not only all human understanding, but all human effort as well; it is God's love for us that is precisely the primary and transforming gift of grace. Maritain famously refers to this unique form of love as "mad love" (*amour fou*): "the *mad love* that Wisdom Itself [God] has for each and all of us...."[14] It is a transforming love that unites us, in the imperfection of this life, with the very source of Love Itself: "love unites us in our heart to [the triune God] who is hidden...."[15] Under the loving care, protection, and guidance of the Holy Spirit, we are able to experience "the Divine things imbedded in us by charity, [and] God becomes ours by charity.... This secret wisdom which secretly purifies the soul attains God as a hidden God, a saving God, one who is the more a savior the more hidden He is."[16]

This form of wisdom is a divine grace, a supernatural gift that manifests itself in many ways and in varying degrees, depending on the

---

[12] Ibid., 7.

[13] Ibid.

[14] Ibid.

[15] Ibid., 12.

[16] Ibid.

unique personality of the person who receives it and in whom it resides. The distinguishing mark of this gift of divine grace in which the saints (ordinary and heroic) participate and with which they cooperate, is that they "do not contemplate [in order] to know, but to love. They do not love for the sake of loving but for the love of [God] whom they love. It is for the love of their first beloved, God, that they aspire to that very union with God that love demands.... [I]t is by forgetting all else so that they do not live, but the Beloved lives in them."[17]

Maritain admonishes philosophers who too readily forget the part that love plays in human life: how could we neglect love, he asks, since "it is the very thing that does accomplish everything."[18] And yet, in another of those seemingly limitless theological paradoxes, divine love accomplishes all that it does through us only to the measure that we open ourselves up to it and allow it to work through us. Only sin is truly our own; it is the "nothing" which, without Christ, we are able to do on our own and without Him. Maritain's friend, Thomas Merton, ratifies, reaffirms, and reiterates this paradox when he writes: "...we cannot find [God] unless He has first found us. We cannot begin to seek Him without a special gift of His grace, yet if we wait for grace to move us, before beginning to seek Him, we will probably never begin."[19]

And so, in order to read Maritain's essay, "The Majesty and Poverty of Metaphysics," correctly and completely, we will do well to keep in mind the following three points: 1) after their conversion, the Maritains' primary devotion was and remained an abiding commitment to grow in the depths of their faith and spiritual lives; 2) Jacques' early 1908 insight about the role that God's grace plays in human life and thought sustained him throughout his personal life as a man of faith and his professional life as a Catholic philosopher; and 3) as a Catholic philosopher, the ideas Jacques expressed in his 1925 essay reflect his unwavering commitment to making clear the philosophical underpinnings of the truths of the Catholic faith.

---

[17] Ibid., 10–11.

[18] Ibid., 11.

[19] Thomas Merton, *No Man Is An Island* (Garden City, New York: Image Books, A Division of Doubleday & Company, Inc., 1967), 13.

Admittedly, being receptive to divine grace is not an easy thing to do. Maritain knew that, and he warned us of this essential risk: whether for the poet or the metaphysician, the answer to the call offered through those poetic and metaphysical gifts of intuition requires the consent of the recipient that involves some very difficult acrobatics indeed. The majesty of metaphysics is that it takes us "to the door," as Maritain writes; it cannot go through it. The poverty of metaphysics is that, in the end, it is still nothing more than a human approach to the divine; it is not the revelation to us of the divine itself. For, as sublime as a natural knowledge of God is, it is still only as great as our human limitations allow. It is not, however, as great *as is possible for God*. Fortunately for us, and aided by the wisdom and prayers of the saintly Jacques and Raïssa, the love and grace of God make the impossible possible, even in this life, since they enable us "to gravitate, head first, to the midst of the stars...."[20]

---

[20] Jacques Maritain, "The Majesty and Poverty of Metaphysics," in *The Degrees of Knowledge* (Notre Dame, Indiana: University of Notre Dame Press, 1995), 4.

# IN DEFENSE OF THE INTUITION OF BEING

JAMES G. HANINK

*The intuition of being was lived in* actu exercito *by St. Thomas [...] but I do not know (and this is perhaps due to my ignorance) of a treatise or* disquisitio *where it has been studied [...] in* actu signato.

—*Jacques Maritain,* Untrammeled Approaches[1]

## I. INTRODUCTION

For John Paul II, a Thomistic personalist,[2] metaphysics is at the heart of philosophy; and the act of being, *actus essendi*, is at the heart of metaphysics. "[T]he philosophy of being," he writes, "is based upon the very act of being itself, which allows a full and comprehensive openness to reality as a whole, surpassing every limit to reach the One who brings all things to fulfillment" (*Fides et Ratio* #97).

Jacques Maritain is a key source for any exploration of the *actus essendi* and, indeed, a thinker whom the Holy Father thanks for his broad contribution to philosophy (*Fides et Ratio* #74). Maritain insists that an intuition of being is vital to an appreciation of the *actus essendi.* He places this intellective intuition in the judgment that follows abstractive apprehension; this prior apprehension itself depends on sense perception. In distinguishing between apprehension and judgment, he takes pains not to undermine the unity of the intellect. Yet only in judgment, he claims, does idealism (the thesis that to be is to be present to the perceiver) give way to realism (the thesis that to be is to be the subject of an act of existing). Judgment, he writes, "affirms or posits in the mind" the *suppositum*; and it does so "as that subject

---

[1] Jacques Maritain, *Untrammeled Approaches*, trans. Bernard Doering, Preface by Ernst R. Korn (Heinz R. Schmitz) (Notre Dame, Indiana: University of Notre Dame Press, 1997), 222, n. 32.

[2] Karol Wojtyła, "Thomistic Personalism," in *Person and Community*, trans. Theresa Sandok, O.S.M., Introduction by Stefan Swiezawski (New York: Peter Lang, 1993), 165-75.

itself is posited...in extra-mental reality." To make this judgment is "to grasp intuitively, or *to see*, the being, the existence, the extra-mental *esse* of that subject."[3]

This is the intuition of being. Its object, the *actus essendi*, drives the actualization of whatever is real in accord with its potentiality. An intuition of this act of being leads one to the intelligibility of being, its *ratio entis.* One grasps particular existents as having the act "to be," or "*quasi habens esse.*"[4] One appreciates that everything *is* in its own analogous way.

But is there, on a close analysis, such an intuition at the core of metaphysics? In what follows, I state what some take to be the strongest objection to the thesis that there is such an intuition and explore what prompts it. Then I argue that the objection is not persuasive. Lastly, I suggest that other objections might be equally problematic.

## II. THE SENSORY LIMIT OBJECTION

For ease of reference, we can call the objection at issue "the sensory limit objection." It claims that, given our epistemic limitations, we can have no such intuition of being. For us, the act of existing is restricted to sensible objects, for example, wine and roses—and those who enjoy them. But metaphysics, the study of being as such, cannot limit itself to physical things and their sensible properties. Metaphysics treats of *ens inquantum est ens.* So whatever we find at the core of metaphysics must itself transcend the material. Thus, a friend of the thesis that an intuition of being is at the core of metaphysics faces a formidable task. He or she must show how, for us, this intuition could have bearing not just on physical things but on both possible beings and super-sensible beings as well.

---

[3] Jacques Maritain, *Untrammeled Approaches*, 220.

[4] In his *Being and Some Twentieth-Century Thomists* (New York: Fordham University Press, 2003), 131, n. 1, John F. X. Knasas cites Aquinas: "Nam ens dicitur quasi esse habens, hoc autem solum est substantia, quae subsistit" (*ST* I, q. 44, a. 2).

Both Étienne Gilson[5] (famously) and John Knasas[6] (recently) argue that such a showing is impossible. Gilson says that an intuition of *esse* would be an intuition of God, and we can have no such intuition. Any intuition that we might have would be of the *esse* of sensible objects. From the knowledge of such contingent beings, we might then argue for the existence of *esse ipse subsistens*. But an argument is not an intuition. Moreover, we cannot think without initial images, yet we have no such image of existence *as* existence.

John Knasas, for his part, frames his objection in terms of the structure of analogy. That structure involves a sameness understood in terms of differences. We can term such analogical concepts "analogons" and their instances "analogates." But for us the analogates of *esse* are always sensible. So they cannot give us the range of cases requisite for us to grasp *immaterial* analogates of *esse*. He writes that "we only know the analogon of analogous *esse* through its analogates, and these are sensible. This locus for the apprehension of the analogon fails to provide sufficient insight into the analogon to grasp possible immaterial instances of analogous *esse*."[7] Regrettably for us, then, analogy has inescapable and empirical limits.

We have before us, then, two distinct forms of the sensory limit objection to the intuition of being. The first, that of Gilson, claims that such an intuition is tantamount to an intuition of God, and this is impossible. The second, that of Knasas, claims that an analogy of being cannot extend beyond the sensible beings upon which our knowledge is based.

---

[5] Étienne Gilson, "Propos sur l'être et sa notion," *San Tommaso e il pensiero moderno*, ed. Antonio Piolanti (Citta Nuova: Pontificia Accademia Romana di S. Tommaso d'Aquino, 1974), 8-10. John F. X. Knasas calls attention to this passage.

[6] John F. X. Knasas, "How Thomistic Is the Intuition of Being?" in John F. X. Knasas, ed., *Jacques Maritain: The Man and His Metaphysics* (Mishawaka, Indiana: The American Maritain Association, 1988), 83-92. Knasas refers us to this passage in his more recent *Being and Some Twentieth-Century Thomists*, 131, n. 1.

[7] John F. X. Knasas, "Gilson vs. Maritain: the Start of Thomistic Metaphysics," *Doctor Communis* 43 (1990): 263.

## III. A PRELIMINARY ABOUT NATURAL PHILOSOPHY

In answering the sensory limit objection, there is a preliminary point to make about the division of labor within philosophy. The point is this: the intuition of being does not displace natural philosophy as an approach to metaphysics. Benedict Ashley, O.P., among others, fears some such displacement, perhaps on the part of those with differing views on the place of Aristotelian foundations in science.[8] This fear is unnecessary. Without natural philosophy, we cannot make sense of generation and corruption *nor* of matter and form. In setting the stage for a causal inquiry into the coming to be of matter and form, natural philosophy prepares us for the intuition of being. "[M]etaphysical intuition," Maritain writes, "is formally independent of the philosophy of nature" and yet "materially and as to us, it presupposes the philosophy of nature [...]."[9] In affirming *esse*, moreover, we can scarcely forget essences and natures. Maritain rightly warns us that "[I]f you abolish essence, or that which *esse* posits, by that very act you abolish existence, or *esse*."[10]

Beyond this preliminary point about natural philosophy, however, three additional factors help us counter the sensory limit objection. The first is our experience of a wide range of irreducible singularities which transcend the empirical. The second is the role of the free and cognitive acts which characterize our capacity to transcend the material. The third is the very richness of sensation which itself provides for an analysis that, in leading to the metaphysical, can trigger an intuition of being.

## IV. IRREDUCIBLE SINGULARITIES

What, for a start, are these irreducible singularities? Consider a rose that attracts our gaze. Through sense perception, and an abstractive process, we know that a rose *is present* to us. But we need to move to the

---

[8] Benedict Ashley, *The Way toward Wisdom* (Notre Dame, Indiana: University of Notre Dame Press, 2006), 65-66.

[9] Jacques Maritain, *The Philosophy of Nature* (New York: Philosophical Library, 1951), 3-4.

[10] Jacques Maritain, *Existence and the Existent*, trans. Lewis Galantiere and Gerald B. Phelan (Garden City, New York: Image Books, 1959), 13.

judgment that the rose *exists*. In making this judgment, we might have an intuition of being, and in various ways.

For the philosopher, perhaps rather an odd sort, the intuition might come in the course of thinking through the structure of judgment. For other people, the sense of self in sensory or intellectual acts might be its catalyst. For some the sheer wonder at an object of grace—a red, red rose—might occasion it. Or perhaps the bloom of the rose calls to mind the vitality of nature, or its fading underscores the passing of time, or its fragility the press of our own anxiety. In each case, we might experience the catalyst for an intuition of being. And for those who do not stop to smell the roses? For such as these we might commend the wonder that there is something rather than nothing. It, too, might trigger an intuition of *esse*. Reflecting on such varied experiences, Maritain finds that it is "on the occasion of some individual reality grasped in its pure singularity" that one might enjoy an intellectual intuition of being.[11] This intuitive "leap," in turn, is an avenue to the structure of the real.

To be candid, many philosophers themselves might never experience an intuition of being. If so, it is unfortunate. After all, it seems that anyone could have such an intuition. A poet is among the more promising candidates. Czeslaw Milosz, for example, writes that we sometimes realize "that what we are seeing, all that reality, is beyond words ....From reality which is homely, perceived in a most ordinary way, something else, autonomous and enclosed in language, has come unglued."[12] Whether poet or plain man, once given an intuition of being, one could by an act of apprehension return to its object. Thus, one could form a *concept* of being; and, by analogy, one could apply it to particular existents.

It falls to the philosopher, however, to articulate and explore the concept of such an intuition. As Maritain notes, "if a child or a poet can

---

[11] Jacques Maritain, *Untrammeled Approaches*, 225. For a sampler of such occasions, see W. Norris Clarke, *The One and the Many: A Contemporary Thomistic Metaphysics* (Notre Dame, Indiana: University of Notre Dame Press, 2001), 27-28.

[12] Czeslaw Milosz, *Road-side Dog* (New York: Farrar, Straus and Giroux, 1998), 163.

have...the intuition of being, nevertheless such concepts of abstractive origin, and formed at the third degree of abstraction are proper to the metaphysician."[13] Here a comparison comes to mind. Even a child, St. Thomas teaches, has some grasp of the ultimate end of every moral act, that is, some grasp of union with God.[14] But the child must yield to the metaphysician for a reflective understanding of what a union with God involves.[15]

In any case, while existential singularities are empirical in their inception, they can help us counter the sensory limit objection. The existential impact of such experiences reaches beyond their empirical starting points. Thus, they draw our attention to a range of distinctive experiences that can trigger the intuition of *esse.* But as epiphanic as these varied singularities are, they are perhaps less critical than the everyday free and cognitive acts of the human person. The significance of these everyday and yet extraordinary acts lies in their nature, to which I now turn.

## V. FREE AND COGNITIVE ACTS

The second factor to which we turn for help in countering the sensory limit objection builds on the first. Suppose we reflect carefully on our mental acts. Consider, say, taking joy in the richness of existence, including our own, and giving thanks for it. Neither these acts nor their object are reducible to the empirical, unless we are willing to embrace a materialism that evacuates the richness of human subjectivity.[16] We can, moreover, experience such acts with a singular intensity that might trigger the intuition of being. Such acts call into play our human freedom. So, indeed, do all human acts. Nor are we likely to imagine any human experience with more enduring power

---

[13] Maritain, *Untrammeled Approaches*, 233.

[14] Thomas Aquinas, *ST* I-II, q. 89, a. 6 ad 3.

[15] Benedict Ashley, O.P., no friend of the intuition of being, indirectly suggests this comparison. See his *The Way toward Wisdom*, 150.

[16] For an extended argument to this effect, see Peter Geach, "What Do We Think With?," in *God and the Soul* (London: Routledge & Kegan Paul, 1978), 30-41.

than the ongoing, day-by-day experience of freedom, most especially in its gradually forming the human character.

St. Thomas, whom we might well consult on the question, does not simply assign the will and the free choices that shape our lives to the sphere of metaphysics; but neither does he assign them to natural philosophy. In the view of Lawrence Dewan, O.P., "The study of the intellect and the will belongs in part to that topmost flight of natural philosophy that considers the human soul, but mostly it belongs to metaphysics."[17] To support his verdict, he directs us to Thomas's *Commentary on Aristotle's Physics*. There Thomas comments:

> [S]o the last things considered by natural science are forms which are, indeed, in some way separated, but which have existence in matter. [R]ational souls are forms of this sort.... But how forms are totally separated from matter, and what they are, or even how this form, i.e., the rational soul, exists insofar as it is separable and capable of existence without a body and what it is according to its separable essence, are questions which pertain to first philosophy.[18]

Thomas, one might add, makes a like observation in his discussion of the division of the sciences.[19]

In discussing Thomas's metaphysics of evil, Maritain supports Dewan and does so from a surprising perspective. He reminds us that the Angelic Doctor, in a reference to angelic knowledge, distinguishes between the universe of freedom and the natural world it presupposes. Maritain writes:

---

[17] Lawrence Dewan, O.P., *Wisdom, Law, and Virtue* (New York: Fordham University Press, 2008), 125.

[18] *Commentary of Aristotle's Physics*, trans. Richard J. Blackwell and Richard J. Spath (New Haven, Connecticut: Yale University Press, 1963), Bk. 2, l. 4 (no. 175).

[19] See Aquinas's *Commentary on Boethius' On the Trinity* in Aquinas, *The Division and Methods of the Sciences: Questions v and vi of his Commentary on the De Trinitate of Boethius,* translated by Armand Maurer, 4th revised edition (Toronto: Pontifical Institute of Mediaeval Studies, 1986), v, 2 ad 7.

> [I]t is because of this distinction that St. Thomas teaches that the free act as such, being not of this world, is beyond the grasp of the natural knowledge of the angels (to which, however, is due everything *of this world* considered as God's work of art; for the free act is not a part *of this world*, but of an original universe of its own, the universe of freedom.)[20]

Angelic Doctor, indeed!

Given their distinctive nature, then, might we not see these free choices of ours as forming a personal path to the unrestrictedly real? To be sure, we cannot divorce human freedom from our sensory operations or from the empirical. But the data of the senses are *preconditions* for the exercise of our freedom. Freedom itself begins with an act of the will, a power of the soul. This act of the will, moreover, does not depend on the data of the senses as constant concomitants.

Such an act of the will does, of course, require that one has the intellective power to distinguish among various possible actions. It is notable, then, that neither does Thomas assign our intellective acts to natural philosophy. In their distinctive nature, they also seem to form a personal path to the unrestrictedly real. Cognizing, of course, is an act of the intellect, itself a power of the soul. Yes, nothing is in the intellect without first being in the senses. But sensation is not intellection. Nor do our cognitive acts depend on sensory data as constant concomitants. Often, as experience shows, we need to suppress sense data that either impedes us from acting freely or from thinking clearly.

Of course, we couldn't know that we act freely and intelligently without a sensory grasp of our actions. But free and cognitive acts have a reality that goes beyond that of sense reception. This reality differs sharply, we know, from that of a mathematical abstraction, a mere *ens rationis*; such abstractions *do* nothing.[21] In contrast, each free and

---

[20] Jacques Maritain, *St. Thomas and the Problem of Evil* (Milwaukee, Wisconsin: Marquette University Press, 1942), 10.

[21] Of note here is Thomas's broader claim that some things do not *by nature* exist in matter and motion, and "[i]n this way being, substance, potency and act are separate from matter and motion, because they do not depend on them for their existence, unlike the objects of mathematics which can only exist in matter" (*In de Trin.* v, 4).

cognitive act has its own way of existing. Such acts are *not* substances. Yet action is so central to reality that it is a most basic avenue to *what is*. W. Norris Clarke, S.J., sees Thomas's *agere sequitur esse* as recognizing in action "the self-revelation of being."[22] Thus our free and cognitive acts play a critical role in expanding the data from which we can form a concept of *esse* that transcends the physical.

Our freedom and intelligence are intertwined. Absent an intellective grasp of possible states of affairs, we could not act freely or responsibly. We could not shape our lives. Absent free choice, we could not think for ourselves; we could only register our sensations. For us, free and intelligent action is an avenue to transcendence. Our quest for transcendence depends on both a cognitive and volitional capacity to go beyond the present moment.

Again, no free and intelligent human act is itself a substance. But it is through free and intelligent acts that we know the human person.[23] Such acts have their own way of existing; each has its own unity, and we can know each directly. Thus, each act, rightly understood, displays a kind of *habens esse*. When we direct our attention to the "*esses*" of such acts, themselves the objects of intuition, we can form a richer concept of *esse*. It is richer because, in forming it, we are not restricted to drawing from the limited data of physical objects. In light of this fuller process, we can see how the intuition of being begins in a judicative grasp of the "to be," or *esse*, of sensible things; and yet this intuition is not limited in its realization to things wholly restricted to the sensible.

Here we should anticipate an objection of the following sort. The proper objects of the intelligence, insists the critic, are mind-independent material objects. But our volitional and cognitive acts are mind-dependent; their existence depends on intellect and will as powers of the soul. Insofar as one appeals to such acts in order to

---

[22] W. Norris Clarke, *The One and the Many*, 35.

[23] In his *The Way toward Wisdom*, 480, n. 69 and 492, n. 7, Benedict Ashley distinguishes between a substance's having an accidental property and substance as, specifically, "transcendentally relative," thus indicating that relation is "transcendental," i.e., pertaining to a thing as "the thing itself according to its requirements for actual existence and intelligibility." One might equally well speak of free and intelligent action as "transcendental."

initiate metaphysics, one falls into mistaken idealism. We can advance to a study of being as such only by drawing analogies with that way of being with which we are most familiar, that is, physical objects as we experience ourselves in causal relationships with them.

In reply to such a critic, two key points call for attention. The first is that while we could not make sense of our world without the sense experience of the properties of mind-independent material objects, neither could we make sense of our world without our experience of human beings as persons. Such persons, to be sure, are objects of sensory experience insofar as they are physical. But they are experientially distinct from mere material objects in that persons are free and intelligent. Persons, too, are the proper, if often mysterious, objects of our intelligence. Indeed, it is because persons, in their freedom and intelligence, transcend material objects, that political science can never be a natural science—to the chagrin of many of its practitioners.[24] The human person, rather, is an epistemic and metaphysical bridge linking the physical with the spiritual. Our distinctive status enables us to mediate between the material universe and its Divine source.[25]

The second point that calls for attention is that we do not come to understand either efficient or final causality by reflecting on the patterned interchange of mere material objects. Rather, we form our understanding of such causality through the cumulative experience of our personal agency. We experience our own agency before we learn to register descriptive causal patterns. Thus, John Henry Newman writes:

> One of the first experiences of an infant is that of his willing and doing; and as time goes on, one of the first temptations of the boy is to bring home to himself the fact of his sovereign arbitrary power, though it be at the price of ...disobedience. And when his parents...begin to restrain him...then he has a second

---

[24] James V. Schall, S.J., made this point in his "Science and Faith" (a paper presented at the American Maritain Association's Thirtieth Annual International Meeting, Nashville, Tennessee, November 3, 2006).

[25] W. Norris Clarke highlights this mediation in his *The One and the Many*, 306. Benedict Ashley notes a like point in his *The Way toward Wisdom*, 197.

> series of experiences of cause and effect, and that upon a principle or rule.[26]

Is there not an Augustinian sobriety in this account of the human learning curve?

Here it is also notable that Benedict Ashley, ever a realist, observes that "for any created mind, the existence of beings is independent of their knowledge of them, except when a creature by a free act of will makes something and hence has a productive knowledge of it, as God has for all creation."[27] Surely here there is an ethical corollary. Are we not, as participants in creative production through our freedom, charged to realize God's providence through our human prudence?[28]

## VI. BEING AS *HABENS ESSE*

The role of free and intelligent acts in the second response to the sensory limit objection directs us to the realist's interest in "*habens esse*," that is, in having a distinct way of being. This interest grows in identifying a third factor to consider in meeting the sensory limit objection. John Knasas, indeed, links his account of how to begin metaphysics with "*habens esse.*" Why suppose, he asks, that we must begin metaphysics by enlisting the immaterial in the range of entities from which we might then grasp the *actus essendi*, the act of being? Might we not, instead, proceed by deepening the analysis that everyday sensation makes possible? As we move from apprehension to judgment, we also move from *ens*, i.e., being, to *habens esse*, i.e., having a distinct way of being. In coming to grasp being as *habens esse*, we will grasp it as act rather than as form. (On this point Knasas notes: "If *esse* were itself a form, it would be existence-neutral, and so judgment would always be

---

[26] John Henry Newman, *An Essay in Aid of a Grammar of Assent*, ed. I. T. Kerr (Oxford: Oxford University Press, 1985), 49.

[27] Benedict Ashley, *The Way toward Wisdom*, 485, n. 17.

[28] St. Thomas finds an etymological link; see *ST* II-II, q. 49, a. 6 ad 1. In his "The Divine Law and the Modern Project," *Modern Age*, 51, No. 1 (2009): 29-30, Mark Shiffman notes the key connection between God's providence and human prudence in Rémi Brague's *The Law of God*, trans. Lydia G. Cochrane (Chicago: University of Chicago Press, 2007).

chasing after reality."[29]) The deepening analysis that he proposes might well show that such an act is in principle free from physical limitation. By way of comparison: in natural philosophy, we define the soul in relation to the body; and yet we argue for the immateriality of the soul; in the ascent to metaphysics, we begin with sense experience and its objects, and yet we need not limit ourselves to the objects of sense experience in deepening our understanding of being.

This deepening analysis might itself serve as the catalyst of an intuition of being. Wonderment prompts philosophy, and finding joy in sheer existence is the realist's birthright. Such reflection on the *actus essendi* might well lead us beyond physical determinants to the self-subsistent. In support of such a deepening analysis of what sensation offers, Knasas cites Thomas on the historical steps that led to metaphysics: the analysis of being as this or that sensible body, its further analysis in terms of form and matter, and lastly a consideration of the cause of being as being, regardless of any determinant aspect.[30] The proposed third factor, then, for meeting the sensory limit objection is that we can indeed deepen our grasp of the sensible to reveal a dynamic that escapes the limits of the sensible.

## VII. A QUESTION RENEWED

The three considerations I've sketched—the role of irreducible singularities, the transcendence of free and intelligent acts, and an understanding of being as *habens esse*, regardless of any determinant aspect—give us reason to think that the sensory limit objection is not persuasive. The thesis that there is an intuition of being at the core of metaphysics remains a promising and provocative one.

That thesis, of course, faces other objections. Some critics are skeptical about *any* appeal to intuition, but without intuitive knowledge discursive reasoning simply cannot get a start. Some are skeptical about the veridical character of sense perceptions that precede abstraction and judgment, but without the shared reality such perceptions provide one falls into solipsism. Still others, of an analytic bent, argue that the supposed act of being, *actus essendi*, rests on a

---

[29] Knasas, *Being and Some Twentieth-Century Thomists*, 212.

[30] Aquinas, *ST* I, q. 44, a 2.

logical muddle about instantiation. But arguably their case depends on a Fregean refusal to define existence for individuals.[31] Perhaps, then, these further objections are less formidable than many suppose. If so, Jacques Maritain's signature thesis about the intuition of being more than holds its own as a worthy *questio disputata*—and, in our time, a pressing one.

Both the personalist and the Thomist, after all, will want to underscore the import of the intuition of being, initiated by our experience of free and intelligent agency, for the moral life. Given the convertibility of transcendentals, moreover, this intuition leads to both the *ratio entis* and the *ratio boni*. To grasp the *esse* of the person is to become open to the dignity of the person and, in turn, the ground for a culture of life. Nor need this life be merely temporal. For personhood, shown in our creativity, makes us *capax Dei*. In our creativity, we confront the most revealing analogate of the analogon that is *ipsum esse subsistens*, in time revealed as the Trinitarian *communio personarum*.[32] As Karol Wojtyła writes, "[we] are creators because we think," and in creating "we also fill the external material world around us with our own thought and being." To this he adds, "there is a certain similarity here between ourselves and God, for the whole of creation is an expression of God's own thought and being."[33]

---

[31] See Gyula Klima, "On Kenny on Aquinas on Being: A Critical Review of *Aquinas on Being* by Anthony Kenny," *International Philosophical Quarterly* 44 (2004): 567-80.

[32] John F. X. Knasas brings together the elements of this grounding in his *Being and Some Twentieth-Century Thomists*, 248.

[33] Karol Wojtyła, "Thomistic Personalism," in *Person and Community*, 171-72.

# How Maritain May have Bridged the Gap between Metaphysics and Activism[1]

## Raymond Dennehy

In this essay, I explore the possibility that the intuition of being provided the intellectual continuity for Maritain's lifelong dedication to both philosophical contemplation and activism. In Part I, I formulate the problem of Maritain's affinities for metaphysics and activism; in Part II, I enumerate examples of his activism,[2] which turn out to make for a very impressive list; in Part III, I set forth the evolution of Maritain's conception of being and show how the parallel growth in importance that the intuition of being assumes in his writings offers a plausible bridge between his metaphysics and his philosophical activism.

### I. AN IMPROBABLE ALLIANCE

Since my earliest years as a student of Maritain, I have remained fascinated with a short passage in Raïssa Maritain's memoirs. There she writes that during their student years at the Sorbonne, Jacques sought to resolve his frustrations at finding truth by an unseemly coupling of the works of Spinoza and Nietzsche.[3]

Not surprisingly, he eventually tired of that cobble. For one thing, the respective philosophical contents are mutually incompatible and, for another, neither is anything like the Thomism that would finally capture Maritain's mind and heart. Yet there are features of this

---

[1] A somewhat shorter version of this was published in *Notes et Documents*, 20 (May-August, 2011): 69-78.

[2] This enumeration first appeared in my *homage* to Maritain on the occasion of his death in "A Tribute to Jacques Maritain: Philosophical Activist," *Social Justice Review* June (1973): 77-78.

[3] Raïssa Maritain, *We Have Been Friends Together* and *Adventures in Grace. The Memoirs of Raïssa Maritain*, trans. Julie Kernan (Garden City, New York: Image Books, 1961), 63.

curious alliance between Spinoza's rigorous metaphysical essentialist monism and Nietzsche's existential integrity that remained constant throughout Maritain's life; each enshrines a commitment to which Maritain was drawn since his youth: the search for absolute truth and a public witness to those truths in the face of injustice.

With regard to the latter, consider that, when only sixteen, Maritain would come home from his philosophy course at the Lycée Henri IV and, in despair of finding answers to his philosophical questions, throw himself on the rug.[4] And Spinoza's solitary life dedicated to study and the pursuit of truth does not differ much from Maritain's own inclination. According to those who knew him well, Maritain always preferred a life of solitude and study.[5] Not only did he regard himself first and foremost as a metaphysician,[6] he also valued contemplation as the highest of all activities[7] and had, in fact, pursued a life of religious contemplation so far as circumstances permitted.[8] In 1961, he entered the Little Brothers of Jesus, a religious order in Toulouse, for a life of study and contemplation:

---

[4] Ibid., 60.

[5] Ibid., 353; Helen Iswolsky, *Light Before Dusk* (New York: Longmans, Green and Co., 1942), 184.

[6] This preference comes through powerfully in the following of Maritain's works: *The Degrees of Knowledge*, trans. Gerald B. Phelan (New York: Charles Scribner's Sons, 1959), 1-7; *Existence and the Existent*, trans. Lewis Galantiere and Gerald B. Phelan (Garden City, New York: Doubleday and Company, Inc., 1959), 31; *The Person and the Common* Good, trans. John J. Fitzgerald (Notre Dame, Indiana: University of Notre Dame Press, 1966), 14.

[7] Jacques Maritain, *Scholasticism and Politics*, trans. and ed. Mortimer J. Adler (Garden City, New York: Doubleday and Company, Inc., 1960), ch. VII, esp. 173.

[8] For evidence of Maritain's early attraction to religious contemplation, see Raïssa Maritian, *We Have Been Friends Together* and *Adventures in Grace*, 171-72 and 179-80. His own writings on the subject reveal a love and insight into the topic that could only come from one who practiced contemplation. See, e.g., *Degrees*, chs. VI to IX, *Prayer and Intelligence* (in collaboration with Raïssa Maritain), trans. Algar Thorold (London: Sheed and Ward, 1928), and *Liturgy and Contemplation* (in collaboration with Raïssa Maritain), trans. Joseph W. Evans (New York: P. J. Kennedy and Sons, 1960).

> He has long loved the Little Brothers, who pursue an essentially contemplative life in the very midst of the world, and 'at the core of the masses'; he attended their Mass of foundation in the Basilica of Sacré-Coeur in 1933, and from the beginning he has had a great influence on their intellectual and spiritual formation. In October of 1970 Maritain himself became a Little Brother.[9]

In regard to any affinity Maritain may have had for Nietzsche's existential integrity, consider two early examples of his activism. The first is Raïssa Maritain's account of how she and Jacques first met at the Sorbonne:

> I was leaving M. Matruchot's plant physiology class one day in a rather downcast frame of mind, when I saw coming toward me a young man with a gentle face, a heavy shock of blond hair, a light beard and a slightly stoop-shouldered carriage. He introduced himself and said he was forming a committee of students to start a movement of protest among French writers and university people against the ill-treatment to which Russian Socialist students had been subject in their own country.... And he asked me to join this committee. Such was my first meeting with Jacques Maritain.[10]

The second example is more dramatic. Having abandoned his commitment to the philosophies of Spinoza and Nietzsche and despairing of ever finding truth, Jacques and Raïssa entered into a suicide pact: if they could not find truth in the world within one year, they would kill themselves.[11] Fortunately for them and for us, they discovered the lectures of Henri Bergson before the year ended.[12]

On the face of things, it admittedly seems implausible that Maritain could have been drawn to both philosophers in the belief that he saw

---

[9] Joseph W. Evans, "Jacques Maritain," *The New Scholasticism* XLVI (1972): 5.

[10] Raïssa Maritain, *We Have Been Friends Together and Adventures in Grace*, 41.

[11] Ibid., 66-68.

[12] Ibid., 72, 80; Jacques Maritain, *Bergsonian Philosophy and Thomism*, trans. Mabelle L. and J. Gordon Andison (New York: Philosophical Library, 1955), 286-87, 304.

some doctrinal unity between their philosophies. What is plausible is that each one spoke to him about things that were important to the already disheartened student: transcendental truth and the call of the concrete, here and now, world. I will go even further and suggest ("argue" seems a bit too strong here) that the young Maritain's passion for each *plausibly* generated a logic that unified them, each to the other: one without the other is impossible; therefore, somehow the transcendent realm of unchanging universal truth and the worldly realm of concrete, changing, particular things are kindred. By this kind of unity I do not mean the obvious ontological relation between universals and particulars exemplified in the syllogism, "Every deliberate killing of an innocent human being is immoral; Socrates is an innocent human being; therefore, the deliberate killing of Socrates is immoral" or as exemplified in moderate realism's account of the same essence existing in things as concrete and particular and in the intellect as abstract and universal. If not these, one might ask, "What's left but Maritain's satisfaction with the two philosophical theories as the most defensible ones he knew at that early stage of his career?" But that would mean that the glue joining the philosophies of Spinoza and Nietzsche was merely a psychological unification of the two. The trouble with this is that it would substitute a merely subjective sense of unity for an objective unification that leads to a philosophical account that integrates one's metaphysics and behavior in the concrete situation. Instead, what I have in mind is the possibility that all along Maritain experienced intuitive moments of the continuity of the transcendent and the concrete. But how?

I do not think that what may seem to be the answer to that question, to wit, Maritain's theory of connatural knowledge, is the correct answer. Though his descriptions of this way of knowing do have their mystique:

> In this knowledge through union or inclination, connaturality or congeniality, the intellect is at play not alone, but together with affective inclinations and the dispositions of the will, and is guided and directed by them. It is not rational knowledge, knowledge through the conceptual, logical and discursive exercise of reason. But it is really and genuinely knowledge,

> though obscure and perhaps incapable of giving account of itself, or of being translated into words.[13]

This knowledge derives its name, "connatural," insofar as it is *co-natured* with the individual human being's actions, manifesting itself in primal human strivings, such as the urge to preserve one's life, to know the truth, to live with one's fellow human beings in society. Although connatural knowledge expresses itself in mystical experience and poetic knowledge,[14] Maritain looks to moral experience for "the most widespread instance of knowledge through connaturality."[15] To be specific, "...it is in experiential—not philosophical—knowledge of moral virtues that Thomas Aquinas saw the first and main example of knowledge through inclination or through connaturality."[16] Whereas one can boast a masterful knowledge of moral science, possessing a conceptual and rational grasp of the virtues, and still lead an immoral life, another can lack a conceptual and rational knowledge of the moral virtues, but act in accordance with them, because one possesses them in one's own powers of will and desire.[17] Connaturality, Maritain insists, is foundational to Natural Law: "...the judgments in which Natural Law is made manifest to practical Reason do not proceed from any conceptual, discursive, rational exercise of reason; they proceed from that *connaturality* or congeniality through which what is consonant with the essential inclinations of human nature is grasped by the intellect as good; what is dissonant, as bad."[18]

All of which makes clear that connaturality for Maritain is an operation of practical intellect, knowledge for the sake of acting. That is why he excludes knowledge through connaturality as a consideration of metaphysics.[19] But, in this essay, I wish to explore the possibility of

---

[13] Jacques Maritain, "On Knowledge Through Connaturality," in *The Range of Reason* (New York: Charles Scribner's Sons, 1953), 23.

[14] Ibid., 24-25.

[15] Ibid., 26.

[16] Ibid.

[17] Ibid., 23.

[18] Ibid., 27.

[19] Ibid., 29.

explaining his dual affinity for metaphysics and activism as an operation of speculative intuition, knowledge for the sake of knowing, that directly unveils the connection between transcendental being and concrete, particular being.

Strange as it may seem, Spinoza's doctrine of intuition may have been the voice, albeit muted, that bespoke its coherence with Nietzsche's philosophy. Consider Harald Hoffding's representation of Spinoza's view of intuition:

> The highest form of knowledge according to Spinoza, is the intuitive, in which the particular phenomenon is immediately perceived to be, as it were, interpenetrated by the general order of things, as e.g. I immediately perceive that the two lines are parallel to one another if they each run parallel to one and the same third line; or, as I, in the knowledge which I have of a subject, at the same time immediately perceive what it is to know a subject. *The difference between the universal and the individual has here entirely disappeared; the unity of the two is perceived at a single glance.* It is Spinoza's highest aim to understand as much as possible in this immediate and intuitive manner. In the last book of his *Ethica* he seeks to understand individual minds in their inner unity with the eternal essence: *an intuition which forms the consummation of his theoretical and practical endeavours.*[20]

Of course, even if Spinoza's doctrine of intuition exerted an influence on Maritain's early thinking, specifically by awakening his intuitive sensibilities and thereby enabling an objective unification of "his theoretical and practical endeavours," that intuition had to be profoundly different from the intuition of being about which Maritain would write years later as a Thomistic philosopher. For one thing, and most importantly, the intuitions of Spinoza were of logical entities, effects *implied* by the formal causality of infinite substance, whereas Maritain's intuited entities were unique and dynamic effects of the First Efficient Cause, *entia ut exertia* (see Section III, below).

---

[20] Harald Hoffding, *A History of Modern Philosophy*, trans. B. E. Meyer (London: Dover Publications, Inc., 1955), vol. I, 306 (italics added).

## II. ACTIVISM, THICK AND THIN

"...[A]mong those of my contemporaries still living as I write these lines, I see in the Western World no more than three revolutionaries worthy of the name—Eduardo Frei in Chile, Saul Alinski in America...and myself in France, who am not worth beans, since my call as a philosopher has obliterated my possibilities as an agitator..."[21] Maritain may have had "tongue in cheek"[22] when he wrote these lines about himself as revolutionary and agitator, but there can be no doubt about his approval of the vocation of public agitator, as is clear from his correspondence with Saul Alinski.[23]

At the same time, there can be no doubt that Maritain took his "call as a philosopher" seriously. As noted above, he gave pride of place to metaphysical study and contemplation. Maritain insists that the search for truth and goodness in themselves transcends utility and, in so doing, reminds society of the supreme importance of what are not means to ends but ends in themselves, things worth aspiring to just for themselves[24]: "What we need is not truths that serve us but a truth that we may serve."[25] We must live our lives by values and realities that transcend time, things that are worth knowing simply for themselves; for that is the knowledge that leads us to understand that means that serve us are, in the end, empty without the knowledge of our "very reasons for living and suffering and hoping."[26] By his witnessing in society to the "supreme dignity of thought," the philosopher calls attention to "what is eternal in man," thereby creating in us a thirst for knowledge that is pure and disinterested (knowledge for the sake of knowing). This is a knowledge of the nature of things, of mind, human

---

[21] Jacques Maritain, *The Peasant of the Garonne* (New York: Holt, Rinehart and Winston, 1968), 23.

[22] Bernard Doering, *The Philosopher and the Provocateur: The Correspondence of Jacques Maritain and Saul Alinski*, ed. Bernard Doering (Notre Dame: University of Notre Dame Press, 1994), xiii.

[23] See the work just cited in #21.

[24] Jacques Maritain, *On the Use of Philosophy* (Princeton, N. J.: Princeton University Press, 1961), 6-7.

[25] Maritain, *Degrees*, 4.

[26] Maritain, *On the Use of Philosophy*, 7.

nature, and God. Such knowledge is superior to anything we can produce, for the simple reason that thought precedes action and nothing can place boundaries on thought. All of which tells us that our practical decisions "depend on the ultimate questions that human thought is able to ask." Here Maritain cannot resist pointing to the irony of the philosopher's calling: The impact that philosophy has on human history results from the fact that philosophy addresses questions that have no practical use.[27]

Even so, Maritain is just as insistent that the call to eternal verities must not blind the philosopher to the reality that he is a member of society with duties to the latter that his calling imposes on him:

> ...[T]he philosopher cannot—especially in our time—shut himself up in an ivory tower; he cannot help being concerned about human affairs, in the name of philosophy itself and by reason of the very values which philosophy has to defend and maintain. He has to *bear witness* to these values every time they are attacked, as in the time of Hitler when insane racist theories worked to provoke the mass murder of Jews, or as today before the threat of enslavement by communist despotism. The philosopher must bear witness by expressing his thoughts and telling the truth as he sees it. This may have repercussions in the domain of politics; it is not in itself, a political action—it is simply applied philosophy.[28]

Besides the moral injunction to give public witness, Maritain also recognizes what might be called organic integrity: "...Thought and action are inseparable; and the action of a philosopher, which is to say, the judgment that he makes about events, is only the concrete realization of his thought, and a way to give witness to truth."[29] These

---

[27] Ibid.

[28] Ibid., 14-15.

[29] My translation from the French: "...la pensée et l'action ne sont pas séparables; et l'action d'un philosophe, c'est-á-dire le jugement qu'il porte sur les évenéments, n'est que l' aboutissement concrete de sa pensée, et une manière pour lui de render temoignage a la vérité" (Jacques Maritain, *Lettre Sur l'Indépendance* [Paris: Desclée de Brouwer, 1936], 7-8).

words are emblematic of his lifetime view of the relation between philosophy and activism.

But what kind of behavior by a philosopher counts as philosophical activism? The agitator is by definition an activist, but the activist is not necessarily an agitator. Yet both share a passion for the world of real people and events. Does writing articles and books that address moral and socio-political problems in a strictly conceptual way, such as the idea of slavery or the idea of just and unjust homicide, count as activism? These would be contributions on the level of practical philosophy, and, as such, are applications of speculative philosophy to human affairs. Unlike the dichotomy that separates the two levels in Kantian philosophy, Thomism acknowledges a continuity between them, since they belong to that category of practical philosophy that Maritain calls "speculatively practical science."[30] As important as such writings are, it is hard to see how they could count as examples of activism. Philosophical activism implies the philosopher's confrontation with a contemporary, moral or socio-political evil in the world, against which he publicly identifies himself as an agent of specific action, such as initiating or at least signing a petition of complaint against a person, institution, or practice. Because a speculatively practical science, like ethics, operates, in contrast, entirely on the conceptual level, it requires no immediate actual evil to confront.

What about speculatively practical examples that, while not directly addressing existing injustices, do nevertheless pertain to them and move readers to act for their abolition? Perhaps writings and lectures in this second category can qualify as examples of philosophical activism and their authors' as philosophical activists. If so, we might characterize them as examples of activism in the *thin* sense and say that Maritain compiled an impressive record as a philosophical activist in that sense. For despite his preference for the solitary life of study and contemplation, Maritain had, over the years, consistently attempted to relate his philosophy to the problems of human affairs. Few have written more searchingly and persistently on the relation of

[30] Maritain, *Degrees*, 346.

the person to political society,[31] the basis of human rights,[32] capitalism and communism,[33] the nature and goals of democratic society,[34] pluralism and freedom of conscience,[35] Church and State,[36] and the role of the Christian in modern society.[37]

These writings have had enormous influence in Europe and in North and South America.[38] Not only have they provided ideological sustenance for social action and workers' groups,[39] they have also inspired the formation of at least one major political party, Eduardo Frei's "democracy of the left" party, and contributed to far-reaching social and economic changes, such as the land and industrial reforms initiated by Frei while President of Chile[40] and by Rafael Caldera during his presidency of Venezuela.[41] Maritain's emphasis on the need for a free society to be progressive, i.e. to make its social, economic, and political institutions increasingly democratic and open to participation by all its members, has had some success in persuading conservative

---

[31] See, e.g., Maritain, *The Person and the Common Good* and *Man and the State* (Chicago: University of Chicago Press, 1956).

[32] Jacques Maritain, *The Rights of Man and Natural Law*, trans. Doris C. Anson (New York: Charles Scribner's Sons, 1943).

[33] Jacques Maritain, *True Humanism*, trans. Margot Adamson (London: G. Bles, The Centenary press, 1938), 37-42, 107-09.

[34] Jacques Maritain, *Christianity and Democracy*, trans. Doris C. Anson (New York: Charles Scribner's Sons, 1944).

[35] See, e.g., Maritain, *On the Uses of Philosophy*.

[36] Jacques Maritain, *The Things That Are Not Caesar's*, trans. J. F. Scanlon (New York: Charles Scribner's Sons, 1931).

[37] Jacques Maritain, *Scholasticism and Politics*, ch. VIII.

[38] James D. Collins, "Maritain's Impact on Thomism in America," in *Jacques Maritain: The Man and His Achievement*, ed. Joseph W. Evans (New York: Sheed and Ward, 1963), 25-45.

[39] Iswolsky, *Light Before Dusk*, 104-17.

[40] Leonard Gross, *The Last and Best Hope: Eduardo Frei and Chilean Democracy* (New York: Random House, 1967), 89, 92, 231.

[41] Rafael Caldera, "Personal Testimony" and Alceuj Amorosa, "The Influence of Maritain in Latin America," *The New Scholasticism* XLVI (1972): 81.

Catholics, both in Europe and Latin America, that Christianity has no special connections with nationalism or with "order for the sake of order."[42] In contrast, he chose as the motto for his first book in political philosophy, "There is order even among the demons."[43] At a time when the privileged classes and many of the clergy in these countries were leaning increasingly toward fascism in their fear of socialism and communism, Maritain's "democracy of the person"[44] provided them with a viable alternative. Viable because it seeks to protect traditional rights and initiatives in the individual,[45] while calling for the elimination of socio-economic inequities through social reconstruction.[46]

But when practical philosophy delves more deeply into the realm of applied philosophy, it enters the category of "practically practical science."[47] And it is here that one can appreciate the young Maritain's affinity for Nietzsche's existential integrity—living according to one's principles—and where we see him as a philosophical activist. Nietzsche wrote, "The only critique of a philosophy is this, whether one can live according to it."[48] Taken by itself, this statement is broad, for it can just as easily refer to one who simply lives his daily life according to his principles. But it would be a clarion call for one with Maritain's passion for justice. His impressive record of speaking out against specific instances of what he regarded as injustice and error in the world

---

[42] Jacques Maritain, *Pour La Justice* (New York: Editions de la Maison Française, 1943), 64-65; Alfredo Mendizábal, "Catholicism and Politics," in *European Ideologies* (New York: Philosophical Library, 1948), 492; see also 5-6, 12-13, n.1, 28-31, 47.

[43] The motto appears on the frontispiece of some editions of *La Primauté du Spirituel* (Paris: Plon, 1927).

[44] E.g., Maritain, *Scholasticism and Politics*, 85.

[45] E.g., Maritain, *Man and the State*, 103-07.

[46] E.g., Jacques Maritain, *Freedom in the Modern World*, trans. Richard O' Sullivan (London: Sheed and Ward, 1935), 139-51.

[47] Maritain, *Degrees*, 346.

[48] My translation: "Die einzige Kritik einer Philosophie is die, ob man nach ihr leben könne." Friedrich Nietzsche, *Nietzsche Brevier*, ed. Wolfgang Kraus, 3rd edition (Wien und Stuttgart: Georg Prachner Verlag, 1954), 19.

introduces us to Maritain as philosophical activist in the *thick* sense of the term. Not that he involved himself in partisan politics. On the contrary, he stated more than once that in order to preserve his intellectual independence, the philosopher must stay clear of such involvement and offer no philosophical support for any political party. The philosopher *as philosopher* has, in Maritain's judgment, no special commitment to the left or the right. But to the extent that these parties adopt platforms that imply judgments on such things as freedom, rights, justice, and the nature and destiny of man, they are fair game for the philosopher's critique, regardless of their political stripe.[49]

For example: During the Spanish Civil War, Maritain refused to take sides. Instead, he worked with groups whose aim was to provide relief to Spanish political refugees.[50] He also wrote a criticism of both the Loyalists and the Communists for their excesses and challenged Franco's claim that he was waging a "holy war" against the Communists. In the same essay, he laid much of the blame for the war itself on the materialism and greed of the Spanish privileged classes and on the traditional identification of the hierarchy of the Spanish clergy with the aristocracy, rather than with the poor.[51] Maritain, along with others, also signed a manifesto condemning the destruction of Guernica by German bomber planes. His position on the war resulted in misunderstandings and hard feelings, as in the cooling between himself and Paul Claudel,[52] and also subjected him to criticism by the Rightist press and by those whom Maritain referred to as the *bien pensants*, i.e., well-meaning but misguided people.[53] But at the same time, it earned him lifelong friends among Spanish political refugees.[54]

---

[49] Maritain, *On the Use of Philosophy*, 14-15; *Lettre sur L'Independence*, 8-9.

[50] Yves R. Simon, "Jacques Maritain: The Growth of a Christian Philosopher," in *Jacques Maritain: The Man and His Achievement*, ed. Joseph W. Evans (New York: Sheed and Ward, 1963), 18.

[51] Maritain's criticism appeared in his introduction to Alfredo Mendizabal's *The Martyrdom of Spain*, trans. Charles Hope Lumley (New York: Charles Scribner's Sons, 1938).

[52] Iswolsky, *Light Before Dusk*, 195.

[53] Ibid.

[54] Ibid.

When anti-Semitism began to spread throughout Europe in the wake of Hitler's propaganda, Maritain did not remain silent. In 1938, he gave a public lecture in Paris in which he vigorously denounced the persecution of the Jews in Germany and exposed the falsifications in the defamatory stereotype of the Jew.[55] Once again, his activism earned him the criticism from the rightist press and the *bien pensants,* many of whom regarded Hitler as their savior against Communism.[56]

Nor did Maritain hesitate to speak out against Marshall Pétain and the Vichy regime for its anti-Semitism, its betrayal of the French people, and for its slavish obedience to the Nazis.[57] When the outbreak of World War II made it impossible for him and Raïssa to return to France from his lecture tour in Canada and the United States, he continued to support his countrymen by working with the Free French in New York City; through radio addresses and publications, he called the attention of the Americans to the condition of his people and appealed for food and money for French relief.[58] Throughout the war, he also worked with the New School in New York City, producing works of a more philosophical and scholarly nature on subjects such as democracy, totalitarianism, and human rights.[59] Miniature editions of one of these works, *Christianisme et Démocratie,*[60] were dropped by British Royal Air Force planes over France in 1944.[61]

In 1947, Maritain, then French Ambassador to the Vatican, served as a member of the UNESCO symposium on human rights. The aim of the symposium was to investigate the theoretical problems generated by a universal declaration of human rights, such as the Human Rights

---

[55] Ibid., 197.

[56] Ibid.

[57] Jacques Maritain, *France, My Country, Through the Disaster* (New York: Longman's Green and Co., 1941), 109.

[58] Jacques Maritain, *Messages (1941-1944)* (New York: Éditions de la Maison Française, Inc., 1945).

[59] E.g., Maritain, *The Rights of Man and Natural Law.*

[60] Maritain, *Christianisme et Démocratie* (New York: Éditions de la Française, Inc., 1943).

[61] Alfredo Mendizábal, "Catholicism and Politics," 492.

Commission of the United Nations was undertaking at the time. Other members of the symposium were Aldous Huxley, who was its chairman, E. H. Carr, Richard McKeon, Harold Laski, Benedetto Croce, and P. Teilhard de Chardin.[62] Maritain wrote the introduction to the book, *Human Rights*,[63] which contains the positions of the members.

To the charge of multiplying examples, I plead guilty. In my defense, I can only say that I thought it necessary to do so for the sake of showing how much a part of Maritain's life activism was and why, therefore, it deserves scrutiny in the light of his commitment to contemplation and speculative philosophy. Thus, back to the question that I raised at the outset of this essay. Is there by any chance a continuity between Maritain's metaphysics and his philosophical activism? Experience offers an abundance of intellectuals and scholars who are vigorous social activists, but their activism doesn't necessarily flow from an articulated intellectual justification. Instead, it's just temperament. They're simply confrontational: "you push me, I push you back." Other cases of activism by intellectuals indicate a continuity between the conclusions of speculative intellect and the justification for the activism. But here is where the difficulties begin. Applying an ethical or political theory to a concrete situation is, as noted earlier, to enter a realm of increasing variables and opaqueness. But the question asked of Maritain is different, as different as the relation between a rule of behavior, such as "Do not steal," and taking the property of a given person is from the relation between Maritain's metaphysics and signing a letter against Franco. The question is: can some continuity exist between the latter two terms? This returns me to the question I raised above: What kind of unity joins Maritain's speculative philosophy with his activism? Objective? Pragmatic? Or merely subjective?

## III. CLOSING THE GAP BETWEEN METAPHYSICS AND ACTIVISM

As noted, what saved Jacques and Raïssa from executing the terms of their suicide pact was their introduction to Henri Bergson's philosophy at the Collège de France.[64] Bergson showed them that it was

---

[62] Maritain, *Man and the State*, 76-80.

[63] Jacques Maritain et al., *Human Rights* (London: Allan Wingate, 1949).

[64] Raïssa Maritain, *We Have Been Friends Together and Adventures in Grace*, ch. 4, esp. 69-84.

possible for the human mind to transcend matter not only in knowledge but also in freedom. Eventually, Jacques' Bergsonian discipleship failed to hold his allegiance, as he went from the status of Bergson's prize pupil to stern critic. What was at stake was the status of the concept. For Bergson, concepts distorted reality by reducing what was always in flux to a series of frozen depictions as in the frames of a motion picture.[65] A true-to-life knowledge of reality was achieved not by the analytic procedure of conceptual thinking but by intuition, which Bergson construed as a supra-rational faculty whereby the will turns in on itself to create a "sympathy" that opens oneself to a knowledge of the real.[66]

Maritain's discovery of Thomas Aquinas' writings introduced him to a construal of the concept that protected the intelligibility of our knowledge of the real from distortions caused by representations, not knowledge, of extramental things. The concept was not what the mind knows, but rather *that by which it knows.*[67] As Maritain's career as a Thomistic philosopher unfolded, his writings revealed a growing emphasis on being as diverse and multiple. This represents a significant change from his *Bergsonian Philosophy and Thomism*, where the emphasis was on being as "the most common and most abstract concept" and an important departure from his friend and teacher, Garrigou-Lagrange, who very clearly conceived of being as a general concept, in effect an essence:

> This first knowledge is truly an apprehension, a mental perception, an imperfect intuition, associated with abstraction. The intellect considers, in sensible things, intelligible being and its most general aspects, without actually considering the sensible qualities...[68]

---

[65] Henri Bergson, *Creative Evolution,* trans. Arthur Mitchell (New York: The Modern Library, 1944), 331-34.

[66] Ibid., 34-35, 8-9, 172.

[67] Maritain, *Degrees,* 127-28.

[68] Reginald Garrigou-Lagrange, *God: His Existence and His Nature*, 2 vols. (Saint Louis and London: Herder, 1949), vol. I, 113-14; Sister M. Elizabeth, I. H. M., "Two Contemporary Philosophers and the Concept of Being," *The Modern Schoolmen* 25 (1948): 224-37.

Maritain uses the term, "trans-objective being" to refer, in the case of being, to both a unity and a multiplicity; i.e., although the concept of being contains what is common to all beings, viz., that they exist, it nevertheless also refers to being, not as known, not as an object of thought, but as existing in diversity and multiplicity outside the mind.[69] In other words, our knowledge of a thing's being never exhausts its being.

Another important aspect of this new emphasis is that it brings Maritain closer to Bergson than when he wrote *Bergsonian Philosophy and Thomism*. Not only is there an emphasis placed on multiplicity and diversity, but also on the energy and dynamism, of being:

> Observe that being presents two aspects. One of these is its aspect of *essence* which corresponds particularly to the first operation of the mind [simple apprehension]. For we form concepts primarily in order to apprehend, though in many cases blindly, essences—which are positive capacities of existence. The other is the aspect of *existence*, the *esse* in the strict sense, which is the end in which things attain their achievement, their act, their "energy" *par excellence*, the supreme actuality of whatever is.... It is the second operation of the mind, in the judgment, by composition and division, that the speculative intellect grasps being, not only from the standpoint of essence but from that of existence itself, actual or possible. Existence is here apprehended *ut exercita*, that is, as actualized by a subject; not merely presented to the mind, as in the case with the simple concept of existence, but as possessed potentially or actually.[70]

Being is not, as Maritain presented it in *Bergsonian Philosophy and Thomism*, a concept, but it is now an act exercised by a subject. And as the emphasis on the act of existence grows in Maritain's thought, so does the emphasis on the role of intuition grow. For even though existence is grasped *ut exercita* through the conceptual functions of judgment, it remains that the concept—insofar as it grasps the essence of things—cannot grasp being as multiple, diverse, and dynamic.

---

[69] Maritain, *Degrees*, 93-94.

[70] Maritain, *Existence and the Existent*, 28.

Is it plausible that within Maritain's Thomism one can look for an understanding of the intuition of being that could serve as an integrating principle in the sense of deepening the philosopher's understanding of his or her obligation to give public witness? Consider the following from his writings:

> A philosopher is not a philosopher if he is not a metaphysician. And it is the intuition of being... that makes the metaphysician.[71]

> It is not enough to teach philosophy, even Thomist philosophy, in order to possess this intuition. Let us call it a matter of luck, a boon, perhaps a kind of docility to the light. Without it man will always have an opining, precarious and sterile knowledge, however freighted with erudition it may be; a *knowledge about.* He will go round and round the flame without ever going through it. With it, even though he stray from the path, he will have the added privilege of solitude and melancholy. If the poet can be called a seer, the philosopher is no less entitled to this name, though in his own way. He may at times be the victim of some bewilderment; but at other times he will know the joy of discovery; and for all of the knowledge he will have got out of books, for all of his knowledge of life, he will owe both bewilderment and joy to the fact that he remains enraptured with being.[72]

Going "...round and round the flame without ever going through it." This line is reminiscent of Bergson's criticism of what he viewed as the rationalist model of knowledge that dominated modern European thought and immured the human mind with concepts. Truly, the investigation of being could not stand as a science (*scientia*) if it were not the investigation of being *as being.* But without the intuition of being, that investigation would, insofar as it studies only the concept of being, restrict the study to *possible* being. That is, of course, inevitable because what stamps being as real is being as *to be,* being as it actually exists; but, as Gilson writes, "in a certain sense, it must be said that *being* is always *conceived* by us apart from existence, for the very simple

---

[71] Ibid., 19.

[72] Ibid., 21-22.

reason that existence itself cannot possibly be *conceived*."[73] Without the intuition of being, the study of being *insofar as it is being* reduces being to a mere concept, thereby leading the student into rationalism and pedantry. That is why Maritain insists that one cannot be a philosopher without being a metaphysician and that one cannot be a metaphysician without having the intuition of being.

There is an incalculable difference between an existent being and a merely conceptual being, but the liability of the pedant is the tendency to lose sight of real things in favor of a fascination with the neat and tidy world of concepts and abstractions. There is the *idea* of oppressed human beings and the *reality* of oppressed human beings. Is it possible that for the pedant, the one whose conception of the world is derived from books alone, the difference between *the thing* and the *idea of the thing* gradually fades? Maritian's temperament seems to have protected him from pedantic liabilities, for he apparently did not associate as much with professors and students as with artists—usually of the vanguard sort, e.g. Rouault, Cocteau, Satie, and Stravinski; with philosophers, such as Berdyaev and Marcel, writers like François Mauriac, those interested in mysticism, and with missionaries.[74] He was an early defender of Satie's music and of Rouault's painting, even to the point of writing *Art and Scholasticism*[75] in defense of the latter's radical change of painting style, which offended the sensibilities of the academy artists.

When we are told that we cannot be metaphysicians unless we have the intuition of being, we surely are entitled to know what that intuition is like. Maritain obliges us with a description. Always ready to defend the integrity of rational knowledge, he insists, contrary to Bergson, that the intuition expresses itself within the conceptual

---

[73] Étienne Gilson, *Being and Some Philosophers* (Toronto: Pontifical Institute of Medieval Studies, 1961), 3.

[74] Simon, "The Growth of a Christian Philosopher," 7; Iswolsky, *Light Before Dusk*, 85-86.

[75] Maritain, *Art and Scholasticism: With Other Essays*, trans. J. F. Scanlan (New York: Charles Scribner's Sons, 1930).

functions of judgment.[76] Yet, his description of the experience borders on the mystical:

> ...[It] is a very simple sight, superior to any discursive reasoning or demonstration. It is a sight whose content and implications no words of human speech can exhaust or adequately express and in which in a moment of decisive emotion, as it were, of spiritual conflagration, the soul is in contact, a living, penetrating and illuminating contact, with a reality which it touches and which takes hold of it. Now what I want to emphasize is that it is being more than anything else which produces such an intuition.[77]

> I have often experienced in a sudden intuition the reality of my being, the profound first principle which makes me exist outside nonentity. It is a powerful intuition whose violence has sometimes frightened me and which first revealed to me a metaphysical absolute.[78]

Although satisfied with the term being as the correct expression of what the intuition beholds, Maritain reminds us of the term's poverty insofar as it cannot reveal all the riches banked in the intuition. It would, he avers, demand all our metaphysical elaborations, past and future, to know all the treasures contained in the concept of being. By conjoining a mental word with reality, the intellect forges the concept of *being as such*, the formal object of metaphysics.

Our senses deliver up to us diverse realities that, at a given moment, unlock the "intelligible mystery" that was hitherto concealed in them. In the introductory chapter of *A Preface to Metaphysics*, Maritain explains what he means by "intelligible mystery." The term is not self-contradictory. Mystery and understanding are not mutually incomepatible terms; to think so is to fall victim to the Cartesian legacy of

---

[76] Raymond Dennehy, "Maritain's Reply to Gilson's Rejection of Critical Realism," in *A Thomistic Tapestry: Essays in Memory of Étienne Gilson*, ed. Peter A. Redpath (Amsterdam/New York: Rodopi, 2003), 72-74.

[77] Jacques Maritain, *A Preface to Metaphysics* (New York: Books for Libraries, 1979), 46.

[78] Ibid., 47.

uncompromising rationalism. To the extent that the full meaning of "being" is not a problem to be solved, it is a mystery. But it is an *intelligible* mystery, the contemplation of which provides an ever deeper understanding of being and its riches.[79] This is a crucial point in the assessment of the intuition of being. An intelligible mystery, just because its ontological depth can never be plumbed, is food for contemplation and thus wisdom. What the contemplative learns about the object of his contemplation will never be falsified or revised by the discovery of new data, for there are no new data, only the reality of the object, whether it be being, beauty, truth, love, or personhood. Unlike objects of contemplation, objects of discursive reasoning are held hostage by the empirical data that constitute evidence. The discovery of new data can cause a revision of a scientific theory, say, or even lead to its falsification. For example, until recently, it was supposed that all dinosaurs were reptiles, but today there is mounting support for the claim that at least some dinosaurs were warm blooded.[80]

Contrast someone whose knowledge of Mahler's Third Symphony is limited to an occasional listening over the years with one who regularly listens to it, contemplates it, focusing his attention on this or that chord or rhythm. On a given evening, both are present at the performance of the symphony; each hears the same notes; and yet, the lover of Mahler grasps its treasures in a way that the dilettante cannot. Granted, intuition has levels of penetration, and the higher the object of intuition, the greater, more profound, are its ontological treasures. But even humbler objects will evade our desire for complete and final knowledge. As Maritain, paraphrasing Aquinas, observed, "We shall never know everything there is to know about the tiniest blade of grass or the least ripple in a stream."[81] Because everything is reducible to being, it follows that being is the profoundest, and most dazzling of all the intelligible mysteries. Being is the highest of the transcendentals; beauty, goodness, and truth are simply manifestations of being. This revelation is an intellectual shock, but it is not the sole preserve of the metaphysician, for one's soul may experience a flash intuition of her

---

[79] Ibid., 3 ff.

[80] http://dinosaurs.about.com/od/dinosaurcontroversies/i/warmblooded.htm.

[81] Maritain, *Existence and the Existent*, 66-67.

own existence. Sometimes, this intellectual perception is like a "mystical grace." If the intuition of being is not always a kind of mystical grace, it is, at all events, "a gift bestowed on the intellect." Not everyone, including philosophers, receives it. Maritain states that Kant never had it. He dismisses the possibility that this unevenness in distribution occurs because it is a technique hard to acquire. On the contrary, nothing could be simpler to perform. Maritain claims that it was precisely because Kant tried to acquire it by a technique that he failed to attain it.[82]

All of which is not to say that the intuition of being comes without any difficulty. There is a difficulty, one of attaining a degree of intellectual purification that leaves the intellect sufficiently disengaged and empty so that it listens, instead of giving answers:[83]

> We must attain a certain level of intellectual spirituality, such that the impact of reality upon the intellect—or to use a crude metaphor, the active attentive silence of the intellect, its meeting with the real—gives the objects received through our senses (whose *species impressa* is buried in the depths of the intellect) a new kind of presence in us; they are present in a mental word, another life, a living content which is a world of trans-objective presence and intelligibility. Then we are confronted within ourselves with the object of this intuition, as an object of knowledge, living with an immaterial life, with that burning translucence of intellectual nature in act.[84]

The intuition of being can be attained, not only by means of confronting the things in the world, but also by the experience of duration (Bergson), anguish (Heidegger), and fidelity (Marcel). But no matter which path one travels, one must cross the threshold, take the decisive step. Maritain tells us that this is achieved by letting go of the concrete psychological and ethical facts whose immersion in matter renders opaque our vision of the "strictly metaphysical values" concealed by them. Then we behold the reality of things, which reality can only be called "being." What makes the experience of the intuition

---

[82] Maritain, *Preface to Metaphysics*, 48.

[83] Ibid., 49.

[84] Ibid.

of being inexpressible is that it is primordial and simple, and thus at the root of our intellectual life.[85]

Images of "crossing the threshold" and taking the "decisive step" echo the words of Plato where, in the *Republic*, the young men and women who were to become the philosopher kings must make the leap to behold the one thing that their teachers were unable to communicate to them, the Absolute Good. The vision of this, the ultimate reality, allowed them to see all things in their proper light and nature: goodness, the virtues, preeminently justice, how to deduce from it the best laws for the city-state, etc. Did the intuition of being allow Maritain to see and understand the world, its people and their actions in a truer light, the light of being? As shown above, his own words offer that possibility.

## IV. CONCLUSION

What does it mean to say that the philosopher *seeks the truth*? If he is in the tradition of Aristotle and Thomas Aquinas, as Maritain was, he would be a moderate realist, one whose philosophizing rests, to borrow from John Wild, on three principles: (1) Things exist in the world independently of our knowledge of them; (2) we can know these things, not perfectly, but truly; (3) from this knowledge we can derive objective principles of ethical conduct. And as such, he would seek to know the truth about existence, real things, not simply the truth about mere propositions and theories. So the integrating principle between Maritain's metaphysics and his activism can arguably be the intuition of being. Earlier it was observed that the attempt to unify two philosophies as disparate as those of Spinoza and Nietzsche, respectively, could at best result in a subjective unification, a psychological cobble, organized by dual commitments, the former an affinity for the absolute truths of metaphysics and the other a passion for the embodiment of truth and justice in the world. It was also noted earlier that a considerable difference separates practical philosophy (speculatively practical science) from philosophical activism (practically practical science). The former addresses *concepts* of human nature and dignity, justice, freedom, human rights, and political society, etc., not their actually existing counterparts. The latter

---

[85] Ibid., 52-53.

addresses existing situations, but not as the result of a metaphysical deduction, and surely not as a deduction from Spinoza's essentialist metaphysics to Nietzsche's anti-system pro-vitalism! Still, at that stage of his fledgling philosophical career, these were the only two philosophies that Maritain found acceptable.

But perhaps the intuition of being is by its very nature a bridge between the highest metaphysical principles and existing finite individuals. Maritain attests to the connection between his sudden knowledge of the metaphysical absolute and of knowledge of his own self "existing outside nonentity" when experiencing the intuition of being. Now, given the reasonable belief that Maritain's search for truth embraced real things, and given that the intuition of being powerfully confronted him with a knowledge of his own existence "outside nonentity," is it not plausible that the intuition also confronted him with the existence "outside nonentity" of people and events in the world? And not only their existence, but the reality (existence "outside nonentity") of the dignity of human beings, and the reality ("existence outside nonentity") of injustice also confronted him with the power of the intuition of being?

Maritain writes that the formal object of metaphysics flows from an "eidetic visualization" of a transcendental (being) that floods everything with an intelligibility that involves "irreducible proportionality or analogy": *a is to its own act of existing (esse) as b is to its own act of existing (esse)*. In the operation of judgment (*ut exertia)* we discover "the actuation of a being by the act of existing, grasped as extending beyond the limits and conditions of empirical existence, grasped, therefore, in the limitless amplitude of its intelligibility."[86]

Existence (*esse*) adds nothing constituent to a being's essence, but it makes it real. Aquinas reminds us that an existing donkey is more valuable than an imaginary lion; and we know from our individual experiences that when we need a dollar to buy a ticket for the bus ride, a real dollar is more valuable than the mere idea of a dollar and even of the idea of a million dollars, simply because it is real and the ideas are not. If the intuition of being shows us the reality of ourselves and others more profoundly and richly than it could otherwise be known,

---

[86] Maritain, *Existence and the Existent*, 29-31.

then is it not worth our time to wonder if Maritain's long and impressive record of activism was fueled by his intuitive vision of the reality of things? And maybe all this was prefigured when, as a young student at the Sorbonne and protégé of Bergson, Maritain "...bore aloft through the classrooms the revolutionary torch of a passionate socialism and of the philosophy of intuition."[87] If so, that would still not necessarily establish a conceptual continuity between his metaphysics and his activism, but it could arguably establish an intuitive continuity between them. This would provide a sturdier connection than that of a subjective or psychological, continuity of what could be, at best, no better than a merely diplomatic alliance between the philosophies of Spinoza and Nietzsche. And it would have conferred an internal, ontological—as opposed to Spinoza's merely formal—logic between his metaphysics and activism to replace his admiration for the integrity of two men whose philosophies could not be farther apart.

---

*87 Raïssa Maritain, *We Have Been Friends Together and Adventures in Grace*, 80.

# MARITAIN, RATZINGER AND THE NEW ERA OF INTELLECTUAL CULTURE[1]


## JOHN DEELY


### I. THE EPISTEMOLOGY/ONTOLOGY DIVIDE OF MODERN PHILOSOPHY

In *The Degrees of Knowledge,* without fully explaining himself, Maritain insists that "if unreasonable prejudices" against the idea that "a philosophy of being could...also be a philosophy of mind" can be turned aside, we "might well...see a new dawn break upon a new and glorious scientific era", one "putting an end to misunderstandings engendered in the realm of experimental research by the conflict between Aristotle and Descartes", and inaugurating a new era wherein "the divine good of intellectual unity, shattered for three centuries now, would...be restored to the human soul."[2]

How so? Beyond claiming that this "new era" would "quite clearly suppose the supreme regulation of metaphysical wisdom"—among the chief concerns of *The Degrees of Knowledge*, to be sure—Maritain in this work gives us no straightforward indication of *where*, in modern terminology, ontology (or "philosophy of being") and epistemology (or "philosophy of mind") come together.

### II. A DIGRESSION ON THE PROBLEM OF "CLASSIFYING MARITAIN"

In this regard, permit me to voice my suspicion that *The Degrees of Knowledge*, even though it is the work of Maritain's many that is most explicitly devoted to the problem of how to get beyond the modern 'turn to the subject', actually does not represent Maritain's best 'guess at the riddle' of how to overcome the modern opposition of studying

---

[1] [Editor's Note: At the author's request, the Editor has altered the style otherwise used throughout this book to place punctuation marks (commas, periods, etc.) outside of quotation marks, when these do not appear in the secondary source being quoted.]

[2] Jacques Maritain (1882-1973), *The Degrees of Knowledge*, trans. Gerald B. Phelan (New York: Charles Scribner's Sons, 1959), 66-67.

the process of knowing (epistemology) to attaining a knowledge of being (ontology).

My companion Brooke (with respect to whom Maritain—actually both of the Maritains, but Jacques in particular—we consider our 'patron saint') once wrote a book that asked in its title whether Jacques Maritain was "modern" or "ultramodern".[3] But what she meant by "ultramodern" was actually what came later[4] to be defined rather as "*post*modern": for the work of Maritain, itself quintessentially involved with modernity and/or rather the *overcoming* of modernity, was not modernity at its extreme (which is what "ultramodern" best indicates) but rather modernity in the depths of its dissatisfaction with the 'turn to the subject' and the solipsism to which this 'turn'—in spite of the best efforts of its protagonists both before and after Kant—inexorably pushed its adherents.

Maritain considered suicide preferable to the 'final interpretant', the 'inescapable consequent' (in its technical *différance* from 'consequence'), of modernity, or at least so his early pact with Raïssa strongly suggests. It was never the fullest possible development of modernity that Maritain sought ('ultramodernity'), but rather the way beyond modernity, yet without losing modernity's gains. These gains, admittedly, if we contrast philosophy with science, were almost solely on the side of science, although philosophy of old was practical as well as speculative, and it was not only but at least *mainly* as speculative that philosophy in modernity constituted, in Maritain's view, a debacle.

His early work he labeled *Antimoderne*.[5] It was a blunder, this choice of titles, from which in certain circles his reputation never recovered. "Antimoderne" hovered as a cloud from under which, at least for some,

---

[3] Cf. Brooke Williams Smith, *Jacques Maritain, Antimodern or Ultramodern? An Historical Analysis of His Critics, His Thought, and His Life* (Amsterdam: Elsevier, 1976).

[4] Cf. Brooke Williams Deely, "Jacques Maritain's Reflections on 'America': Sign of a New Christendom," in *Semiotics 2003*, ed. Rodney Williamson, Leonard G. Sbrocchi, and John Deely (Ottawa, Canada: Legas, 2005), 219–33, 223, and John Deely, *Four Ages of Understanding* (Toronto: University of Toronto Press, 2001), 611.

[5] Maritain, *Antimoderne* (Paris: Revue des Jeunes, 1922).

Maritain could never emerge. And yet he was the first Catholic thinker to anticipate the emancipation of Vatican II from the pre-Vatican II Vatican view that separation of Church and State and tolerance of non-Catholic versions of Christianity were to be tolerated only where and as long as the Catholics did not form the majority within the given state—not so different from the 'modern' (or at least contemporary) Islamic view: "One man, one vote—one time". Even the declaration of death as the due of one who converts to Islam only afterward to fall away and revert to error has its forerunners in the 17th century France of Pierre Bayle. He had to flee upon deciding that he was wrong to convert from being a Huguenot to being a Catholic, since 'being a Huguenot', like being a 'person of a book' (Jew or Christian), had protected status in the state only so long as the person in error had not 'seen the light' and embraced the 'one true view' of Islam (or, in France of Bayle's day, Catholicism). After that, in "lapsing from the truth", all bets were off.

Maritain was no modern in speculative philosophy, yet in practical philosophy he was a 'thoroughly modern Millie'. Not only was he the first individual philosopher cited by name in a papal encyclical, but he was cited precisely as the first Catholic intellectual worthy of the name to embrace Democracy and the separation of Church and State that democracy requires in order to be real. And when it comes to the beginnings of modern science, he stands alone among prominent Catholic intellectuals in his evaluation of the Galileo affair as the disaster that it was (marking the limit, as Maritain said, of divine patience with the "means of inquisition", themselves a great "stain upon human history" and "grave offense against God"[6]). In matters political, his *Integral Humanism* inspired the Latin American world with

---

[6] Maritain, *De l'Église du Christ* (Paris: Desclée de Brouwer, 1970), trans. Joseph W. Evans, *On the Church of Christ. The person of the church and her personnel* (Notre Dame, Indiana: University of Notre Dame Press, 1973), 181, 211. In the thirteen years spanning 1983–1995, the Cercle d'Etudes Jacques et Raïssa Maritain (in the persons of Jean-Marie Allion, Maurice Hany, Dominique and René Mougel, Michel Nurdin, and Heinz R. Schmitz) established the definitive text of all the Maritain's writings and brought them to publication in 15 volumes entitled *Jacques et Raïssa Maritain. Oeuvres Complètes* (Editions Universitaires Fribourg Suisse et Editions Saint-Paul Paris, 1983–1995). The above work appears in vol. XIII, 9-411. (The *Oeuvrès Complètes* is hereafter abbreviated by "*OC*," followed by volume and page numbers.)

an influence that continues to the present day. In this area, as John Knasas has pointed out,[7] Maritain moves far beyond what a literalist reader of Aquinas might be inclined to endorse. But Maritain, for all his devotion to the work of St. Thomas, looks always to the *consequences*—indeed, the far consequences[8]—of the thought of being, not to the imaginary horizon of the 13th as "the greatest of centuries".

## III. BACK TO OUR PROBLEM CONCERNING THE EPISTEMOLOGY/ONTOLOGY OPPOSITION

In the question before us, the question of how to conceive the actual relation between the two terms whose significates the moderns distinguished as "epistemology", on the one hand (the study of the nature and processes or means of human knowing), and, on the other hand, "ontology" (the study of the being of that which is—provided that we can get beyond the processes of knowing and reach all the way to 'that which is', which can by no means be presupposed after the 'turn to the subject'), we have a question to which Maritain in his work constantly called attention, but never himself, I dare say, quite managed to answer. It tantalized him. He understood its importance. And he did everything he could to make his listeners aware of its import. Yet, if we are to judge by the reactions so far to his work on the role of signs in knowing, although he fell short in his lifetime,[9] yet, like

---

[7] John F. X. Knasas, "Aquinas and the Liberationist Critique of Maritain", *The Thomist* 52.2 (April, 1988): 247–67.

[8] E.g., the opening paragraphs of Maritain's "Letter for the *Basilian Teacher*" (April 7, 1962), in *OC* XII, 1218-25.

[9] Speaking as one who from his student days knew Maritain personally, Thomas A. Sebeok comments that "I have always been perplexed that Maritain remained, in America and elsewhere, essentially unrecognized outside his parochial tradition, and even within, as a serious contributor to semiotics [e.g., *Understanding Maritain: Philosopher and Friend*, eds. Deal W. Hudson and Matthew Mancini (Macon, Georgia: Mercer University Press, 1987) makes no mention of it]....The rich...vein in semiotics...running from Aquinas...through Maritain...has been insufficiently mined by the general semiotics community here or abroad. That mother lode of pure gold is far from exhausted." (See Thomas A. Sebeok "Semiotics in the United States", in *The Semiotic Web 1989*, ed. Thomas A. Sebeok and Jean Umiker-Sebeok, with

every great thinker, he bequeathed to posterity to tease out the further implications of what he was "on to" without being able to finalize the matter.

## 1. Maritain at Princeton: still in the "age of substance"

I am reminded of the tale of Maritain told to me by my former teacher and close friend, the Dominican Friar Ralph Austin Powell. Returned from Louvain in the World War II era, Ph.D. in hand, Powell assumed a teaching position at St. Michael's College at the University of Toronto in the early years of Gilson's establishment of the glorious Pontifical Institute of Medieval Studies. Yet, after a year of teaching there, Powell resigned, because he found that, as far as he was concerned, St. Michael's of the day had no interest in real philosophy, but only in the teaching of history of philosophy, and history with a definite slant. He abandoned his faculty status there and returned to his Washington home, retiring to the attic to read the whole of Plato and Aristotle in their original language. Happily ensconced, he was astonished to be summoned by his father, who admonished him that he, the father, had from the beginning misgivings about his doctoral pursuit of philosophy at Louvain, because a man has an obligation to serve the public—a teacher, a lawyer, a doctor. If you need to go back to university for another degree, the father advised, to make yourself useful to society, by all means I will pay your way once again; but what you cannot do is sit at home and do nothing.

Nothing! For a philosopher to steep himself in the Greek of Plato and Aristotle is to do nothing! Ralph Austin was astonished and chagrined, humiliated. But refuge was at hand. Jacques Maritain that year was teaching at the Princeton Institute for Advanced Study, and the son was able to secure the father's support to go and study with Maritain as an interim solution to the problem of "sitting around the house."

At Princeton at the time, in addition to his lectures, the Maritains would host occasional Sunday gatherings with the students, and these, too, Powell attended until he was a familiar face, and felt comfortable

assistance from Evan P. Young [Berlin: Mouton de Gruyter, 1990], 275–395, 311-12.)

enough to ask for a private meeting with Maritain to present for his assessment his own—Ralph's own—basic philosophical stance. As Fr. Powell tells the tale, the meeting took place in the Maritain's living room, with Jacques and Raïssa seated at opposite ends of a long couch across from Powell's chair.

Powell at the time was a convinced idealist, a student of Jules Lachelier, on whose work Powell's Louvain doctoral dissertation had been based. As Powell held forth, the Maritains listened, with only an occasional question interjected by Jacques. After nearly two hours Powell reached the end of his exposition, and asked for Maritain's overall assessment. Jacques replied that it was clear that Ralph Austin was indeed a philosopher of considerable depth, and Jacques encouraged him by all means to continue to develop his philosophical thought. He, Jacques, had only one suggestion regarding Ralph's philosophical position. "I think," he said, "that you need to introduce into your system the idea of substance."

Powell went away elated. He had been listened to, praised, and encouraged by none less than the great Jacques Maritain! His vocation as a philosopher had been confirmed! A full three days passed before Powell realized that if he followed Maritain's suggestion by introducing into his system the idea of substance, the system, which depended on his own co-creation with God each second of the world, would be utterly ruined! Elation gave way to demoralization, and Powell resolved his problems by deciding to join the Dominican Order, where he was required to undergo doctoral studies all over again, culminating in a second—a Thomistic—doctoral dissertation modestly titled *Truth or Absolute Nothing*, and dedicated "To Rev. Humbert Kane, O.P., who knows more about nothing than anyone I know."

Certainly the idea of substance is central to Maritain's work, as it was to the work of Aristotle and Aquinas; and it became central, too, to Powell's own thinking. "The Problem of Identifying More or Less Absolute Unitary Beings in our World", Powell's most mature statement of the problem, is published posthumously in *The American Journal of Semiotics* 25.3-4 (2009), 77-126, and can be regarded as the finest fruit of his long-ago private meeting with Jacques Maritain.

## 2. The need for a move beyond substance: "back to the future"

But what are we to make of Joseph Ratzinger's thesis that "the undivided sway of thinking in terms of substance is ended; relation is discovered as an equally valid primordial mode of reality"?[10] How does this claim square with the centrality of substance in Thomistic thought, as Maritain so deftly and indirectly led Powell to see?

The answer, I think, is to be found in the work of the man that Maritain identified as his principal teacher after St Thomas himself,[11] namely, John Poinsot, who published his Latin work in philosophy and theology under his name in religion, Joannes a Sancto Thoma.[12] The equiprimordial reality of relation with substance does not appear at all when we approach being principally with an eye to the order of so-called *ens reale*, being as it is independently of whatever human beings think, believe, or feel—hardcore reality. From this standpoint, indeed, relation appears rather as *ens minimum*, with substance comparatively *maximum* in the finite order. But this standpoint, the standpoint of "Thomistic Realism" in the modern context, is inadequate to the problem that Ratzinger envisaged, which is the problem of person and personal identity and which is relatively independent of substance, after all, and certainly irreducible to it. Had your mother surrendered you as a fertilized ovum to be implanted by medical means in a woman

---

[10] Joseph Ratzinger (Pope Benedict XVI as of 19 April, 2005), *Introduction to Christianity*, trans. J. R. Foster (New York: Herder and Herder, 1970), 132; reprinted with a new preface, repaginated and with unexplained minor changes in the English (San Francisco: Ignatius Press, 2004), 184.

[11] See Maritain, *Antimoderne*, 144; *Reflections on America* (New York: Charles Scribner's Sons, 1958), 74–75; and *Le Paysan de la Garonne* (Paris: Desclée de Brouwer, 1966), trans. Michael Cuddihy and Elizabeth Hughes, *The Peasant of the Garonne* (New York: Holt, Rinehart and Winston, 1968), 219. See also Williams Deely, "Jacques Maritain's Reflections on 'America'," 221–22.

[12] The matter of the name of John Poinsot (1589–1644) is fully discussed in John Deely, "Editorial AfterWord" and critical apparatus to *Tractatus de Signis: The Semiotic of John Poinsot*, disengaged from the *Artis Logicae Prima Pars* (Alcalá, Spain) and published in a bilingual critical edition arranged by John Deely in consultation with Ralph Austin Powell (Berkeley: University of California Press, 1985), 391–514, 421-24; electronic version hypertext-linked (Charlottesville, VA: Intelex Corp., 1992).

of a completely different race and culture, your substance today—your genotype, in biological terms—would remain what it first was in your mother's womb; yet your personal identity and name would be completely different from what it is. It is the problem of "the semiotic self", as Sebeok and others[13] have pointed out.

## IV. BEFORE ANY POSSIBLE DISTINCTION OF ONTOLOGY FROM EPISTEMOLOGY

Precisely in the being of relation, ontological relation as indifferent to the difference between *ens reale* and *ens rationis*, do philosophy of being and philosophy of mind find their original unity of subject-matter, prior to any possibility of a distinction (let alone an opposition) between "ontology" and "epistemology" such as the moderns essayed. And the first thinker in the Thomistic tradition, perhaps the first philosopher of any tradition, to point this out was John Poinsot.[14]

Relation, Poinsot demonstrated, is the crossroad of knowledge and being, not only in the Divine Trinity of Persons, as Thomas had pointed out,[15] but as well throughout the order of finite being in its totality, precisely because all knowledge depends upon signs, and all signs consist in ontological relations triadic in type—a thesis associated in our day with Charles Sanders Peirce, without recognition so far that Peirce got the thesis from his study of later Latin thinkers otherwise

---

[13] See Sebeok, "The Notion Semiotic Self Revisited", in *Semiotics 1988*, ed. Terry Prewitt, John Deely, and Karen Haworth, (Lanham: University Press of America, 1989), 189–95; "The Semiotic Self Revisited", Foreword to *Sign, Self, and Society*, ed. Benjamin Lee and Greg Urban (Berlin: Mouton de Gruyter, 1989), v–xiv; and "'Tell me, where is fancy bred?': The Biosemiotic Self", in *On the Borderlines of Semiosis* (Imatra: International Semiotics Institute, 1993), ed. Eero Tarasti, *Acta Semiotica Fennica* 2, 221–28; and Norbert Wiley, *The Semiotic Self* (Chicago, Illinois: University of Chicago Press, 1994).

[14] See, in Poinsot, *Tractatus de Signis*, his"Remarks *Super Libros Perihermenias*", 38/11–39/11; the Second Preamble, Article 2, 93/17–96/36, esp. 94/25–95/4; and Book I, Question 1, esp. 117/28–118/18.

[15] Thomas Aquinas (1224-1274), *Summa theologiae* (1266-73), in *S. Thomae Aquinatis Opera Omnia ut sint in indice thomistico*, ed. Roberto Busa (Stuttgart-Bad Connstatt: Frommann-Holzboog, 1980), vol. 2, 1.28.1; commented on in Poinsot, *Tractatus de Signis*, 93/17–96/36.

universally neglected by the moderns (including the Neothomists),[16] and in particular from his study of Poinsot's teachers, the Conimbricenses, on the subject of signs.[17]

Of course, being and knowing can go their separate ways, when theories accepted as true are in fact false (such as the theological doctrine of Galileo's day that the sun revolves around the earth, as God himself was supposed to have told us).[18] It is only in truth, a Thomist might, with good reason, want to argue, that being and knowing come together, for "truth for finite minds is the correspondence of thought with thing", and such correspondence has to be critically established and verified.[19]

---

[16] See Mauricio Beuchot and John Deely, "Common Sources for the Semiotic of Charles Pierce and John Poinsot", *Review of Metaphysics* XLVIII.3 (March 1995), 539-66. Here again Maritain, particularly in contrast with Gilson—who encouraged neglect of the Latin Thomistic development between the 14th and 17th centuries—stands out as exceptional: see Deely, "Quid Sit Postmodernismus?" in *Postmodernism and Christian Philosophy*, ed. Roman T. Ciapolo (American Maritain Association: Washington, D.C., 1997), 68-96 (an essay on the work of Étienne Gilson and Jacques Maritain in relation to Poinsot).

[17] This seminal treatise (1607) has only now been edited and translated into English as an independent monograph by John P. Doyle—a fitting work to mark the beginning of the first fully postmodern century of an increasingly global intellectual culture: see his bilingual, critical edition, *The Conimbricenses. Some Questions on Signs* (Milwaukee, Wisconsin: Marquette University Press, 2001).

[18] Cf. Deely, *Four Ages of Understanding* (Toronto: University of Toronto Press, 2001), 493–99, for details of the matter, including the scriptural passages (494 n. 11) in which the proper interpretation of the relative motion between sun and earth is directly revealed.

[19] See the first paper in this volume by Steven Jensen, "Why the Senses Cannot Have Truth: The Need for Abstraction."

Yes, but, as Heidegger well asked,[20] what is the ground for the prior possibility of such correspondence? It is in the light of this question that Poinsot's *Tractatus de Signis*—which so fascinated Maritain, but otherwise suffered neglect in the 20th century era of Neothomism—provides the decisive analysis. The being of things is what it is regardless of what anyone thinks, feels, or believes, indeed. This is the hardcore meaning of *ens reale*. But things are knowable, and, when actually known, things exist not only in themselves (ultimately as substances), but now also in relation to some finite knower; and the status of things in relation to being known is not the status of substance as such (*esse in se*), but rather the being of terminus of a cognitive relation, the *aliud*, as it were, of *esse ad aliud*.

## V. THE DIFFERENCE OF OBJECTS FROM THINGS

This understanding of the difference between objects and things was on the way to being systematized among the Latins, but never reached the status of a notion (a distinction) fully thematized. Moreover, the usage among the Latins on this point was not merely left unthematized but quite reversed in the context of the development of modern philosophy. In the modern context, "object" and "thing" come to be regarded as terms lacking in any significant difference of meaning, because objects are all that we know, and so are regarded as an alternative way of saying "thing" by the 'realists', or simply express whatever can be known by the 'idealists' who hold that 'things-in-themselves' are unknowable anyway—so nothing is to be said about them in any case.

Now the generic term for concept in St Thomas is the Latin expression *species expressa*.[21] With this in mind, Maritain notes[22] that "it

---

[20] See Martin Heidegger (1889-1976), *Vom Wesen der Wahrheit* (Frankfurt: Klostermann, 1954)...although actually composed in 1930 and earlier published in 1943. (The English translation by R. F. C. Hull and Alan Crick, "On the Essence of Truth"—in *Existence and Being*. ed. Werner Brock [Chicago: Gateway, 1949], 292-324—was particularly consulted in preparing the present work.)

[21] In *The Degrees of Knowledge*, 115, Maritain asserts that the generic term "*species*", from which the expressions *species impressa* and *species expressa* distinctively derive, "has no equivalent in our modern languages" of

seems that St Thomas was much more concerned with the relation between the *extramental thing* and the *species* thanks to which it [the extramental thing] is made object than with the relation between the *species* and the *object* itself taken as such."

Only when we deal with the relation between the concept and the object itself taken as such (that is to say, as knowable not only when it is a thing but regardless of whether it is also a thing here and now, which sometimes it is and more typically it is not) can we begin to realize the profound implication of the seemingly innocuous statement that the difference between objects and things is that things only contingently, but objects necessarily, involve a relation to some finite knower.

## 1. Modern confusion in the very posing of the question

So we need to ask precisely *how* is an object as such involved in a relation to a knower? The object is not normally the *relation itself*, nor is it the *foundation* of the relation, for the foundation of the relation where concepts are involved in knowing is precisely the concept itself. And concepts are not, according to St Thomas, involved in all knowing. It is indeed only when concepts are involved that knowing can go astray from the truth, as evidenced in Gilson's question, the question that has bedeviled the twentieth century twilight of modern philosophy, for Thomist and non-Thomist philosophers alike: "How can we guarantee the fidelity of the concept to its object?"[23]!

---

philosophy; and it is also a term which has been all but universally misunderstood in the Neothomistic development of the last century, mired down in the ubiquitous "quo/quod fallacy" conflating *species expressa* with the preinterpretive function St. Thomas reserves to the *species impressa.* Clarifying these points in particular, among others relevant to our present theme, has been the effort of my book on *Intentionality and Semiotics* (Scranton, Pennsylvania: Scranton University Press, 2007).

[22] Maritain, *The Degrees of Knowledge*, 389, n. 4.

[23] Étienne Gilson (1884-1978), *Thomism. The Philosophy of Thomas Aquinas* , trans. Laurence Shook and Armand Maurer (Toronto, Ontario, Canada: Pontifical Institute of Medieval Studies, 2002 [= Étienne Gilson Series 24]), 266; this translates the 6th and final edition of this work (Paris: J. Vrin, 1964), the first edition having been published in 1941.

Yet Gilson's very way of putting this question is problematic, and indicative of the modern tendency to equate objects with things, to regard the term "object" and the term "thing" as synonyms first of all. For of the three elements required for a relation, namely, foundation in a subject, the relation itself as provenating from that foundation suprasubjectively, and the 'other' at which the relation terminates, it is clear when we enumerate these elements that the object corresponds always and only to the third element, the terminus.[24] And terminus and foundation of a relation are correlates: there is no problem of a "fidelity" of the one to the other; they are correspective.[25]

So the question Gilson is really asking is one that he himself does not quite realize. The question really is not the *fidelity* of concept to object but the *coincidence* of object with thing. Every object of a concept as terminating the concept pretends to be—that is, presents itself 'as if'—a thing, but only sometimes is it so; and if then the difference between an object and a thing is that an object as such exists as the terminus of a relation, whereas a thing may or may not be terminus respecting a given relation (as when a father is not really the father), we need to ask about the status of a terminus not as thing *or* as object but *as such*.

## 2. Objects as terminus of relations

Every object is terminus of a relation, and every relation has a terminus; yet not every terminus is an object, and not every object is a thing. Let us consider relation in its original locus of philosophical discussion as a category of *ens reale*. This is the notion of relation

---

[24] The point is perhaps too technical to develop properly here, but it is fundamental to the whole question of the singularity of relation as making possible in nature an action of signs (prior even to life or cognition) that only in intellectual knowledge does it happen that relations in their difference from related objects and related things can themselves become termini of objective awareness, as also fundaments of yet further relations: see Poinsot, *Tractatus de Signis*: Second Preamble, Article 3, esp. the "Prima Difficultas", 102/35–105/14; and Deely, *Purely Objective Reality* (Berlin: Mouton, 2009).

[25] See Poinsot, *Tractatus de Signis*: Appendix C.

common to Aristotle and Aquinas[26] that Ockham and all the moderns after him denied,[27] the notion that relation in its positive and proper being does not reduce to being in itself (substance) or to being in another (accident), but only depends on *esse in* in order to achieve its status over and above *esse in* as *esse ad*, terminating at some thing "other than itself" in order for the relation to be a "real relation", i.e., a relation in the order of *ens reale*, thus:

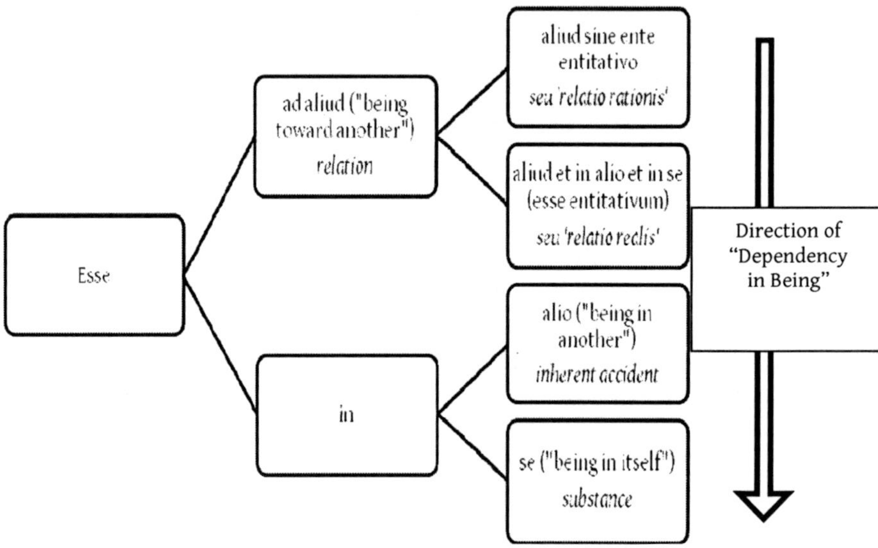


**Diagram illustrating the singularity of relation respecting ens reale**

VI. THE IRREDUCIBILITY OF RELATIONS TO THE ORDER OF *ENS REALE*

But notice that while the existence of the terminus as thing (i.e., the existence of the terminus as terminus in *esse entitativum*) is the essential

[26] See "The Fundamental Architecture of the Treatise on Signs" in Deely, "Editorial AfterWord", 472–79.

[27] Julius R. Weinberg, *Abstraction, Relation, and Induction: three essays on the history of thought* (Madison, Wisconsin: University of Wisconsin Press, 1965).

condition making the relation be a *relatio realis*,[28] the entitative status of the terminus is not at all what makes the relation be a relation (*adesse* is what makes a relation to be a relation ontologically), nor is its entitative status what makes it *as* terminus *be* terminus. For one and the same thing, unchanged in its subjective being, under one set of circumstances will *also* be terminus of a given relation, and not terminus under other circumstances. Two triangular things, A and B, will be "similar" on the basis of their shape only as long as both exist. Their shapes, given their simultaneous existence, are at once the rationale of founding and of terminating, respectively, a relation in this case bilateral. But their respective shapes "in themselves" are subjective properties, part and parcel of the being of the triangular things as things in the order of *ens reale*. Their respective shapes *also* found and terminate a relation of similarity only when and as long as the relation over and above subjectivity ("intersubjectivity", as is commonly said) itself exists. Absent the relation, absent also the being as foundation or fundament as such, and also the being as terminus as such.

These considerations reveal two things crucial for understanding the intersection of being with mind: it is the reality (mind-dependent or mind-independent indifferently) of the relation as relation that lends itself to the being of terminus as such and to the being of fundament as such. So, while a relation in order to belong to the category of *ens reale* (*relatio realis*) must exist intersubjectively, it is the existence of the relation itself that makes a fundament be a fundament as such subjectively and a terminus to be a terminus as such suprasubjectively ("ut aliud").

## 1. The being distinctive of "passions of the soul"

Now, when Maritain says[29] that the Thomistic term *species* "has no equivalent in our modern languages", he has in mind the point that concepts are unique among the accidental forms of *esse in* (or *inesse*) in that they cannot exist without giving rise to, without provenating, *adesse*, relations to objects other than themselves, precisely because the

[28] See Poinsot, *Tractatus de Signis*: Second Preamble, Article 2, esp. 91/12–16; and 94/35–95/17, esp. 95/2–4.

[29] Maritain, *The Degrees of Knowledge*, 115.

concepts as qualities of the soul are elements of *subjectivity* as founding relations to objects, while the *objects* terminate those relations *suprasubjectively* regardless of whether the object is or is not also a thing. So while relations are always suprasubjective in their positive being as *esse ad* (or *adesse*), they are only sometimes *inter*subjective as well, namely, when their terminus *happens also to be* something possessing *inesse*, which need not be the case. So relations, all relations, are necessarily suprasubjective, but only sometimes and contingently intersubjective, namely, when they obtain in the order of *ens reale*.[30] But when the subjective being of the terminus is destroyed by death or some other mishap, the relation, if it is a cognitive relation based on concepts or a cathectic relation based on feelings, unchanged as relation, ceases to obtain in the order of *ens reale* and intersubjectively, yet without in the least ceasing to be a relation or ceasing suprasubjectively to present an object as its terminus.

## 2. The equiprimordiality of relation with substance: a first glimpse

So the fundamental character of relation as equiprimordial with substance begins to impose itself, not only because finite substances cannot exist in fact without being involved in relations with their surroundings, but because experience wholly exists as a network of cognitive and cathectic relations which obtain suprasubjectively not only when they obtain intersubjectively but also even when they do not obtain intersubjectively. And in every case of suprasubjectivity—that is to say, in every case of *adesse*, including the more limited case of intersubjectivity—relations lend to things whatever being as terminus (terminus as such) things have (which is always in the case of objects as such, regardless of whether and when those objects are also things).

---

[30] See Deely, "Why Intersubjecivity Is Not Enough", in *Early Fall School in Semiotics 2004 Tom X* (the *Proceedings* of the International Early Fall School in Semiotics of the Southeast European Center for Semiotic Studies of the New Bulgarian University, Sofia, Bulgaria, 2004), 34-58 (text: 34-55; questions: 55-58). Now also printed as Ch. 9 of *Purely Objective Reality*, 143-64.

## VII. MARITAIN'S CLAIM CONCERNING PHILOSOPHY OF BEING REQUIRES POINSOT'S DOCTRINE OF SIGNS

Yet Maritain's claim concerns how a philosophy of being can also be a philosophy of mind, and so far we have only shown how and why being and knowing can diverge. To show how these two conceptions—"ontology" and "epistemology" in modern terms—come together in a virtual coincidence presupposed to their separation and guaranteeing that their separation cannot be an opposition (as it became in modernity, especially after Kant), we have to press yet further our discovery that the intentionality of consciousness (as being of or about, directed upon, an object) is derivative from the singularity of relation as the only mode of being indifferent to the distinction between *ens reale* and *ens rationis.*

Poinsot points out that the relation between concept and object is a sign relation, that is to say, a relation whereby one thing (in our present case, a concept) presents something other than itself (the object, or what it is that is known) to or for the one knowing—the one whose awareness the concept specifies as being of this rather than of some other object. Many Thomists have claimed to see in this doctrine of concepts as "formal signs", signs which make objects known without having to be *themselves* first objectified, the key to Thomistic realism. But these Thomists are deluded on the point, for Poinsot expressly points out[31] that, were knowledge in "formal signs" or concepts the whole of human knowledge, there would be no direct contact with the order of *ens reale* in human experience. Maritain joins Poinsot on this point,[32] noting that only because *not all* of our awareness of objects

---

[31] Poinsot, *Tractatus de Signis*: Book III, Question 2, 310/37–312/6, esp. 312/2–6.

[32] Maritain, *The Degrees of Knowledge*, 118 n. 1. See also Josephus Gredt (1863-1940) in his *De Cognitione Sensuum Externorum. Inquisitio psychologico-criteriologica circa realismum criticum et objectivitatem qualitatum sensibilium* (ed. altera aucta et emendata; Rome: Desclée & Socii, Editores Pontificii, 1924), iv: "Scripto nostro tamquam unica via ad idealismum vitandum manifestatur realismus naturalis integralis philosophiae thomisticae, cujus cardo in doctrina consistit de sensuum externorum cognitione intuitiva excludente quamcumque speciem expressam."—"The integral natural realism of Thomistic philosophy, the doctrinal heart of which consists in excluding from the intuitive cognition of external sense any least trace of an expressed specifying form, is shown in our writing to be the one and only way of

depends upon concepts are we assured of a partial coincidence between objects as objects and things as things.

Yet, even though not the whole but only that part of our awareness that has a limited indifference to the reality of its objects depends upon concepts, *the whole* of our awareness depends upon signs. As Maritain puts it,[33] "the sign involves the whole extent of moral and human life; it is in the human world a universal instrument, just as is movement in the world of nature." Sign relations in their ontological character as relations are more fundamental than even the intentionality of consciousness involving concepts.

*In these relations at the very origins of awareness* in sensation, prior to any possibility of separating ontology from epistemology, Maritain's thesis—that philosophy of being can also be philosophy of mind, and conversely—finds its demonstration. Sensation, St. Thomas says, consists in the action of the sensible upon the sense, itself an instance of "brute secondness" causal interaction, but an interaction from which thirdness arises, in that the proper sensibles simultaneously present to the animal the common sensibles of shape, movement, position, etc.; and this web of relations constituting sensation, even though they are cognitive relations—that is to say, relations of awareness—yet are at the same time relations which cannot be *entia rationis* (*relationes rationis*).

In other words, the relations of sensation—in its prescissive distinction from perception and intellection alike (alike in that both the higher levels of awareness and experience beyond bare sensation depend upon concepts, and so are relatively indifferent to the reality of their objects apprehended)—are the sign relations that guarantee the partial coincidence of being with knowing especially insofar as it is a pure question of *ens reale*.

---

avoiding idealism" (which is exactly the point of Poinsot at 312/2–6: "Quodsi existat in aliquo sui ut in imagine vel effectu, non immediate videbitur, sed ut contentum in imagine, ipsa vero imago est, quae videtur."

[33] Maritain, "Sign and Symbol," in *Redeeming the Time* (London: Geoffrey Bles, 1943), trans. and ed. Harry Lorin Binsse, 191.

## VIII. SEMIOTICS AS INESCAPABLE IN MARITAIN'S TRANSCENDING OF MODERN PHILOSOPHY

Despite the portentous rhetoric Maritain uses in presenting his essays and retouchings of his essays on sign,[34] few among his admirers to this point have taken with full seriousness Maritain's claim that the sign "involves *the whole extent* of human life and knowing". Yet just this neglected aspect of Maritain's thought, in continuity with the thought of John of St. Thomas and St. Thomas before him, marks the clearest trajectory in which Maritain's thought is more *post*modern than it is simply "antimodern" or even "ultramodern".

Maritain never used the word "semiotics", just as St. Thomas never used the word "epistemology". Yet just as we have been required to present St. Thomas in modern context in terms of "epistemology" and "ontology", even though the terms *do not well fit* his actual thought, so in postmodern context will we have to consider Maritain and St. Thomas alike in semiotic terms—with the vast difference that this time the terms not only postdate the main work of these two philosophers *but also well fit* their thought in all that concerns human life and experience.

Thomas Sebeok, the *Zeichenmeister* of 20th century developments in semiotics, said, as his own life entered its final years, that "I wish I had grasped Maritain's credo" concerning the doctrine of signs "sooner and better, for I have become convinced that the tradition in which he labored mutually harmonizes with and enriches what I have elsewhere termed the 'major tradition' in semiotic studies."[35]

Semiotics, the study of the action of signs, is the study more than any other that reveals at once the postmodern thrust of Maritain's alliance with Thomas Aquinas and John Poinsot together with the justice of Ratzinger's thesis[36] that "the undivided sway of thinking in terms of substance is ended" by the discovery that relation is "an

---

[34] See Deely, "Semiotic in the Thought of Jacques Maritain", *Recherche Sémiotique/Semiotic Inquiry* 6:2 (1986): 1-30, for a comprehensive overview of Maritain's texts on the doctrine of signs, or "semiotic".

[35] Sebeok, "Semiotics in the United States", 311–12; see further Sebeok, *Global Semiotics* (Bloomington, Indiana: Indiana University Press, 2001).

[36] See note #10.

equally valid primordial mode of reality" with substance in the world existing as knowable.

# PART IV
## The Scope of Science

# DISTINGUISHING BETWEEN NATURAL PHILOSOPHY AND SCIENCE: THE CASE OF ANCIENT MECHANICS

JEAN DE GROOT

## I. INTRODUCTION

In his book, *The Degrees of Knowledge*, speaking of philosophy and experimental science, Jacques Maritain says, "The whole structure of the experimental science of the ancients has doubtless crumbled and its collapse may well appear to anxious minds to spell the ruin of everything the ancients had thought."[1] Maritain makes this point several times in the context of separating the science of the ancients from their metaphysics and philosophy of nature.[2] His obituary for ancient science contrasts markedly with a recent judgment of his countryman, François De Gandt, the eminent historian of science, who says that the themes and fundamental concepts of both ancient astronomy and mechanics "*sont passés presque intacts dans la science moderne de la nature.*"[3]

Along with De Gandt, I believe there is continuity between ancient and modern within classical mechanics, not only in concepts but also in

---

[1] Jacques Maritain, *The Degrees of Knowledge*, trans. Gerald B. Phelan (Notre Dame, Indiana: University of Notre Dame Press, 1995), II.28, 64.

[2] Maritain, *Degrees*, II.16, 44–45, especially 49.

[3] François De Gandt, "Force et science des machines," in *Science and Speculation: Studies in Hellenistic Theory and Practice*, ed. J. Barnes, J. Brunschwig, M. Burnyeat, and M. Schofield (Cambridge: Cambridge University Press, 1982), 96. See also Meli's account of how early modern mechanics took its point of departure from ancient texts in mechanics (Domenico Bertoloni Meli, *Thinking With Objects*, [Baltimore: The Johns Hopkins University Press, 2006], ch. 1). It has long been recognized that the Greeks had in hand the basic principles of both steam power and simple machines. On the debate as to why the Greeks did not industrialize, see Helmuth Schneider, *Das griechische Technikverständnis: Von den Epen Homers bis zu den Anfängen der technologischen Fachliteratur* (Darmstadt: Wissenschaftliche Buchgesellschaft, 1989), 1–9, 52–62.

the fundamental framework for perceiving and conceptualizing motion. Indeed, it can also be shown that, in Aristotle's thought, mechanical notions served both in a natural philosophical account, as Maritain would define *physica*, and in an account recognizable to us as scientific. (To make clear the precise connotation of 'mechanics' here, let me specify that, like other contemporary scholars, I distinguish between 'mechanism' understood as the corpuscular philosophy, which is one type of materialist interpretation of the physical world, and 'mechanics,' which is a set of mathematical principles that describe and predict the movement or balancing of weights.[4] It is mechanics in the latter sense that is relevant to Aristotle's natural philosophy.)

The underlying strategy of my paper is roughly this: Let us accept that there is continuity between ancient and modern in practical mechanics. If there is also a connection between ancient mechanics and Aristotle's natural philosophy, then examining that connection may be instructive for approaching how science and philosophy—especially the philosophy of being for sensible things—should be understood in relation to one another in our own time. We can learn from Aristotle how a universal and timeless science, practical mechanics, is fittingly related to a perennial natural philosophy. Accordingly, in what follows, I will sketch how Aristotle made use of the central principle of ancient mechanics, the principle behind the lever, to develop a key concept of natural philosophy, namely *dunamis*, potentiality or power.

From this vantage point, we can evaluate Maritain's very strong division between science and natural philosophy. His division is based on the inability of science to grasp the ontological dimension of nature. One part of my project, which can only be touched upon here, is to show how the difference between science and natural philosophy emerges—perhaps in one of the first instances of this difference, in the Aristotelian *Mechanical Problems* (hereafter *MP*). The most important thing to come out of the line of research described here, however, is a new perspective on Aristotle's concept of *dunamis*. In my sections II and

---

[4] For examples of contemporary scholarship that separate mechanics and the mechanical philosophy, see Sylvia Berryman, "Ancient Automata and Mechanical Explanation," *Phronesis* 48 (2003): 344–69; Meli, *Thinking With Objects*, ch. 1 and 5; and Peter Dear, *The Intelligibility of Nature: How Science Makes Sense of the World* (Chicago: University of Chicago Press, 2006), ch. 1.

III, we see how this concept has a strong physicalistic connotation, and this helps us to understand it as part of the philosophy of nature. Finally, my contention is that there is not as strong a separation between science and philosophy of nature as Maritain believed, at least from the standpoint of Aristotle himself and in the case of the ancient example I will present.

## II. THE LEVER PRINCIPLE IN ARISTOTLE'S TREATMENT OF ANIMAL MOTION

When Aristotle developed his natural philosophy in the 4th century BC, what is called rational mechanics had not yet been separated from the principles of constructing simple machines. The lever, pulley, wedge, and rudder were known to the ancients as devices for moving weights. Probably only a few of the craftsmen who could make such simple machines, however, were familiar with the account of their functioning in terms of the geometry of the circle. Not only the author of the Aristotelian *MP*, but also Aristotle himself, ascribed the power of these devices to one principle, the moving radius (See Figure 1).

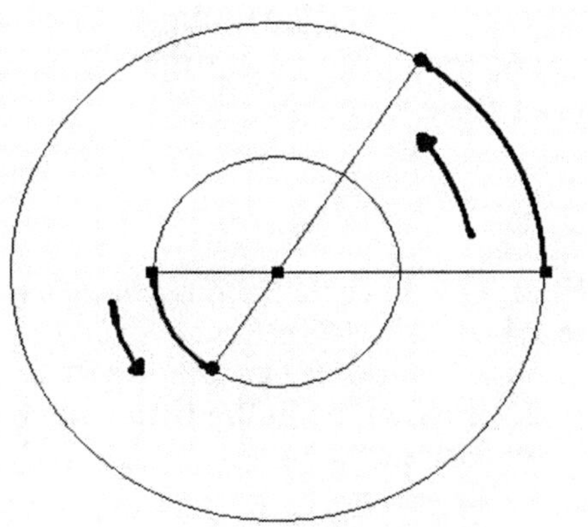

**Figure 1 Points on a moving radius**

POINTS ON A MOVING RADIUS ARE ALL MOVING DIFFERENT SPEEDS PROPORTIONAL TO THEIR DISTANCE FROM THE CENTER. THE MORE DISTANT POINTS ON THE RADIUS COVER A GREATER DISTANCE, A LARGER ARC, IN THE SAME TIME.

The principle is cited by Plato at *Laws* X, 893c–d, by Aristotle in *De Caelo* II.8, 289b34–35, and II.10, 291a35–b1, and in *MP* 1, 849a3–b18.[5] To our minds, it might seem that points moving along the circumferences of larger and smaller circles move with the same speed, i.e. the same angular velocity. As the ancients thought of this state of affairs, however, the arc distance belonging to a segment of a circumference with a longer radius is simply a longer distance. A point on a radius farther from the center moves faster than one nearer the center. Arcs of larger and smaller concentric circles were compared only indirectly, in terms of the lengths of their radii.[6] The greatest interest of the principle comes when we consider opposite arcs of larger and smaller circles. Applied to opposite arcs, the principle provides an explanation of why a lever can move a weight unmovable by human effort alone (See Figure 2).

A small force applied at the end of the longer arm of a beam will move a great weight at the end of the shorter arm, a weight that could not be moved by that force if applied to the object directly. The movements at ends of the lever are arcs of circles with the same center, the fulcrum. The ancient formulation is that, depending on placement of the weight along the beam, the same force would move the weight shorter and longer distances in the same time.

---

[5] I use the recent edition of *MP* by M. E. Bottecchia Dehò (*Problemi meccanici. Introduzione, testo greco, traduzione italiana, note; Minor Works*. Soveria Mannelli [Catanzaro]: Rubbettino Editore, 2000). I follow the chapter divisions of the Teubner edition, which are followed also by Hett in the Loeb edition of *MP* (Aristotle, Minor Works, trans. W. S. Hett [Cambridge, Massachusetts: Harvard University Press, 1980]).

[6] The role of π in determining the area and circumference of circles did not play a role in the Greek understanding of the circle until Archimedes' *Measurement of the Circle* (3rd century BC). Archimedes derived the ratio between the circumference and diameter of a circle. An approximation of π appears in the Rhind Papyrus (2nd millennium BC). Thales is said to have shown that the diameter divides the circle in half and Anaxagoras devoted attention to the squaring of the circle. On these topics, see Thomas L. Heath, *History of Greek Mathematics* (New York: Dover, 1981), vol. 1, 220–35, and E. J. Dijksterhuis, *Archimedes*, trans. C. Dikshoorn with a new bibliographic essay by Wilbur R. Knorr (Princeton: Princeton University Press, 1987), 222–23.

This principle had great versatility in explanation. The citations of the principle by Plato in *Laws* X and by Aristotle in *De Caelo* II.8 are central to accounts of the different speeds of the planets. In *Laws* X, Plato alludes to the principle being also the source of all sorts of wonders (*thaumata*) outside the realm of astronomy (893b3).

**Figure 2 Opposite arcs of larger and smaller circles**[7]

A SMALL FORCE APPLIED AT THE END OF THE LONGER ARM OF A BEAM WILL MOVE A GREAT WEIGHT AT THE END OF THE SHORTER ARM.

The author of the Aristotelian *MP* makes the principle underlie a host of natural and craft phenomena. Unlike movement in the heavens, these other applications involve exertion of force. The principle explains why it is easier to raise water from a well with a windlass—a crank and axle—than simply pulling on a rope (*MP* 13), and why the helmsman trims his sails in order to control his craft better in heavy weather (*MP* 7). By means of the principle, Hero of Alexandria provided instructions for how to translate movement from one plane to another so as to make figures above a platform simulate life-like movements.[8]

---

[7] The figure is from Pseudo-Juanelo Turriano, *Los Ventiun Libros de los Ingenios y de las Maquina*, 1595 (image jt519a posted on Database Machine Drawings of The Archimedes Project of the Max Planck Institute, http://dmd.mpiwg-berlin.mpg.de).

[8] Hero of Alexandria, *Automatopoiêtica*, in *Opera Omnia*, vol. 1, ed. Wilhelm Schmidt (Leipzig: B. G. Teubner, 1899), ch. vii–viii (362–65). Automata were artificial figures designed to be capable of a range of movements, usually the movements belonging to living things. Hero of Alexandria (AD 1st century) describes the apparatus for simulating animate movements as part of an automatic theater conceived as a whole. Whether or not Plato and Aristotle

The principle lies behind the modification of speed possible by means of gears, which are basically different-sized wheels in contact.[9] In the automatic theater, wheels linked by cables and turning in different planes become the basis for a variety of useful or surprising alterations in speed and direction of movement.

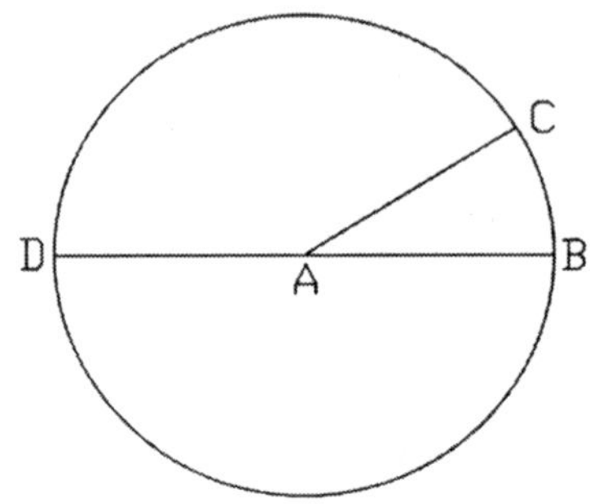


**Figure 3 Aristotle's description of limb movements**

ARISTOTLE UNDERSTANDS THE MOVEMENT OF A LIMB AS AN INSTANCE OF THE LEVER. IF A IS AN ELBOW, THEN THE FOREARM MOVES FROM B TO C.

knew the entire automatic theater of Hero's design, they both speak of apparently jointed figures moved by sticks or wires attached to limbs of the figures. Both allude to or address directly the principle behind the mimetic effects. Simple and complex devices were made in accordance with the same few principles. Note that Homer refers to *automatoi* as heat-driven self-moving cauldrons (*Iliad* XVIII, 373–77).

[9] *MP* 1 presents the principle of wheels in contact moving in opposite directions (848a20). The discovery of the Antikythera device established that the Greeks had a capability for precision gearing not previously known to historians. The device is a set of gears in a metal box that tracked the position of heavenly bodies by display on a cover surface like a clock-face. It is dated to the 1st century BC. See E. C. Zeeman, "Gears from the Greeks," *Proceedings of the Royal Institute of Great Britain* 58 (1986): 139–56, and Derek de Solla Price, "An Ancient Greek Computer," *Scientific American*, June 1959: 60–67.

In *Movement of Animals* (*MA*) 1, Aristotle describes the movement of a limb as the action of a moving radius, where the moving force is applied near the center of the circle[10] (See Figure 3). If A is an elbow, then the forearm moves from B to C.

That Aristotle understands the movement of a limb as an instance of the lever is clear from his use of the moving radius principle later in the treatise in a general account of the powers of animal movement. In *MA* 7, he wishes to explain how a sense percept or imagining causes such great changes as the coordinated movement of an entire animal body to attain an object of desire, or the shivering and shuddering produced by a terrifying thought (701b16–22). He cites the amplification of effect accomplished by a slight shift in a ship's tiller in the hands of the pilot. There is a very great change in the position of the prow of the ship (b24–28). The author of *MP* gives a more extended treatment of the rudder in similar terms, making the rudder a lever moved by the slight movement of the tiller (*MP* 5, 850b28–34). For both authors, it is important that the tiller lies near the fulcrum (*hupomochlion*) of the lever and that the tiller's movement is small but correlated to another movement larger by some proportion. Aristotle makes the point explicit in connection with his tiller example: "It is not difficult to see that a small change occurring at an origin produces great and numerous differences at a distance" (701b25). Aristotle takes the moving radius principle as describing a kind of vector, a line of amplification of effect of a single cause. Aristotle says that the alteration in the body caused by perception and imagination, though small, produces greater alterations and different kinds of effects in the parts of the body.

He makes clear in *MA* 7 that the multiplier effect of the lever principle is not to be taken as the means of reducing all movement to a species of locomotion (701b10–16). He says that what distinguishes living things from non-living things is precisely that living things have capacities (*dunameis*) for genuine growth, increase, and alteration (b13). In the passage, whatever is the species of 'greater effect' produced by

---

[10] The text used is Martha Nussbaum, *Aristotle's De Motu Animalium. Text with Translation, Commentary, and Interpretive Essays* (Princeton: Princeton University Press, 1978).

an initial change, Aristotle ascribes the greater effect to underlying *dunamis.*

We see from this consideration what Aristotle believes to follow from the principle of the lever if we apply it more generally to all kinds of change, namely an explanatory scheme for increase and diversification of effect. This point is made more vividly in another part of *MA* 7, where Aristotle speaks of *automata*—puppets, marionettes, or figures in an automatic theater. In accounting for the response of an animal to an object of desire or imagination, he says:

> The movement of animals is like that of automatic puppets, which are set moving when a small motion occurs: the cables are released and the pegs strike against one another; and like that of the little cart (for the child riding in it pushes it straight forward, and yet it moves in a circle because it has wheels of unequal size: for the smaller acts like a center, as happens in the case of the cylinders) (701b1–6).

It has been puzzling to scholars that Aristotle seems to take the *automata* to illustrate the same thing as the toy wagon (*hamaxion*).[11] The toy wagon is a cart with either two or four wheels in which the wheels are smaller on one side than the other. The cart is a very simple device compared to the complexity of the wheels, cables, and moving figures of an automatic theater. Elsewhere I have shown that the *automata* and the *hamaxion* both refer to the moving radius principle as exemplified in the rolling cone.[12] (See Figure 4.) The rolling cone has circles in its surface perpendicular to its axis that are mapped onto the plane surface on which it rolls.

---

[11] In general, scholars have read into the reference to *automata* the modern understanding of a mechanism as an arrangement of material parts transmitting movement from one part to the next by contact. See Nussbaum, *De Motu*, 347; David Furley, *Two Studies in the Greek Atomists* (Princeton: Princeton University Press, 1967), 216; Berryman, "Ancient Automata," 359; Mohen Matthen, "The Four Causes in Aristotle's Embryology," *Apeiron* 22 (1989), 176–77. From this standpoint, the similarity Aristotle assumes between the toy wagon and the *automata* is puzzling because the toy wagon is such a simple device. There is not a succession of movers.

[12] Jean De Groot, "*Dunamis* and the Science of Mechanics: Aristotle on Animal Motion," *Journal of the History of Philosophy* 46, no. 1 (2008): 43–68.

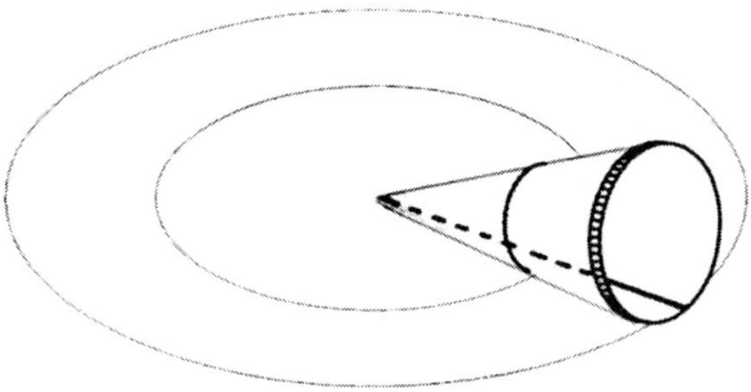

**Figure 4 A rolling cone on a plane surface**

THE ROLLING CONE HAS CIRCLES IN ITS SURFACE PERPENDICULAR TO ITS AXIS THAT ARE MAPPED ONTO THE PLANE SURFACE.

At its points of contact with the plane surface, the rolling cone describes a rotating radius. In his *Automatopoiêtica* (AD 1st century), Hero of Alexandria uses the rolling cone, and the different speeds of the concentric circles located on its surface, to explain how a hidden apparatus can translate the movement of a descending plumb-weight into circular movements proceeding in different directions at different speeds. He speaks of wheels located within a cone and extends the trope to a wheel in a different cone related to the first cone. As Hero uses it, the rolling cone is a shorthand expression for the amplification of effect produced by means of different-sized wheels in contact and connected by axles. This shorthand expression incorporates the translation of circular motion from one plane to another, which is so important for the surprising effects associated with *automata.*

Aristotle's *hamaxion* with its different-sized wheels illustrates in very simple terms the moving radius principle; the *automata* illustrate the same principle applied within an arrangement of interlocking wheels. Aristotle brings this understanding of practical mechanics to bear on the question of why animal movement proceeds without continual contact with an agent cause and why change in living things can so far outstrip the magnitude of the initial impulse to change. The moving radius is a model for the relation between the soul's initial action in the body—sensing—and the consequent responses to imagination and desire. His account of these responses is what he takes to be a very real condition of pent-up activity that shows itself in natural phenomena and simple machines. He characterizes this condition as *dunamis.*

Aristotle makes an explicit connection between *automata* and the concept of *dunamis* in *Generation of Animals* (*GA*) II.1. He explains how embryological development continues apace, after the initial effect of the parent sperm is spent. He says it is due to the potentiality resident in the materials contributed by the female. Making an analogy to the principle of the automatic puppets, he says:

> For the parts of such puppets while at rest have a sort of potentiality of motion in them (*echonta gar pôs huparchei dunamin ta moria êremounta*), and when any external force (*ti tôn exôthen*) puts the first of them in motion, immediately the next is moved in actuality (734b10–13).

This is a striking and significant use by Aristotle of the *automata* analogy. He says development of the embryo depends on pent-up power resident in matter, the female contribution, and in whatever parts of the embryo are already present. Aristotle has a vivid sense of the locomotive energy held in reserve because of a principle of mechanics. Something similar is at work in embryological development, he says, though the potentiality is not simply for movement from place to place.

### III. ARISTOTLE'S *DUNAMIS* AND MECHANICAL ADVANTAGE

Let us consider more carefully the notion of power, or potency, that Aristotle draws from the mechanical devices he mentions. *Dunamis* is often understood as a kind of invisible characteristic belonging to something already fully actual on another level. E.g., water is clear and liquid, but it has the power to nourish living things. Usually, *dunamis* is a passivity that supports additional action or essence, upon the reception—in an appropriate time, place, and way—of a robust enough form from something other than the *dunamis*. E.g., blood and bone become a vertebrate body. On this conception, only what acts on *dunamis* has the form that the potentiality comes to possess when actualized. Other causes besides *dunamis* are determinative of what *dunamis* becomes. *Dunamis*, then, is passive power.

*Dunamis* conceived on the model of the lever does not fit this characterization. With the lever, the power itself is exerted or activated and is manifest in action. *Dunamis* in the case of the lever does not receive form but rather a push or initiating impulse, and the latency immediately issues in action of a distinctive sort. At the same time, this activity comes out of a receptivity harbored in an arrangement and structure of materials. The power of the lever is power in both a receptive and active sense.

Does this understanding of form as present in *dunamis* fit Aristotle's account of power and potentiality in *Metaphysics* Θ, the *locus classicus* for the meaning of potentiality in Aristotle? In *Metaphysics* Θ.1, Aristotle says the original meaning of potentiality is its meaning in relation to motion (1046a2). *Dunamis*, he tells us there, is a principle productive of movement in *some other thing* or *in the thing itself* possessing the potency but *qua another* (1046a11). These two senses have generally been understood as active and passive potency respectively.

This assumption is closely linked with another received view, namely, that capacities are either for motion or for being something. Both these divisions are given in *Metaphysics* Θ.1, it is said.[13] In regard to active and passive powers, *dunamis* is defined in *Metaphysics* Θ.1 as "a principle (*archê*) of change in another or [in the thing itself] *qua* another" (1046a11). Aristotle immediately explicates this definition in terms of change of the second sort residing in what undergoes change (*tôi paschonti*) (a13). So, here is passive potency, contrasted to active, as the ability to receive action and be changed.

As for the division between potencies for change or for being, Aristotle says in *Metaphysics* Θ.1 that, although the prior meaning of *dunamis* is in reference to motion, it is not the most useful for his present purposes (1045b36). This has been taken to signal his greater interest in potencies for being. The development of Book Θ, although perhaps not the first five chapters, in general bears out this interpretation. The two contrasts have a textual basis, then. Nevertheless, both dichotomies—between active and passive potencies and between potency for motion or being—have been under revision in recent scholarship.

Michael Frede addressed the two oppositions together, as he sought to re-center the meaning of *dunamis* as defined by action, whether the

---

13 Ross, *Metaphysics*, 240–41. Frede criticizes the interpretations of both Ross and Bonitz in "Aristotle's Notion of Potentiality in *Metaphysics* Θ," in *Unity, Identity, and Explanation in Aristotle's Metaphysics*, ed. T. Scaltsas, D. Charles, and M. L. Gill (Oxford: Clarendon Press, 1994), 173-93, at 179.

capacity is for change or for being.[14] Frede believes the division between active and passive potencies, as well as the discernment of potentiality (*potentialitas*) as a "a kind of item in the ontology, a distinct, somewhat mysterious kind of possibility," are both accretions of centuries of commentary on Aristotle in changing philosophical contexts.[15] Neither common interpretation of *dunamis* is a compelling reading of the original text. He believes, contrary to the standard interpretation, that being-capacities get their meaning from change-capacities. Capacities are real, but within a much more pedestrian ontology than the one developed within the Aristotelian tradition. Frede's formulation of this position is clear and useful: "Aristotle thinks that there are truths of the form 'A possibly is F,' in some special sense of 'possibly,' which cannot be reduced to truths of the form 'A is actually G.' " The physical world just is characterized by this fact, that there are *dunameis* as well as *energeiai* or *entelecheiai*, actualities.[16] In this context, Frede points out the artificiality of separating potencies for change or for being. Without existing, a thing can no more *be changed* than it can change something else. So, potencies are not merely conceivable possibilities, but exist. Let us consider a particular example that can illustrate Frede's point about *dunamis*, an example also relevant to the relation of small and large changes.

---

[14] See Frede, "Potentiality." Most other treatments of *dunamis* in *Metaphysics* Θ.1 focus on potencies for motion as a springboard to potential being, which lacks sense without reference to its prior actuality (*energeia*). See, for instance, L. A. Kosman, "Substance, Being, and *Energeia*," *Oxford Studies in Ancient Philosophy* 2: 121–49; Stephen Menn, "The Origins of Aristotle's Concept of *Energeia* and *Dunamis*," *Ancient Philosophy* 14 (1994): 73–114; and Charlotte Witt, *Ways of Being: Potentiality and Actuality in Aristotle's Metaphysics* (Ithaca: Cornell University Press, 2003).

[15] For an interpretation of *Metaphysics* Θ.1 that contrasts markedly with Frede's, see Witt, *Ways of Being*. It is questionable how different, in the final analysis, Frede's interpretation is from the traditional one. He understands *dunamis* as a mode of existing of forms of sensible things, so his interpretation is rooted in substance.

[16] Frede, "Potentiality," 173. For another statement of capacity as real because of its relation to change, see Stephen Makin, *Aristotle: Metaphysics Book Θ. Translated with an Introduction and Commentary* (Oxford: Clarendon Press, 2006), 18.

Aristotle's treatment of 'oily' (*to liparon*) as a passive power illustrates the close relation of receptivity and action for *dunamis*. Something oily is what can burn (*kauston*) (1046a24). Oiliness is a power that requires some agent in order for the power to act. So, "oily" is a receptivity. Yet, oil's flammability shows that even a capacity conceived as passive is an active power when it shows itself by the impulse of some external agency. A warehouse fire started from a match dropped in oil is destructive in multiple ways, threatening even to take calamitous control of all the surroundings. More oil burns and the warehouse is set ablaze. It is hard to say that the passive *dunamis*, in the way it exists in this case, simply follows along behind the power that acts on it, as a weaker double.[17] The match is not "more" than the fire it caused. The flammability of the oil is the more powerful active power of the two contributors, agent cause and capacity. Someone might counter that there is a clear transition from passive power to active exercise in this case, since the flammability turns into actual burning. Furthermore, the match is actuality and to that extent "more," being already alight before it hits the oil. In contrast, I would point out that by the burning power of the oil, the oil burns. Combustion spreads through the body of the oil by the oil's own power. Oil has the power to burn itself, which is something active. In this case, so-called passive power and active power are very closely allied.[18] Passive power might be better called something's "*receptivity* to exertion of its own active power." Indeed, the present analysis supports Frede's suggestion that passive and active powers should not be separated into two.

In many Aristotelian contexts, "passive" is a poor English translation for the Greek *pathêtikos* which has a connotation of "undergoing." In *Nicomachean Ethics* II.5, *pathê* is often translated as

---

[17] Makin treats the puzzles of correlating passive and active powers in his commentary on *Metaphysics* Θ.1 (Book Θ, 29–34).

[18] I am not unmindful of the tenet of Aristotle's philosophy, which has drawn much attention in recent years, that any motion has an unmoved mover, in this case the match already alight or the parts of oil already aflame setting other parts on fire. See, for instance, *Physics* VIII, 258a5–12. For now, I wish to draw attention to a neglected part of Aristotle's natural philosophy, the structure of active capacities and their connection to latent power. In this context, Aristotle conceives of motion as having some version of agency.

"emotions," but *pathê* are really the non-rational side of our responses to things that happen to us, i.e., responses to our "undergoings." The undergoing of a trial or bad experience is also the expression of anger or sadness coming from the experience. *Pathê* are emotions that are expressed because they are evoked. We have *dunameis* for *pathê* (1105b25). It is by virtue of *dunameis* that we are said to be *pathêtikos* (b26). The ethical virtues and vices are not *dunameis* but states (*hexeis*) we are in relative to *pathê*, when our responses have been formed to the stable and predictable by repetition in behavior. *Dunamis* needs a translation that connotes both receptivity and response. The word "reactivity" for *pathêtikos* has too much of a connotation of stimulus-response or action due to irritability in the subject. The neologism "ractive," though ugly, at least illustrates the seamless combination of receptivity and activity most appropriate to *dunamis* as Aristotle develops its meaning for animal motion in *MA* 1–7.

Let us consider this more detailed sense of *dunamis* in Aristotle's account of embryological development in *GA* II.1. This is the passage where Aristotle compares embryological development to the movement of *automata*. Here, Aristotle insists that neither the animal nor any complete part of it is contained in the sperm, but that the sperm does play a role as agent (the *huph'hou*) of form, a role that it passes on to another part of the developing embryo later in the process. The agent depends upon the *dunamis* in the materials acted upon, in order for development to proceed. Aristotle in effect says that the male seed has the parent's form as part of the parent's body and not as a 'carrier' of the form to the offspring. Aristotle says, "If, of soul, there is nothing which is not in some part [i.e., if every part of a living thing has soul in it], also this part (the seed) would be straightaway ensouled" (734a14–15). So, the male seed shares in the soul of the true agent cause, the parent. Aristotle emphasizes that this secondary agent is partial, not a whole. Yet, its partialness includes the ability to sustain a process that will achieve substantial form in actuality. So, the substantial form of the developing embryo, the form it will have when development is completed, depends on a condominium of the *dunamis* in matter and the resident active agent. This means that matter must be very specific to form. It also means embryological growth is a system and that the teleology governing the development is spread throughout the entire system.

This understanding of power and agent is consistent with the way that, in a simple machine, mechanical advantage passes into actuality by means of a blow or pressure applied at the end of a balance arm. In this case, the mover is a cause that does not itself possess the form of what is accomplished. How much more so, then, may the seed, which shares in soul, be an agent that brings about an amplified effect, the offspring. This understanding of power and agent helps to understand *Metaphysics* H.6. In this chapter, Aristotle asks what accounts for 'what is potentially' (*to dunamei on*) existing actually (1045a30–31). In the case of things subject to generation, he says, there is no other cause beyond the agent. This is because of how matter and form make up a unity, he says. They are the same thing, the one (matter) potentially, and the other (form) actually (1045a23, b18). This view makes the form present in the condition of actuality something that belongs to the matter as well.

The approach to understanding *dunamis* that I have articulated adds physical content to the *dunamis* concept without making it into some already actual thing. Indeed, the defining of *dunamis* in terms of motions and proportional relations shows that not all realities should be looked for in the realm of finished substances whose quiddity is already given. Originally, *dunamis* has content based on universal scientific and pre-scientific experience. This pre-scientific experience validates the reality of *dunamis* while also establishing the overall context for a deeper causal account.

To this extent, *dunamis* is a notion of natural philosophy in a way that a kindred mechanical idea, *rhopê*, is not. The concept of *rhopê*, force or impetus, treats the same phenomena as Aristotle's *dunamis* but in a way that makes the power of mechanical advantage like a fully actual being, an entity. In this contrast, we see the beginning of science as different from natural philosophy. I can give some indication of what I mean by returning to the Aristotelian *MP*.

In his account of larger and smaller balances, the author of *MP* introduces a concept, *rhopê*, to compare the faster and slower movements of different concentric circles. The problem is why larger balances are more accurate than smaller ones. He says the degree of advantage (*to megathos tês rhopês*) brought about by the same weight (*hupo tou autou barous*) is greater in larger circles, and this is why the same force causes a greater distance to be covered in the larger circle

(849b33–34). Here, *rhopê* is closely allied to the manifestation of latent power in movement itself. Aristotle had used the term *rhopê* in *DC* IV.1 in connection with the natural movement of the elements. He says that weight and lightness are defined by their power to be moved physically (*tôi dunasthai kineisthai physikôs pôs*). If there is a name for the corresponding actualities, he says, it might be *rhopê* (307b31). So, *rhopê* is the actuality of movement.

In the *MP*, *rhopê* is given a more expansive explanatory role but at the same time a narrower meaning. In chapter 8, the author asks why curved shapes are the easiest of all shapes to move. He offers reasons having to do with resistance from a contacting surface, and how a weight at the end of a radius will be inclined to move, given its position on the circle (851b21–33).[19] Finally, he suggests that larger circles are related to smaller ones somehow by mutual resistance (*dia to antereidein*), so that a larger circle can move great weights, "on account of the angle of the larger circle having a certain *rhopê* in relation to the smaller, and the *rhopê* being in the proportion that the diameter of the longer has to the smaller" (851b38). If a circle has *rhopê* in relation to another, it is moved more easily (than the other) (852a1–2). The author does not say that both circles have *rhopê*, but one has *rhopê* in relation to the other. This advantage comes about by the system of factors, especially length of diameter, by which one circle overmatches the other in ability to move. Clearly, power latent in the arrangement underlies there being *rhopê*. The problem is that we are now inclined to ask "what is *rhopê*?" since the author ascribes to it a generalized causal power.

The author treats this causal power as entering into some relation of quantitative exchange with blows and taps. Yet the connotation of the term shifts between description of the realm of real phenomena and a realm of more permanent underlying forces and powers. He gives no indication that these forces and powers are anything other than entitative, like the elements of the phenomenon being treated. From what we have come to understand about *dunamis* in Aristotle's thought, *rhopê* should be a mode of being, an underlying power for actuality. The

---

[19] At the top of a vertical diameter, a weight has no greater inclination to move to one side or the other, but moved slightly off the vertical, the weight will move more in the direction of its inclination (*eph'ho rhepei*) (851b27–33).

author does not present his accounts within that horizon of explanation, however. The power of mechanical advantage is acquiring entitative status and with that, its manner of being becomes obscure.

Much more needs to be said to flesh out the contrast of *dunamis* and *rhopê* here suggested. The point is, however, that in Aristotle's own account natural philosophy and science shared a resort to potentiality or power that could be allied to metaphysics. As an effort is made to give a more complete treatment of a phenomenon and one that defines causes with the greatest perspicacity, a limitation of vision sets in. The scientist, as in *MP*, takes for granted the being of what he seeks to explain. This leads him to multiply beings on the same level as ordinary existent things and to deconstruct original phenomena into these beings rather than to seek knowledge of principles across many cases by analogical reasoning. The explanatory advantages of *dunamis* as a mode of being are not lost (and will figure in the later history of mechanics) but are poorly understood by the practitioner himself.

This seems to be an instance of the limitation of human science that is described by Maritain in *The Degrees of Knowledge*. He says, "By a kind of natural necessity, abstraction, the lot of all human science, brings with it, along with a multiplicity of partial and complementary insights, the rigid law of logical movement, the slow elaboration of concepts...."[20] The multiplication of accounts and the elaboration of concepts bring with them a constriction of philosophical perspective. For example, *dunamis* as a principle of natural philosophy becomes *rhopê*, a theoretical entity in mechanics. Nevertheless, the problem Maritain has described is both less acute and easier to diagnose in the ancient context I have presented than it is in the contemporary sciences Maritain sought to understand.

## IV. CONCLUSION

The following points emerge from the line of research I have sketched so very briefly here. In contrast to Maritain, it seems to me reasonable to argue for two types of continuity in connection with science: (1) a continuity between ancient and modern science and (2) a continuity between some aspects of perennial science and a perennial

[20] Maritain, *Degrees*, I.5, 5.

natural philosophy. Granted, continuity in both areas is not universal to all the sciences or even to one entire science, like mechanics. Nevertheless, we should not overlook the fact that some basic sciences, like practical mechanics, do not change in their fundamentals. There are aspects parallel to practical mechanics in this regard in other sciences.

In his strategy for recovering Aristotelian philosophy of nature, Maritain is adamant that there can be no continuity, ontologically, between physico-mathematical theories and philosophical knowledge.[21] This claim, of course, arises primarily from his evaluation of the different manners of conceiving the objects of physics, mathematics, and metaphysics. It is reinforced, however, by his judgment on the ancient sciences. My suggestion, based on the evidence presented, is that Maritain gave up too quickly on the continuity between natural philosophy and science, both for antiquity and the present day.

Aristotle did not think of natural philosophy and science as different endeavors. This was not simply a failure of vision on his part, since a basic physico-mathematical notion of his own time was integral to his natural philosophy. Aristotle provides us an example of the continuity between *physica* and science. Nevertheless, as Maritain saw, science in the modern age labors for the most part without the benefit of natural philosophy's perspective on subjects and attributes, the necessary and accidental, abstraction and hylomorphism. The ancient example I have presented suggests that modern science's detachment from natural philosophy is not due entirely to the exceptionalism of modern science but rather to the way scientific concepts developed (and to some extent are bound to develop) out of natural philosophy. This is at least a start on an important task of our own time: to bring into relief the value of philosophy of nature in lending self-understanding to the scientific enterprise.

---

[21] Maritain, *Degrees*, II.29, 64.

# FAITH, PHYSICAL DETERMINISM, AND SCIENTIFIC METHOD

PETER A. PAGAN

In recent years, some high-profile debates over Darwinian theories of evolution have proven useful in bringing to light important divisions within the Christian community on certain fundamental questions. Two of the more notable participants in these debates are Christoph Cardinal Schönborn, O.P., Archbishop of Vienna, and Stephen M. Barr, a Catholic physicist and member of The Bartol Research Institute, a research center in the Department of Physics and Astronomy at the University of Delaware. The differences between their respective views are as instructive as they are significant. For instance, they differ in their views concerning the proper explanatory reach of modern science. Cardinal Schönborn holds that modern science is competent to "explore [quantitatively] measurable and mechanical causes," which fall within the scope of modern science's "purely quantitative-mechanical methods."[1] Moreover, he endorses the claim that, as long as one does not exceed the proper methodological limits of modern scientific inquiry, one cannot deal directly with or explain supersensible objects such as mind, purpose, God, and the "natures or essences of things."[2] Barr, in contrast, denies that modern science "deals only with sensible phenomena rather than with the reality underlying them, or that it studies just the accidental quantitative aspects of things rather than their essences."[3] He adds: "All such views, whether they stem from nominalism, Humeanism, Kantianism, instrumentalism, or positivism, involve a gross underestimation of the

---

[1] Christoph Cardinal Schönborn, "Reasonable Science, Reasonable Faith," *First Things* (April 2007): 24-25.

[2] Ibid., 23.

[3] Stephen Barr, "Quantifying Quantum," *First Things* (June/July 2007): 6.

explanatory successes of modern science and the power of human reason."[4]

These Catholic thinkers differ also as regards their respective conceptions of randomness. In accord with his Christian understanding of divine providence, Cardinal Schönborn appears to endorse what I call the "ignorance interpretation" of randomness—the strictly epistemological claim that an admission of randomness is no more than an admission of the limits of human knowledge of the underlying causes of natural phenomena at both the macroscopic and the submicroscopic levels of reality. The ignorance interpretation is consistent with the thought of Thomas Aquinas, whom Cardinal Schönborn cites often in support of his own stance. Barr, in contrast, appears to endorse a more radical view of randomness, what I call the "acausal interpretation" of randomness—the ontological stance that natural events, at least at the submicroscopic level of reality, cannot be understood within the framework of classical determinism.[5] Arguing in favor of the Copenhagen interpretation of Heisenberg's principle of uncertainty,[6] he believes it to be "quite congenial to the worldview of

---

[4] One should note that Cardinal Schönborn has consistently held that the power of human reason extends far beyond the methodological boundaries of modern science. Indeed, he has criticized scientism or the philosophical view that modern science constitutes the supreme or the only form of genuine human knowledge of reality.

[5] Stephen Barr, "Faith and Quantum Theory," *First Things* (March 2007): 21-25.

[6] According to one formulation of Heisenberg's uncertainty principle in quantum theory, it is impossible in principle to measure simultaneously and with perfect accuracy the values of two magnitudes, namely, the position and momentum of a subatomic "wavicle," inasmuch as the precision of the measurement of the value of one of these magnitudes will be proportionate to the imprecision of the measurement of the other value. According to the Copenhagen (philosophical) interpretation of that principle, which jumps from an epistemological premise to a metaphysical conclusion, perfectly accurate measurements of the values of such magnitudes taken conjointly and simultaneously necessarily elude the grasp of mathematical science, *because*, in the case of a subatomic "wavicle," it does not possess *simultaneously* an exact position and an exact momentum. Stated differently, and more generally, a perfectly accurate measurement of any past or present state of physical reality is impossible in principle because any past or present

the biblical religions," partly because it sweeps away the putative error of physical determinism, which he regards as incompatible with an essential preamble of the Christian faith, namely, the doctrine of free will.[7]

Barr's view of randomness and his opposition to physical determinism fuel his attempts to answer Cardinal Schönborn's criticism of neo-Darwinian orthodoxy.[8] In opposition to Barr's stance, I shall attempt to defend the following two propositions: (1) it would be a mistake to hold that, in comparison with physical determinism, the Copenhagen interpretation of Heisenberg's uncertainty principle is more congenial to the Christian faith, and (2) physical determinism poses no real threat to human freedom properly understood. In my attempt to answer Barr's criticism of physical determinism in the name of faith (and freedom), I shall also comment on what I deem to be an overreaching conception of the proper compass of modern science.[9]

---

state of physical reality is inherently indeterminate. Thus, according to this ontological interpretation, no future state of nature could in principle be foreknown or predicted with strict certitude, but only probabilistically, because the present (or past) state of nature is not determinate *per se*. The dispute surrounds the *ontological* assertion of physical indeterminism and the associated denial of universal causality. As Barr puts it, opponents "regard the Copenhagen interpretation as an abandonment of scientific realism, disbelieve in the kind of wave-particle duality that would have, say, a single particle going through two windows at once, and see the probabilities of quantum theory as reflecting the operation of hidden causes, as they do in classical physics, rather than any true indeterminacy." Stephen Barr, "Correcting Quantum," 16. See Stanley Jaki's valuable essay, "Determinism and Reality," in *Patterns or Principles and Other Essays* (Bryn Mawr, Pennsylvania: Intercollegiate Studies Institute, 1995), 114-44.

[7] See Barr, "Correcting Quantum," 25.

[8] See my reply to Barr, "Neo-Darwinism and Catholic Teaching," *The National Catholic Bioethics Quarterly*, Vol. 6, No. 4 (Winter 2006): 622.

[9] To anticipate, the overreaching conception that I have in mind is inconsistent with the indispensable need of philosophy of nature and metaphysics. As Cardinal Schönborn correctly emphasizes: "If we are going to bring more clarity to the modern debate by employing the means of natural philosophy, several steps are necessary. We must first and foremost recover an understanding of what the modern scientific method is able to explain and

Let us begin by turning to Barr's own understanding of physical determinism. In his view, if the physical universe unfolds in precisely the manner required by classical physics, there would be no place for free will. As he puts it:

> [I]f the state of the physical world were completely specified at one instant, its whole future development would be exactly and uniquely determined. Whether a man lifts his arm or nods his head *now* would (in a world governed by classical physical laws) be an inevitable consequence of the state of the world a billion years ago.[10]

With that view in mind, Barr proceeds to argue against classical determinism in favor of the Copenhagen interpretation of Heisenberg's uncertainty principle, which, in Barr's eyes, unlocks nature's door to free will.[11] He notes that the Copenhagen interpretation of Heisenberg's

---

what it is intrinsically unable to explain. We must recognize that by its method it cannot deal directly with top-down causation or with the natures or essences of things. It proceeds instead by means of mathematical and mechanical explanations that, in the old expression, 'save the phenomena'... *Scientism*—by which I mean the philosophy (usually implicit and unrecognized) that modern science is the only way of gaining objective knowledge of reality—must be overcome." Christoph Cardinal Schönborn, "Reasonable Science, Reasonable Faith," 23.

[10] Barr, "Faith and Quantum Theory," 23.

[11] "Most of those who suggest that quantum indeterminacy may have something to do with free will are saying something quite different. They do not say that quantum indeterminacy explains free will, but rather that it provides an opening for free will. Free will is conceived of as a faculty arising, at least in part, from something that is non-physical. However, in order for the non-physical to have room to operate, matter—in particular the human brain—must not be completely under the rigid control of physical cause and effect.... The laws of physics... must be flexible enough that more than one outcome is possible in a particular situation: for free will to be possible, the laws of physics must have indeterminacy built into them. The key point is that quantum indeterminacy allows free will, it does not produce it." Stephen Barr, *Modern Physics and Ancient Faith* (Notre Dame, Indiana: University of Notre Dame Press, 2003), 179. The foregoing excerpt from Barr's book is part of a chapter devoted to the question of "Determinism and Free Will," 175-89. Such a discussion falls outside the compass of modern

uncertainty principle "implies that even if one had all the information there is to be had about a physical system, its future behavior cannot be predicted exactly, only probabilistically."

Acknowledging that not all scientists, including believers and agnostics, share his positive assessment of the Copenhagen interpretation, Barr observes that some contemporary scientists would endorse the less common view that "God does not play dice," that is to say, they reject the Copenhagen interpretation in favor of classical determinism. One such scientist cited by Barr is Peter Hodgson, a believer who, according to Barr, "insists that Bohmian theory is the only metaphysically sound alternative [to the Copenhagen interpretation]."[12] Barr notes that the Bohmian interpretation does not employ the hotly disputed concept of a particle-wave duality, which necessitates the insertion of probability theory into quantum theory. This insertion of probability theory into quantum theory is required, according to Barr, because "in no other way can one make sense of *the same entity* being both a wave and a particle."[13] Bohmian theory, in contrast, which preserves the older view that "waves are waves and

science. See Peter A. Pagan, "Darwinian Ideology or Universal Teleology? Science, Causation, and Providence," *The National Catholic Bioethics Quarterly*, Vol. 6, No. 2 (Summer 2006): 303, n. 36. The same can be said of the legitimate intellectual endeavor to show that modern science (as opposed to scientism) and revealed religion are complementary, not competing, approaches to truth and being. *Modern Physics and Ancient Faith* must be understood, then, as an extended *philosophical* exercise offered by a theorist with expertise in modern physics.

[12] Stephen Barr, "Faith and Quantum Theory," 25. In a subsequent correction printed in *First Things* (August/September 2007), 16, Barr retracts his earlier claim that Hodgson is among those scientists who *both* reject the Copenhagen interpretation *and* maintain that "Bohmian quantum theory is 'the only metaphysically sound alternative to the Copenhagen interpretation.' " One can consistently reject the former without embracing the latter. Barr adds that Hodgson regards another theory, "stochastic electrodynamics," as perhaps more promising than the Bohmian view. In comparison with Barr, Hodgson seems to adopt a more provisional stance, at least as regards what we may *affirm* scientifically. Hodgson's *denial* of the Copenhagen interpretation, in contrast, is not in the least tentative.

[13] Barr, "Faith and Quantum Theory," 25. Italics in original.

particles are particles," is more consistent with classical determinism. Barr regards Bohmian theory as a fundamentally new alternative to, not merely an interpretation of, quantum theory. He rejects Bohmian theory because it unravels what he takes to be "one of the great theoretical triumphs in the history of physics: the unification of particles and forces," and because "it brings back Newtonian determinism and mechanism," which, in Barr's view, undermines human freedom.

It is not my purpose here to defend or refute Bohmian theory. I wish to focus, instead, on the argument that, because classical determinism necessarily undermines human freedom, and the Copenhagen interpretation is the only *reasonable* option that seems to undermine classical determinism, one may safely conclude that the Copenhagen interpretation is presently the scientific option most in accord with a biblical faith perspective.[14] Surely the denial of free will cannot be reconciled with Christian orthodoxy, a point I shall assume in this context. The affirmation of free will, however, does not obviously bolster a purely scientific argument in support of the Copenhagen interpretation that Barr favors. With respect to the position I would endorse in opposition to Barr's more common stance, I suggest that

---

[14] Barr also discusses the many-worlds interpretation of quantum theory, which is favored by Don Page, among other theorists. The many-worlds interpretation is not deterministic, which appeals to Barr, but he considers its philosophical ramifications to be essentially irrational ("Faith and Quantum Theory," 24). Here I must concur with Barr. One should note that in his now famous op-ed piece, "Finding Design in Nature" (*New York Times*, 7 July 2005), which has elicited numerous illuminating exchanges, Cardinal Schönborn is no less critical of the many-worlds interpretation or, as he puts it, the "multiverse hypothesis in cosmology." I might add that it seems fair to say that Barr's "Faith and Quantum Theory" casts significant light on his own understanding of the scientific concept of randomness, a central issue in the academic dialogue initiated by Cardinal Schönborn, who defends global teleology in opposition to the idea of randomness as it is typically conceived within neo-Darwinian circles (e.g., Stephen J. Gould, Kenneth Miller). On the idea of randomness as it is ordinarily conceived, see Peter A. Pagan, "Darwinian Ideology or Universal Teleology?" 296-98, 304-06; idem, "Darwin and Design," in *Truth Matters*, ed. John Trapani (Washington, D.C.: American Maritain Association, 2004), 120-21.

believers critically examine two basic questions. First, would believers be well advised to endorse a scientific theory that does away with classical determinism? Second, does classical determinism really undermine the doctrine of free will, a doctrine that is indispensable from the perspective of Christian orthodoxy?

In response to the first question, let us consider the view held by Peter Hodgson. Consistent with modern science's methodological limits, Hodgson rightly observes that "[p]hysics can take no account of Divine intervention or of acts of free will, so in the course of scientific research the world is assumed to be strictly determined."[15] That is not to say, however, that Hodgson advocates Laplacian determinism. Hodgson's methodological stance is more nuanced than Barr's published statements indicate. As Hodgson observes:

> First of all, the world is not just a completely determined world. We are in the world, and we have free will....If this were not so we would be just robots....It is not only ourselves, but also God who can act on the world. *Everything, ultimately, is caused by God.* Aquinas distinguished two types of divine causality, primary and secondary. By primary causality God causes everything, but He also acts by secondary causality when he creates matter and gives it certain definite properties. Thereafter the matter behaves in accord with these properties. *This does not happen by unbreakable necessity,* because God has complete power over nature and can suspend or alter the laws of nature....This means that Laplacian determinism is unacceptable...both God and human beings can cause...effects [that Laplacian determinism cannot explain].[16]

Classical determinism has proven to be a valuable methodological assumption within the domain of physical theory. Without that assumption, modern science would scarcely have attained this point in its history. This important working assumption, however, need not be extended to cover the whole range of being, if reality cannot, in mechanistic fashion, be reduced to matter in motion. Moreover,

---

[15] Peter E. Hodgson, *Science and Belief in the Nuclear Age* (Ann Arbor, Michigan: Sapientia Press, 2005), 127.

[16] Hodgson, *Science and Belief*, 126-27; italics added.

believers who appreciate the importance of a realist metaphysics of being as being may, within the domain of physical theory, safely employ a mechanistic model of physical reality without falling into the error of thinking that such a scientifically fruitful model could yield a fully adequate knowledge of nature, which includes corporeal beings made in the image of God: human persons.[17]

If, however, one holds that modern physical theory by itself can supply a proper demonstrative grasp of the hidden but intelligible essences of things, as Barr seems to believe,[18] then a mechanistic model of the physical world, even as it is filtered through the specialized lens of modern science, cannot but prove to be problematic from a Christian faith perspective. In that event, one would be forced to choose between modern science and revealed religion. Such a choice would be most unfortunate, but this choice is unnecessary. One must resist the temptation to increase the scope of modern physical theory beyond its proper borders. By resisting this temptation, one can avoid the false choice between the deliverances of faith and those of modern scientific

---

[17] See, for instance, my reply to Barr in "Neo-Darwinism and Catholic Teaching," 623-24.

[18] Barr comments on "the thorny question of instrumentalism and the relation of quantum theory to reality. Many people have said that the traditional [Copenhagen] interpretation of quantum physics necessarily entails an instrumentalist view of science. That depends on what one means by instrumentalism. I believe that science, including quantum physics, makes objectively true statements about the real world and helps us to understand that world as it really is in itself. I reject views that say that modern science is merely useful or successful in manipulating (as opposed to understanding) the world, *or that it merely 'saves the appearances,'* or that it deals with sensible phenomena rather than with the reality underlying them..." Stephen Barr, "Quantifying Quantum," 5-6; emphasis added. Certain phrases used here by Barr signal clearly that his criticism is aimed at the position espoused by, among others, Cardinal Schönborn. In this connection, see the cardinal's essay, "Reasonable Science, Reasonable Faith," 23. Further insight is offered in "Intelligence and Design," *First Things* 175 (August/September, 2007): 14-6. The latter contains Cardinal Schönborn reply to letters written in response to "Reasonable Science, Reasonable Faith."

rationality.[19] It does not appear that either Barr or various contemporary intelligent design theorists, whose views he rejects, have managed to overcome this serious temptation. Hodgson, however, has not succumbed to this temptation. Thus, in accord with Hodgson's understanding of the value of classical determinism as a working assumption within the domain of modern physical theory, one may rightly deny the non-scientific claim that "[w]hether a man lifts his arm or nods his head *now* would (in a world governed by classical physical laws) be an inevitable consequence of the state of the world a billion years ago." This denial is not so readily available to those who, in accord with the doctrine of philosophical materialism (e.g., Charles Darwin), do not recognize the reality of immaterial principles such as the human intellect.

Barr might still continue to insist that Hodgson's approach does away with "the mysteriousness of quantum theory by sacrificing much of its beauty."[20] The underlying value of beauty in science was expressed by Barr in his book, *Modern Physics and Ancient Faith*:

> In the classical [deterministic] case, a deviation from the behaviors predicted by the physical laws due to a non-physical influence would show up as a *violation* of those laws. The laws would say that an atom should move a certain way, and it would move in a different way...it will never be possible to know if such violations of the laws of physics go on in the human brain. But the idea that they do is, to many people, rather ugly and philosophically unsatisfying. On the other hand, in a quantum process, several alternative outcomes are truly allowed to

[19] Another solution is offered by fideism, which dissolves the speculative union between the supernatural light of faith and the natural light of reason, but that solution is unequivocally rejected by Catholic orthodoxy. A third solution is to reinterpret the entire deposit of faith so as to make it conform to the uncompromising demands of modern science. That is the path of rationalism, also rejected by Catholic orthodoxy. What both solutions have in common is the failure to grasp the proper methodological limits of modern science.

[20] Barr, "Faith and Quantum Theory," 25.

> happen by the laws of physics, and so a choice can be made without a 'violation' of physical law.[21]

Setting aside the question whether suspensions of physical laws are truly inconsistent rather than more consonant with the beauty and mystery of creation, which includes images of God, one may doubt the assertion that these violations are philosophically unsatisfactory. Arguing from the uninterrupted constancy of physical laws, David Hume famously denied the empirical possibility of miracles. The natural order would seem to preclude miracles if it were true that physical laws are absolutely inviolable, which is something Hume could hardly argue consistently, for he rejected something indispensable to experimental science, namely, the ontological principle of causality. Yet perfectly reasonable believers opposed to fideism, such as Thomas Aquinas and Peter Hodgson, affirm the reality of supernatural miracles. Here one might quote the latter:

> The foregoing has shown that the success of quantum mechanics does not imply that the world is indeterminate and so does not provide the means whereby God can intervene. Even if it did provide those means, they would not be able to account for all recorded interventions, since they violate other physical principles. For example, the feeding of five thousand [via the miraculous increase of loaves and fish] is contrary to the law of the conservation of matter... It is an impoverished conception of God to suppose that he is bound by his own laws. God is the supreme lord of nature, who can make and unmake its laws and bring it into being... It is unnecessary to think of God trying to change the course of events by keeping within the limits of quantum indeterminacy.[22]

Although miracles imply violations of physical laws recognized in modern science, persons who embrace a perfectly rational faith, i.e., a faith that is fully consistent with the truths within the range of unaided

---

[21] Stephen Barr, *Modern Physics and Ancient Faith,* 181; italics in original.

[22] Peter Hodgson, *Science and Belief,* 220. For additional nuances, see Thomas Aquinas, *Summa Theologiae*, Ia, q. 105, aa. 6-7; Ia-IIae, q. 93, a. 5; q. 113, a. 10.

human reason, need not deny supernatural miracles.[23] For the violations in question aren't necessarily contrary to philosophical reason. Such violations are deemed irrational by philosophical materialists, agnostics, and by victims of heterodox religious catechesis. By way of contrast, Hodgson, who admits the reality of supernatural miracles, cannot justly be accused of supporting a deformed theology worthy of a clever deist or a Humean positivist. Indeed, Hodgson's reflections on natural science exhibit an admirable coordination of the wings of faith and reason without diminishing either one.

The fact that physical laws are broken does not mean that scientists must abandon the methodological assumption of physical determinism. For scientists as such cannot pretend to supply a complete explanation of everything without stepping outside the proper boundaries of physical science. It is true that physical science can lead scientific investigators to what are sometimes called "boundary questions,"[24] but the adequate answers to such questions must be left to metascientific forms of knowledge, including metaphysics and sacred theology.

If physical *indeterminism* actually obtained at the very foundations of material nature, it would seem necessary to adopt an essentially new conception of miracles, one that does not recognize the fact that physical laws can be and have been broken. Surely a most unusual understanding of miracles would be required. The transmutation of water into wine, for example, would need to be understood in terms of statistical probabilities; a miracle would be construed not as a truly

---

[23] By way of clarification, one should mention that when we say that divine miracles violate the laws of nature, we do not intend to suggest that God actually violates the natures or laws established by God Himself. For it makes no sense to hold that God can act against Himself. What we mean, rather, is that when a miraculous action occurs, such as the multiplication of loaves and fish, the act wholly transcends the natural order of operation of finite secondary causes. Thus, a divine miracle is neither according to nature nor contrary to nature, but beyond nature—"supernatural." This is one sense of the supernatural that is not admitted by those who favor philosophical naturalism. See Thomas Aquinas, *Summa Theologiae*, Ia-IIae, q. 113, a. 10.

[24] See Mariano Artigas, *The Mind of the Universe: Understanding Science and Religion* (Philadelphia and London: Templeton Foundation Press, 2000), 13-25.

*supernatural* event, but only as a highly *improbable* one. Indeed, if we were to adopt the Copenhagen interpretation of quantum mechanics, we could no longer consider the affirmation of a miraculous event to be logically inconsistent with the doctrine of philosophical naturalism, which strictly precludes the reality of supernatural causes. A first-rate theologian such as Augustine or Thomas Aquinas, however, would have considered a purely naturalistic conception of miracles to be quite foreign to an authentically Christian vision of reality. A miracle compatible with philosophical naturalism is a miracle in name only. If one admits genuine miracles, it is unclear how one could find "rather ugly and philosophically unsatisfying" the idea that physical laws are broken through the insertion of free human acts. The recognition that physical laws have been and continue to be broken in no way contradicts the claim that natural scientists as such should prefer the methodological assumption of physical determinism rather than the Copenhagen interpretation, which is not a purely scientific conjecture anyway.

Here I would pause to note that Barr emphasizes that the Copenhagen interpretation concerns "someone's (the observer's) *knowledge*,"[25] the imperfect knowledge of created human minds. We must not forget, however, that scientists transcend natural science's proper boundaries the moment they explicitly introduce human reason into the subject matter of modern scientific discourse.[26] If such emphasis on the mind of the human observer is an essential feature of quantum theory as construed by the currently dominant Copenhagen school of thought, then one could hardly deny that the Copenhagen interpretation is inherently metaphysical in nature, exceeding the proper scope of modern science. This is not to deny, of course, that the practice of modern science invariably depends on philosophical assumptions (e.g., that there is an inherent order in nature, that every effect demands an antecedent cause, that nature is inherently knowable, etc.). But these assumptions cannot be proven within the

---

[25] Barr, "Faith and Quantum Theory," 24.

[26] Darwinians, of course, typically fail to grasp the radical and naturally unbridgeable ontological gap between non-rational animals and free moral agents, which is why the Catholic Church cannot abide Darwinian orthodoxy (e.g., *The Descent of Man*).

proper domain of modern science, which is concerned with explaining sensible objects or, as it is sometimes said, "saving the phenomena."[27]

As regards the methodological assumption of physical determinism, I wish to emphasize that it need not be treated as an absolutely universal assumption without exception. A methodological assumption can be considered true within a limited domain of inquiry, without implying that the same assumption must be applicable beyond the domain of inquiry in which the assumption is considered true. Thus methodological naturalism, according to which a scientific researcher as such must seek only natural explanations of observed events, need not imply philosophical naturalism, according to which observed events could have nothing but purely natural explanations, inasmuch as philosophical naturalism positively denies even the logical possibility of supernatural causes. Philosophical naturalism makes no allowance for genuine miracles like the multiplication of loaves and fish. In other words, methodological naturalism does not deny the reality of supernatural causes. It simply doesn't consider them. Philosophical naturalism, in contrast, absolutely precludes supernatural causes. In similar fashion, physical determinism can be employed as a valuable methodological assumption in physical theory, without necessarily implying that such determinism is applicable at every level of reality. That is to say, physical determinism does not logically imply metaphysical determinism or strict necessitarianism. If one recognizes that human persons are free moral agents, then one can hardly deny that even an exceptionally powerful created mind, e.g., an angelic intelligence, in possession of an exhaustive scientific knowledge of the actual state of the material universe and its vast web of physical causes at a particular historical instant, could not predict with infallible accuracy the exact state of the same universe tomorrow morning, let alone a billion years from now.

Metaphysical determinism does not obtain because we are free agents, and the proof that we are free agents lies beyond the reach of modern science. The truth that we are free agents is a scientifically

---

[27] See, for instance, Cardinal Schönborn, "Reasonable Science, Reasonable Faith," 23: "Modern scientific method] proceeds...by means of mathematical and mechanical explanations that, in the old expression, 'save the phenomena.' "

indemonstrable assumption of modern science. If we were not free agents, genuine scientific activity among human persons would not be possible. As I pointed out some years ago to a hard-core determinist with an advanced degree in physics, if it were true that we are absolutely determined in all of our actions, then there would be no real point to arguing over whether determinism is true even at the level of human action. For our past, current, and future beliefs and mental activities would be wholly beyond our control. Genuine human rationality involves far more than does an artificially intelligent computer system. Unlike the spiritual exercise of human rationality, an artificially intelligent machine is strictly determined in all of its operational functions. The reality of human action, which is necessarily rooted in human reason, and the assumption of absolute determinism are mutually incompatible. Of course, the metascientific recognition *that* we are free agents does not explain the inner nature of freedom itself. Such an explanation requires metaphysical analysis. In terms of explaining the reality of human freedom properly understood, which is not to be equated with freedom of indifference, the Copenhagen interpretation of Heisenberg's uncertainty principle is useless. Here Barr is simply mistaken when he claims that indeterminism opens the way to free will.[28] For the intellectual path to true freedom was never obstructed by physical determinism. Barr seems to assume that the exercise of genuine freedom must be consistent with the inviolable operation of physical laws. In the context of physical determinism, however, the exercise of human freedom would entail the regular violation of physical laws, which in Barr's view would be ugly and philosophically unsatisfying. Within the framework of physical indeterminism, however, no such violations would obtain. So, in Barr's view, physical *indeterminism* is aesthetically pleasing and philosophically satisfying.

We must be careful to note, however, that there is a significant ambiguity associated with the common scientific defense of physical *indeterminism*, which relies heavily on probability theory and the idea of randomness. Not a few believe that the universal principle of causality is undermined by Heisenberg's uncertainty principle in quantum

---

[28] See Barr, *Modern Physics and Ancient Faith*, chap. 20: "Determinism and Free Will."

theory. It is said that "an event is causally conditioned if it can be foretold with certainty."[29] Such a view of causation is certainly held by writers like David Hume, who reduced causation to the idea of constant conjunction acquired through cognitive habituation. (How such habituation could be acquired without genuine causation is another question.) Given such an understanding of causation, if we cannot discern that a particular sort of effect is regularly preceded in time by a particular sort of causal mechanism, then it would seem that the effect must be without a cause. Nevertheless, one need not understand the principle of causality in terms of the perception of constant temporal conjunction. The repeated failure to identify an adequate causal explanation underlying an observed event does not logically entail a complete absence of causation. A "billiard-ball" model of causality will not suffice for those interested in pursuing a deeper, less superficial, level of explanation. We must go beyond a shallow mechanistic or Humean understanding of causality and develop a metaphysically robust conception of causation, such as that employed in the writings of Aristotle and Thomas Aquinas.

As long as one refuses to allow within natural science the dubious importation of mechanistic philosophy or philosophical materialism, upon which the ideology of global evolutionism depends, the methodological assumption of physical determinism need not bar the metaphysical recognition of intellect and free will. Physical determinism is a vital working assumption within the circumscribed conceptual topography of empiriometric science. Contrary to the metaphysically immodest claims of scientism, however, one must constantly be mindful of the fact that modern science is not competent to deal with the whole range of reality, which cannot properly be reduced to material beings within reach of our own faculties of sensory perception.[30] Being in all of its intelligible fullness and depth falls properly within the domain of metaphysics, not that of physical science.

---

[29] Vincent E. Smith, *Science and Philosophy* (New York: Bruce, 1965), 88, quoting Planck, *Where is Science Going* (New York: Norton, 1932), 45.

[30] Compare Mariano Artigas, *The Mind of the Universe,* 10-12, 108-12, 35-44.

One can hardly overemphasize this vital philosophical truth today, and it is particularly relevant in the present context. For Barr's *philosophical* position in this regard is wide of the mark. In comparison with the views he expressed in his essay, "Faith and Quantum Theory," aspects of Barr's underlying philosophy of science are made more explicit in his subsequent reply to letters. As noted earlier, Barr denies that modern science "deals only with sensible phenomena rather than with the reality underlying them, or that it studies just the accidental quantitative aspects of things rather than their essences."[31] Such a denial stands in marked contrast to Pope John Paul's position on the proper reach of natural science:

> Scientific proofs in the modern sense of the word are valid only for things perceptible to the senses, since it is only on such things that scientific instruments of investigation can be used.

---

[31] Stephen Barr, "Quantifying Quantum," 6. One should note that the grammar of essences as conceived by thinkers such as Aristotle and Thomas Aquinas is not properly a feature of the language of modern science. It is true, of course, that modern scientists employ the term "species" when discussing differences among the varieties of animals (and plants), but the idea of species used in modern evolutionary biology is not the same as the philosophical concept of species. In the modern biological sense, the term "species" refers to a population of individuals capable of interbreeding. Biologists typically draw the line of demarcation between one species of animal and another at the point where no interbreeding among individuals can occur and reproductive isolation is observed. The differences between species are rather superficial differences in degree, not radical differences in kind. The boundaries between various species are fluid, not definite and unchanging. In short, modern evolutionary biology presupposes a nominalist understanding of species, and there is no recognition of extramental essences. When one employs the philosophical concept of species, in contrast, one enters the ontological realm of definite and unchanging essences, and the presence of formal causes is central. Cf. Dennis Bonnette, *Origin of the Human Species* (Amsterdam; Atlanta, Georgia: Editions Rodopi B.V., 2001), 19-26, 43-47, 87-91. Since Barr has previously argued in favor of neo-Darwinian evolutionary theory, one must ask whether he and Cardinal Schönborn are using the term "essence" in precisely the same sense. If Barr does not share the cardinal's concept of essence, then Barr should clarify what exactly he has in mind when he asserts that modern science goes beyond sensible appearances and studies the underlying essences of things.

> [...] Science must recognize its limits and its inability to reach the existence of God. It can neither affirm nor deny his existence.[32]

Cardinal Schönborn's position is perfectly in accord with that particular view of the methodological limits of modern science. The late Mariano Artigas expresses a closely related view on those very same limits. "Empirical science, by its very nature, is limited to those aspects of reality that can be studied using experimental control."[33] Even if one does not take Pope John Paul's statements on the limitations of modern science to be the final word on this important methodological question, one must grant that his statements concerning the theories and discoveries of modern science, including evolutionary biology, need to be interpreted within the context of his philosophical understanding of the proper epistemic reach of modern science.[34] Furthermore, if Pope John Paul's understanding of that reach

---

[32] John Paul II, "The Proofs for God's Existence," general audience of July 10, 1985, n. 1, http://www.vatican.va/holy_father/john_paul_ii/audiences/alpha/data/aud19850710en.html.

[33] Mariano Artigas, *The Mind of the Universe,* 8. John Criscione offers a similar observation: "The scientific method, as practiced in the hard sciences, is useful for the rational investigation of repeatable observations or repeatable phenomena, such as the gravitational attraction of two objects. To extend it to cover unrepeatable phenomena, the scientific method has to be weakened....Members of the hard sciences need a method that is strong, and it is imperative that scientists not weaken it. We cannot have it both ways. We either restrict application of the scientific method to appropriate phenomena or it loses its validity....[S]cientists should accept the limits of a potent scientific method rather than dilute it in order to cover the universe [which involves more than can be grasped by the senses alone]." John C. Criscione, "Intelligence and Design,"11-12. Regarding the limits of experimental science, Cardinal Schönborn concurs: "[E]xperimentation on repeatable phenomena has certainly been one of the hallmarks of the scientific revolution, and arguably its single most important feature, providing us with a plethora of knowledge about the natural world unavailable to the philosopher and his method based on common experience alone. So I think Dr. Criscione's point is very well taken and a key element of any reevaluation of the nature and limits of modern science," 12.

[34] To cite Pope John Paul II's public statements on evolutionary theory, for example, in support of one's own evolutionary convictions, while

is correct, then Barr's explicit reference to the human mind as an essential feature of his defense of the Copenhagen interpretation entails that his line of argument is philosophical, not purely scientific, in character. For the reality of mind is not something that falls within the restricted competence of modern physical theory, but is a scientifically indemonstrable presupposition.

Barr would defend his more ambitious conception of the epistemic range of modern science with the charge that the more modest conception endorsed by Cardinal Schönborn "involve[s] a gross underestimation of the explanatory successes of modern science and the power of human reason."[35] One should pause to take note that this charge is not simple, but complex. The first part of Barr's charge asserts that the more modest conception of the epistemic reach of modern science does not adequately represent the explanatory range of modern science. The second part of his charge alleges that the more modest conception fails to do full justice to man's rational faculty. If one distinguishes the two parts of Barr's charge, it becomes apparent that such rhetoric lacks any real logical force. For the first part of his charge begs the question, inasmuch as it assumes that his more ambitious conception of the explanatory reach of modern science is the correct one.[36] His position seems to blur the line of demarcation between

---

repudiating his prior understanding of the limits of modern scientific method, would be to risk a serious distortion of his actual teaching.

[35] One should note that Cardinal Schönborn has consistently held that the power of human reason extends far beyond the methodological boundaries of modern science. Indeed, he has criticized scientism or the metascientific view that modern science constitutes the only or the supreme form of genuine human knowledge of reality.

[36] Here one might object that I, no less than Barr, am begging the question, since I seem to be assuming that the more modest view of the epistemic reach of modern science is the correct one. In response, I would point to the important distinction between the premodern notion of science and the modern conception of physical science. The epistemic reach of the former, which includes philosophy of nature and philosophical psychology, extends far beyond that of the latter. Within the framework of the premodern notion of science, one can indeed deal with deeper questions, such as human freedom and responsibility, which modern scientists typically do not consider to be within the purview of their specialized disciplines. When

science and philosophy, inasmuch as he seems to proceed as if empiriometric science is the modern equivalent of natural philosophy, which does consider the natures of corporeal beings. In addition, the second part of his charge is of special interest. For it appears to insinuate that the proper scope of modern science is equal to that of human reason! If he intended to suggest as much, then his position could not easily be distinguished from that of scientism, which he claims to disavow. Here, the words of Pope John Paul are instructive:

> [While recognizing the significant methodological limitations of modern science], however, we must not draw the conclusion that scientists in their scientific studies are unable to find valid reasons for admitting the existence of God. If science as such cannot reach God, the scientist who has an intelligence, the object of which is not limited to things of sense perception, can discover in the world reasons for affirming a Being which surpasses it. Many scientists have made and are making this discovery.[37]

According to this vital qualification, the scope of natural science is subordinate to the metascientific range of human reason. Whether or not Barr's position implies scientism, his esteem for modern scientific rationality appears to surpass by far the value he places on philosophical reason, including metaphysics.[38] The not uncommon

---

modern scientists do attempt to deal with those more fundamental questions pertaining to the underlying spiritual core of human existence, they tend to run into serious difficulties, as long as they remain within the proper boundaries of modern physical theory. If one ignores the foregoing distinction, one will be prone to commit the sort of Kantian missteps that lead one to undervalue speculative reason. In that regard, see Pope Benedict XVI's highly relevant Regensburg Lecture <http://www.vatican.va/holy_father/benedict_xvi/speeches/2006/september/documents/hf_ben-xvi_spe_20060912_university-regensburg_en.html>.

[37] Pope John Paul II, "The Proofs for God's Existence," n. 1.

[38] "Almost all scientists are instinctively and professionally suspicious of anything that smells like 'teleology'... For almost two millennia this kind of [teleological] thinking prevailed in the physical sciences, and it is generally agreed that it led nowhere. *Teleology was found to be a sterile approach to understanding the physical world.* Many accounts of the history of science

failure to appreciate the fundamental role of metaphysical reason, however, is a central concern both of Cardinal Schönborn and of the Catholic Church's magisterium: as reflected, for instance, in the teachings of Pope John Paul II and Pope Benedict XVI.[39] Barr wishes to

---

emphasize that the Scientific Revolution occurred only when scientists abandoned teleology in favor of investigating the physical mechanisms that underlie phenomena. That is why any talk about how certain features of the physical world are necessary in order for human life to exist seems to many scientists like a giant step backward, an attempt to smuggle *discredited teleological notions* back into science. They sincerely worry that people will be led astray from the high road of scientific thinking into the *barren wastelands of fruitless metaphysical speculation*....Teleological thinking can indeed be a showstopper as far as doing real scientific research is concerned. For many centuries it was." Stephen M. Barr, *Modern Physics and Ancient Faith,* 138–39; emphasis added. The irony is that positive opposition to teleological thinking is not a truly scientific posture. Of course, the objective and universal truth of teleology (i.e., final causality) cannot be demonstrated without moving beyond the proper boundaries of natural science; nevertheless, teleology is scientific in the sense that it is an antecedent necessary condition or presupposition of natural science. Cardinal Schönborn appreciates this critical point: "It is true that modern scientists have typically rejected these notions [formal and final causes], but they haven't eliminated them, only ignored them. More precisely, they have *presupposed and relied upon* them while simultaneously claiming their nonexistence. Yet the very best scientists do not limit themselves to purely reductionistic, 'bottom-up' explanations. They know that things are not exhaustively explained by explanations of their parts. They may not use the old terminology, but by their exploration of hierarchy and form such scientists are returning to the tradition of natural philosophy. And natural philosophy leads to metaphysics, to the understanding of being as such" ("Intelligence and Design," 14). On natural science's presuppositions, see Mariano Artigas, *The Mind of the Universe*, 22-23, 27-53. On the theistic, indeed Judaeo-Christian, foundations of modern science, Stanley Jaki's historico-critical work is recognized internationally, although his prolific scholarship is often underrated within scientific circles, especially those under the spell of scientism. Cf. Peter A. Pagan, "Darwin and Design," 103-04.

[39] "The philosopher...does not arbitrarily limit what must be explained, nor the possible modes of explanation. Without doubt [as compared with reductionism], the philosopher's stance is more rational, because he seeks to understand and explain all reality, not an arbitrary subset. The philosopher can explain whatever the 'scientist' can explain (sometime[s] by simply

defend the harmony between scientific truths and truths of theological faith. Yet, in the last analysis, one cannot succeed in this vital task without relying on the bridge supplied by philosophy, especially a realist metaphysics, and this critical bridge is necessarily compromised as long as one elides the real distinction between philosophy and modern natural science.

---

repeating the scientific explanation) and more, but the 'scientist' cannot explain his own starting point. This 'self-limitation of reason,' in the Holy Father's pregnant phrase from Regensburg, is truly one of the great pathologies of the modern West": Cardinal Schönborn, "Intelligence and Design," 15. See also my "Neo-Darwinism and Catholic Teaching," 623.

# INDEX OF NAMES

## CONTRIBUTORS

**Giuseppe Butera** is Associate Professor of Philosophy at Providence College. A native of Toronto and a graduate of the University of Toronto, he earned his doctorate in philosophy from the Catholic University of America in 2001. A Thomist, his research interests include philosophical psychology, virtue ethics, and natural law. Before coming to Providence College, he held postdoctoral fellowships at the University of Notre Dame and The Pontifical Institute of Medieval Studies. He is the editor of *Reading the Cosmos: Nature, Science, and Wisdom* and has published in such journals as *Mediaeval Studies, The Thomist,* and *Philosophy, Psychiatry, and Psychology*.

**John Deely** is Professor of Philosophy at the University of St. Thomas, Houston, Texas. He is the author of a complete history of philosophy from Thales to the Present, *Four Ages of Understanding* (University of Toronto Press, 2001), which defines the term "post-modern" for philosophy in the terms called for by Pope John-Paul II in ¶91 of *Fides et Ratio.* His many publications cover contemporary problem-areas in philosophy, the development of the doctrine of signs or "semiotics", Maritain's thought, especially in relation to John of St. Thomas (John Poinsot), considered by Maritain to be the "last and greatest of the genius's in the Latin Thomistic line". The corrected 2nd edition of Deely's bi-lingual presentation of Poinsot's 1632 *Tractatus de Signis. The Semiotic of John Poinsot*, which was the featured volume in the *New York Times Book Review* of March 30, 1986, has just been published by St. Augustine's Press (South Bend, Indiana; Spring 2013).

**Jean De Groot** is Associate Professor in the School of Philosophy at the Catholic University of America. Her research interests are in the areas of Aristotle's natural philosophy, philosophy of nature, and philosophy of science. Her teaching responsibilities at Catholic University include courses on Aristotle's Categories and Posterior Analytics, as well as courses in contemporary philosophy, including Wittgenstein and 20th century philosophy of science. Prof. De Groot has published two books, one of which is a collection of articles, *Nature in American Philosophy*. She has also published many articles on Aristotle. She is presently working on the nature of Aristotle's empiricism.

**Raymond Dennehy** is Professor of Philosophy at the University of San Francisco. He is the author of *Reason and Dignity, Anti-Abortionist at Large, Soldier Boy: the war between Michael and Lucifer*, and editor of *Christian Married Love.* For the past 25 years he has frequently appeared on university campuses, law schools, and television to debate the topics of abortion, physician-assisted suicide, and same-sex marriage.

**Lawrence Dewan, O.P.** is Professor of Philosophy at the Dominican University College, Ottawa, Canada, and a member of the Pontifical Academy of St. Thomas Aquinas, Vatican City. A native (1932) of North Bay, Ontario, he studied philosophy at the University of Toronto, the University of Paris, and the Pontifical Institute of Medieval Studies (PIMS). His teaching career has included periods at the University of Ottawa, the University of Toronto and PIMS, and the Catholic University of America, Washington, D.C. He is author of *Form and Being: Studies in Thomistic Metaphysics* (the Catholic University of America Press, 2006); *St. Thomas and Form as Something Divine in Things* (Marquette University Press, 2007); and of *Wisdom, Law, and Virtue: Essays in Thomistic Ethics* (Fordham University Press, 2008). Some recent publications are: "St. Thomas, Natural Law, and Universal Ethics", in *Nova et Vetera,* English Edition, Vol. 9, No. 3 (2011): 737–62, and "A Note on Thomas Aquinas and *Virtus essendi,*" in *The Thomist* 75 (2011): 637-51. A group at Sergio Arboleda University, Bogota, Colombia, is currently publishing Spanish translations of his work.

**John Marson Dunaway** is Professor of French and Interdisciplinary Studies at Mercer University, Macon, Georgia. A former Vice-President of the American Maritain Association and winner of the Jacques Maritain Scholarship Award, he has written, edited, or co-edited seven books on French religious writers. Three of his translations are forthcoming: Jean-Louis Chrétien's *Under the Gaze of the Bible* (Fordham University Press) and two of Vladimir Volkoff's recent novels, *The Pope's Guest* and *The Torturer* (both at Mercer University Press).

**William Haggerty** is an Associate Professor in the Philosophy Department at Gannon University. He received his Ph.D. from Boston College. He has published articles and reviews in *Augustinian Studies, Laval Theologique et Philosophique*, and *The Review of Metaphysics*.

**James G. Hanink** is Professor of Philosophy at Loyola Marymount University in Los Angeles, California. His interests center on metaphysics, epistemology, ethics, and political philosophy. He has contributed regularly to publications of the American Maritain Association, most recently: "Does the Philosophy of Nature Need the Intuition of Being? If So, What Is It?" in *Reading the Cosmos: Nature, Science, and Wisdom*, edited by Giuseppe Butera (2011), 99-110. For a recent contribution to the Canadian Jacques Maritain Association, see his "The Metaphysics of Moral Evil: Context, Truth and Character," in *Études Maritainiennes / Maritain Studies*, XXVI, 99-109. Hanink is active in University Faculty for Life. See, for example, his "Jacques Maritain and the Embryo: A Master's Muddle," in the UFL Proceedings, *Life and Learning* XV, 249-62. He and his wife Elizabeth, long active in pro-life advocacy, have five children and four grandchildren.

**Joshua P. Hochschild** is Associate Professor of Philosophy and Dean of the College of Liberal Arts at Mount St. Mary's University. He is the author of *The Semantics of Analogy: Rereading Cajetan's* De Nominum Analogia (University of Notre Dame Press) and co-editor of *Virtue's End: God in the Moral Philosophy of Aristotle and Aquinas* and *Ethics without God? The Divine in Contemporary Moral and Political Theory* (both St. Augustine Press).

**Steven J. Jensen** is an Associate Professor of Philosophy at the Center for Thomistic Studies, University of St. Thomas, Houston, Texas. He received his doctorate in philosophy from the University of Notre Dame. His publications include *Good and Evil Actions: A Journey Through St. Thomas Aquinas* (the Catholic University of America Press, 2010), *The Ethics of Organ Transplantation* (the Catholic University of America Press, 2011), and many articles concerning the ethics and action theory of St. Thomas Aquinas.

**Christopher S. Morrissey** is Associate Professor of Philosophy at Redeemer Pacific College, the Catholic liberal arts college at

Trinity Western University in Langley, British Columbia, Canada, where he also teaches courses in the Latin language and in Greek and Roman history. He studied Greek and Latin at the University of British Columbia and has taught courses in these languages and in other classical subjects at Simon Fraser University. Morrissey specializes in philosophical theology and his recent focus has been on its genesis in the monotheistic speculations of Hesiod and Plato. His book of Hesiod's poetry has been published by Talonbooks. Morrissey has also published book chapters and journal articles on the medieval Latin philosophy of Thomas Aquinas and his commentatorial tradition, which includes John Poinsot ("John of St. Thomas"), from whom we may trace a foundational doctrine of signs for the interdisciplinary field of semiotics. Morrissey's current research explores how Eric Voegelin's philosophical studies of the historical processes of symbolization complement the pioneering interdisciplinary work by the semiotician and linguist Thomas Albert Sebeok towards a global semiotics.

**Peter A. Pagan** is an Associate Professor of Philosophy at Aquinas College, Nashville, Tennessee. He earned his doctorate at Fordham University and has taught previously at Wheeling Jesuit University (West Virginia) and Fordham University (New York). His interests include natural theology, philosophy of God, natural law theory, Catholic social teaching, the thought of St. Thomas Aquinas, and the interface between science and theology.

**Michael D. Torre** is the recently elected President of the American Maritain Association (as of October, 2012). He had previously served as a Vice President of the Institut International Jacques Maritain. He is currently a professor of philosophy at the University of San Francisco. His book *Do Not Resist the Spirit's Call: Francisco Marín-Sola on Sufficient Grace* is soon to be published (in August, 2013) by the Catholic University of America Press. He previously edited the American Maritain Association volume *Freedom in the Modern World: Jacques Maritain, Yves R. Simon, Mortimer J. Adler* (1989, second printing: 1990), and has contributed numerous articles to its series, of which he has been the General Editor since 2009. This book marks the sixth volume under his General Editorship. 2009 also saw the publication of his *God's*

*Permission of Sin: Negative or Conditioned Decree?* by Fribourg University Press.

**John G. Trapani, Jr., Ph.D.** is a Professor of Philosophy at Walsh University in North Canton, Ohio. During his 39 years at the university, he has served as Chair of the Philosophy Department and Humanities Division. In addition, he is also the Founder and Director of the university's annual Philosophy-Theology Symposium, now in its 38th year. John has just completed two terms as President of the American Maritain Association. He was the editor of the 2004 volume of the AMA book series, *Truth Matters*, and his book, *Poetry, Beauty, and Contemplation: The Complete Aesthetics of Jacques Maritain*, published by the Catholic University of America Press, was released in February of 2011. John is also the leader of the 17-piece "John Trapani Big Band," founded in 1977.

**Nikolaj Zunic** is an Associate Professor of Philosophy at St. Jerome's University, Waterloo, Ontario, Canada. He earned his doctorate at the Institute of Philosophy of the Catholic University of Leuven, Belgium. He specializes in modern German philosophy, metaphysics, and philosophical anthropology, especially in the tradition of theistic personalism. He has published articles in various journals, such as *American Catholic Philosophical Quarterly*, *The Heythrop Journal*, and *Maritain Studies/Études maritainiennes.*

CPSIA information can be obtained at www.ICGtesting.com
Printed in the USA
BVOW040631280513

321728BV00003B/6/P